THE THEORY OF THE NOVEL
IN ENGLAND
1850–1870

THE THEORY
OF THE NOVEL
IN ENGLAND

1850–1870

by
RICHARD STANG

Routledge & Kegan Paul

LONDON

TO SONDRA

CONTENTS

vii

CONTENTS

PART THREE

INTRODUCTION

O NE of the most persistent clichés in the history of modern literature, especially the history of the English novel, is that criticism of the novel and discussions of the theory of the novel somehow began *ex nihilo* with Flaubert in France, and that England remained remarkably insulated from these theories until infected or fertilized (depending on one's point of view) by either Henry James or George Moore in the eighties. Until that decade, or for some writers until the late seventies, the English novelist did not consider himself an artist at all; he was merely a popular entertainer. In England, it was not until the modern critics (James was a lonely precursor) 'determined above all to grant their novelists seriousness, and to take the novel seriously, to take it, that is to say, not as amusement but as art' that there was any criticism of the novel at all, according to Mark Schorer.[1] Walter Allen, in the most recent history of the English novel, also states quite categorically that 'the notion of the novel as a literary form having something to do with art . . . is quite new'—that is, this notion begins not earlier than the last two decades of the nineteenth century—and that novelists until quite recently 'interpreted their craft in no very exalted way'.[2]

These misconceptions about the history of the theory of the novel are not confined to men who consider themselves primarily critics relying for their literary history and scholarship upon others. Bradford Booth, a specialist in the nineteenth-

---

[1] John W. Aldridge, ed., *Critiques and Essays on Modern Fiction 1920–1951* (New York, 1952), p. xv.

[2] *The English Novel, a Short Critical History* (New York, 1955), p. xxi.

century novel, writes that in the mid-nineteenth century, criticism of fiction 'remained in its adolescence', marked by 'jaunty and complacent superficiality'. At least Professor Booth concedes us some criticism, even if adolescent (for with other writers on the subject, it is usually childish or non-existent), but he goes on to say that for significant criticism we had to wait 'until the influence of Henry James had made itself felt. For this unhappy state of affairs the novelists were largely responsible, for they regarded their craft as a form of amusement rather than an art.' Even George Eliot, actually a highly self-conscious artist, as we shall see later, remained for Booth in this state of 'critical innocence'. She 'approached criticism, briefly and tentatively', and 'none of the other first-rate novelists made any contribution towards the establishment of a theory of fiction' except Trollope, who, we are told, had 'fixed principles'.[1] According to Desmond Pacey, who investigated Victorian criticism of prose fiction carefully to do his study, 'Flaubert and His Victorian Critics', in the *University of Toronto Quarterly*, 'the novel had been regarded largely as an instrument of superior amusement or of moral elevation; reviews of novels had been but slightly concerned with matters of style and technique, and articles devoted to a discussion of the art of the novel had been unknown',[2] until of course, again, the miraculous eighties. At least Dr. Pacey grants that the amusement afforded by the Victorian novel was superior; for Ford Madox Ford it was a very low form called 'nuvvles',[3] as distinguished from the novel, a work of art.

To quote from only one more sample, to show how widespread this view is, Robert Gorham Davis, writing in the 'Forum on Realism', edited by Harry Levin and filling a whole issue of *Comparative Literature* in 1951, states authoritatively: 'Between the first two and last two decades of the nineteenth century, there was amazingly little extended or serious discussion of the novel as a literary form, either by English critics or by the English novelists themselves. Thackeray's *British Humourists* is hardly an exception.' [4]

---

[1] 'Trollope on the Novel,' *Essays Critical and Historical Dedicated to Lily B. Campbell* (Berkeley and Los Angeles, 1950), pp. 219–20.

[2] XVI (1946), 83.

[3] *The English Novel* (London, 1930), pp. 105–8.   [4] III, 214.

This study will deal with discussions of the novel as a distinct literary form in the years between 1850 and 1870. The time span, however, will be somewhat elastic and include statements by all novelists whose important work falls into this period. Thus the statements by Thackeray, Dickens, Bulwer-Lytton, and Charlotte Brontë, even if they are made in the thirties and forties, will be considered relevant, and those by Meredith, Trollope, and George Eliot, when falling into the seventies and eighties, will also be included. Critics like R. H. Hutton and Leslie Stephen, whose preoccupations remain those of the fifties and sixties, but whose work extends into the seventies and eighties, will not be cut short at the year 1869, for to do so would seem artificial. On the other hand, the ideas of Henry James, Thomas Hardy, George Moore, and George Gissing, since their novels belong definitely to a later period, will be excluded.

In this period, any study of the theory of the novel, or, for that matter, of the theory of poetry, cannot limit itself, as it could in the succeeding period 1870–1914, merely to matters of technique and form. Such matters were indeed important to the Victorians, but as E. S. Dallas, one of the most original literary theorists of the period, wrote: 'After all, the question of supreme interest in art, the question upon which depends our whole interest in art is, what are its relations to life.' [1] Questions such as the use of fiction, the role of the imagination in the writing of fiction, and the correspondence of fiction to life outside the novel were as central to the mid-Victorian novelist, critic and educated reader as more strictly formal questions are to us.

In this book I shall try to show that mid-Victorian criticism of fiction has been very much underrated, that it should be considered as an important part of the history of English criticism as a whole, and that it must further be considered in any study of the mutations of the English novel. The chief reason for the wholesale dismissal of this large literature is that most of it is buried away in the files of Victorian periodicals. On the whole, the most trenchant discussions are not those published in books, and it is unfortunate for the reputation of Victorian criticism that such books as Thackeray's *British Humourists*,

[1] Eneas Sweetland Dallas, *The Gay Science* (London, 1866), II, 287.

which has many excellent qualities, although criticism is not one of them; Trollope's *Autobiography*, wonderfully frank but not very intelligent critically; and a few others, such as Cross' expurgated edition of George Eliot's *Letters and Journals*, together with a few prefaces to novels, have been the basis of too many considerations of the entire subject of the mid-Victorian theory of the novel. The brilliant discussions of the technique and subject matter of novels and the relation of novels to life by such major critics as G. H. Lewes, Walter Bagehot, R. H. Hutton, W. C. Roscoe, Leslie Stephen, George Eliot (or Miss Evans, as she was when sub-editor of the *Westminster Review* and prolific critic from 1851 to 1857 before publishing her first novel), and a host of vigorous minor critics, such as George Brimley, James Fitzjames Stephen, Samuel Lucas, E. S. Dallas—all of these discussions are still unknown even though they appeared in such important periodicals as the *Cornhill Magazine*, the *North British Review*, the *British Quarterly Review*, the *Westminster Review*, the *National Review*, the *Saturday Review*, and the *Leader*.

Since there has not yet been any adequate account of mid-Victorian criticism of the major literary form of the mid-Victorian period, I hope this book will supply a much-needed missing chapter in English literary history.

I would like to thank Professors Jerome H. Buckley, Frederic W. Dupee and Susan Nobbe of Columbia University, and Professor Charles Shain of Carleton College for their valuable criticism. I am especially grateful to Professor Buckley for his close reading of my manuscript and his many careful corrections. But my chief thanks are to my wife for her indispensable help at every stage of my work.

CARLETON COLLEGE,
  NORTHFIELD,
    MINNESOTA

PART ONE

PART ONE

I

THE SACRED OFFICE
The Novelists

I. THE BACKGROUND

FRANCIS JEFFREY, having selected in 1842 what seemed to
him his most significant critical essays to preserve for posterity
from the pages of the *Edinburgh Review*, felt it necessary to write
a preface to the section on novels explaining why he had been
apologetic 'for seeking to direct the attention of my readers to
things so insignificant as *Novels.* . . .' Writings of that sort, he
went on to say, 'were rated very low with us—scarcely allowed
to pass as part of a nation's permanent literature—and generally
deemed altogether unworthy of any grave critical notice'. By
1842, 'all this, however, has been signally, and happily,
changed . . .' through the influence of such novelists as Scott,
Hugo, Balzac, Jane Austen, Manzoni, and Goethe. 'Among
them . . . the honour of this branch of literature has at any rate
been splendidly redeemed;—and now bids fair to maintain its
place, at the head of all that is graceful and instructive in the
productions of modern genius.'[1]

But evidently this startling evolution in the status of the novel
among cultivated readers was not completely accepted by all
the important critics. For we find De Quincey, as late as 1848
—in the two years preceding, *Wuthering Heights, Jane Eyre,*

[1] Francis Jeffrey, *Contributions to the Edinburgh Review* (London, 1844), III,
396.

Vanity Fair, and *Dombey and Son* had been published in England
—echoing almost unchanged Jeffrey's youthful opinions: novels
are an inferior genre as such and necessarily, by their very
nature, ephemeral. 'All novels whatever, the best equally with
the worst, have faded almost within the generation that produced them. This is a curse written as a superscription above
the whole class. . . . It is only the grander passions of poetry,
allying themselves with forms more abstract and permanent'
that can last. 'How bestial and degrading at this day seem
many of the scenes in Smollett! How coarse are the ideals of
Fielding! . . . What a gallery of histrionic masqueraders is
thrown open in the novels of Richardson. . . .' And further
proof of the lowness of the genre may be had in 'the modern
novelists'. dependence on his *canaille* of an audience'.[1] In 1848
this contempt was shared by a small minority, although, as we
shall see, it persisted with a few people until 1870 and probably
after.

But in the early part of the century, it was widespread among
educated readers and was based on the newness of the genre
and the enormous quantity of bad fiction being turned out for
the circulating libraries. The use of prose, a form of discourse
inferior to poetry, helped even more to lower the new genre
in the early nineteenth century when the idea of ranking genres
was still very strong. The chief aesthetic justification for the
attack was that great literature must be based on general truths
and general types and not minute particularities, i.e. it could
not be realistic, and the novel by its very nature forced the
author to imitate the transitory. After all, what was so change-
able as manners? And manners, it seemed, were the novel's
most natural subject matter.

In the eighteenth century most novelists would not have
agreed to these strictures. They insisted, like Richardson and
Fielding, that they were concerned with universal truths and
that their characters were not mere individuals,[2] and Fielding,
the most important theorizer on the new form that he helped
to invent, always insisted that he was portraying 'not an indi-

[1] 'Forster's Life of Goldsmith', *North British Review*, IX (1848), 193–4.
[2] See the two articles by Houghton W. Taylor, 'Modern Fiction and the
Doctrine of Uniformity', *PQ*, XIX (1940), 225–36; and 'Particular Character', *PMLA*, LX (1945), 161–74.

vidual, but a species'.[1] His work, like all high art, did not attend merely to 'the minute accidental discriminations of particular and individual objects . . .' but 'the general and invariable ideas of nature', i.e. the ideal.[2]

In the eighteenth and early nineteenth centuries, novels were suspect on still another ground: they seemed so easy to read. Any piece of literature which gives so much pleasure, according to Coleridge—and he apparently enjoyed novels very much—without 'requiring the exertion of thought' must necessarily be 'intellectually and morally enervating' and if indulged would eventually bring about the 'entire destruction of the powers of the mind'.[3] But though Coleridge disapproved of novels as a genre, he was fascinated by the possibilities being opened for a more exact kind of psychological notation. What had been fitfully attempted in the drama could now be done more continuously in the novel: Sterne and Richardson seemed to follow the mind in action and get at the thought processes themselves.[4]

The principal attack on the new genre, however, had nothing whatever to do with aesthetics. The evangelical wing of the church and most of the dissenters strongly disapproved of all imaginative literature as mere entertainment, as a waste of time that should be spent praising God or making money. Thus for the *Evangelical Magazine* in 1793, novels were 'instruments of abomination and ruin'.[5] Seven years later in the same periodical, there appeared a 'spiritual barometer' on which love of novels is ranked with scepticism, one step below drunkenness and adultery.[6]

This view had certainly penetrated serious literary criticism as early as 1783, for we find in a ninety-page treatise 'On Fable and Romance' by the poet James Beattie, evidently written *con amore*, a palinode in the final paragraph that sounds like a medieval treatise on love by a cleric. 'Romances are a dangerous recreation . . . and tend to corrupt the heart, and stimulate the passions. A habit of reading them . . . fills the mind with

---

[1] *Joseph Andrews* (New York, 1906), Book III, chap. I, p. 166.

[2] Joshua Reynolds, *Discourses* (London, 1887), p. 3.

[3] Quoted from Charles I. Patterson, 'Coleridge's Conception of Dramatic Illusion in the Novel', *ELH*, XVIII (1951), 123.

[4] *Ibid.*, pp. 130–4.

[5] Maurice Quinlan, *Victorian Prelude* (New York, 1941), p. 224.

[6] *Ibid.*, p. 114.

extravagant thoughts, and too often with criminal propensities,' and he would allow his reader to go through only one or two if he wants to 'have something to say on the subject'.[1] When novels were defended from these charges, it was on the ground that they 'show us examples of conduct, superior to those which are to be met with in ordinary life'.[2]

Apologies for the novel had appeared intermittently from the time of Huet in the late seventeenth century. Defending the interminable romances of Mlle de Scudéry and Lá Calprenède against the charge that these books 'exhaust our Devotion, and inspire us with irregular passions, and corrupt our Manners', the good Bishop answered: 'But what can't Evil and Degenerated Minds make an Ill use of?' and he rested his defence on the fact that romances teach us how 'to live and speak'.[3] Of course there had been attacks and defences of poetry and literature in general from the time of Plato, but there were probably never so many at one time as in the years between 1780 and 1820[4] because of the influence of the evangelical middle classes, who were now such an important part of the reading public.

One of the more ingenious strategies for conferring dignity on the newest literary genre was to show that it was not new at all but was in fact one of the oldest genres; and the writers of treatises on fiction set to work to construct impressive genealogies for the novel. Huet traced it from the ancient Near East, making it older than the Homeric epics, and found it entered European literature through Miletus into Greece and Rome. This history, sometimes including the *Odyssey* as a novel, was used by Beattie, Clara Reeve, and Dr. John Moore, and was finally expanded into a very detailed thousand-page,

[1] *Dissertations Moral and Critical* (Dublin, 1783), II, 320.

[2] Hugh Murray, *The Morality of Fiction*, 1805, quoted in John Tinnon Taylor, *Early Opposition to the Novel (1760–1830)* (New York, 1943), p. 92.

[3] Pierre Daniel Huet, *The History of Romance*, trans. Stephen Lewis (London, 1715), p. 142.

[4] See Taylor, *op. cit.*, and Quinlan, *op. cit.* For typical defences see John Moore, 'A View of the Commencement and Progress of Romances' (1769) in *Works*, V (Edinburgh, 1820); Clara Reeve, *The Progress of Romance* (Colchester, 1785), reprinted by The Facsimile Text Society (New York, 1930); Mrs. Barbauld, 'An Essay on the Origin and Progress of Novel-Writing', prefixed to vol. I of *The British Novelists* (London, 1810).

two-volume work published by John Dunlop in 1816 as the *History of Fiction*. This remained the standard work on the subject until the twentieth century, having been reprinted throughout the nineteenth, all the while accruing more and more notes by successive editors. Although his criticism was rather elementary, and often came second-hand from earlier writers, and although much of the book consisted merely of plot summaries, the important thing was Dunlop's implication that fiction was worth such a large expenditure of time and space, and that the novel was one of the great literary forms with an unbroken history from the time of the Greeks. In his introduction, he tried to define the *raison d'être* of prose fiction, and his definition is cast in typical eighteenth-century terms: 'History treats of man . . . in the mass, and the individuals whom it paints are regarded merely . . . in a public light, without taking into consideration their private feelings, tastes, or habits. Poetry is . . . capable of too little detail. . . . But in fiction we can discriminate without impropriety, and enter into detail without meanness.' Its uses are to soothe, please, amuse, and it is a 'powerful instrument of virtue' teaching by example rather than precept.[1]

The man most responsible for raising the status of the novel with the new middle class is universally considered to be Scott. But if he made the form respectable, he certainly did not consider it an important branch of literature, even though he laughed at the widespread prejudice against it. 'One would almost think', he wrote in a review of *Emma* in the *Quarterly Review*, 'novel-reading fell under this class of frailties [drunkenness and debauchery], since among the crowds who read little else, it is not common to find an individual of hardihood sufficient to avow his taste for these frivolous studies.' [2] But even though 'novel-writing is perhaps the most remarkable addition the moderns have made to literature',[3] still the moderns and not the ancients made the addition, and by virtue of its newness apparently it is inferior to all of the older genres. The reviewer of *Waverley* in the *Critical Review* apparently felt the same way when he exclaimed, 'Why a poet of established fame should

[1] John Dunlop, *The History of Fiction* (Philadelphia, 1842), I, xx–xxii.
[2] *Quarterly Review*, XIV (October, 1815), 188.
[3] *Ibid.*, XI (January, 1814), 301.

dwindle into a scribbler of novels, we cannot tell.' [1] Scott himself said repeatedly in the prefaces to his novels, especially to *The Abbot*, *The Antiquary*, *Guy Mannering*, and *The Fortunes of Nigel*, that he did not plan his books beforehand but improvised them as he went along. (This attitude of Scott's is often assumed to be that of the Victorian novelists as well, but as we shall see, most of them had very different views on the dignity of their art.) In the prefaces to the volumes of Ballantyne's Novelists' Library, which Scott later collected into the *Lives of the Novelists*, where he had the chance to expatiate at the greatest length on his own art, he defended the novel as an 'opiate, baneful, when habitually and constantly resorted to, but of most blessed power in those moments of pain and of languor, when the whole head is sore and the whole heart is sick'. [2] Here is an impressive tribute to the power of novels to help readers escape from their troubles, but it hardly helped to raise the prestige of the form. (Apparently Coleridge had a proper fear of what this opiate could really do to a man's mind.)

In another passage on the effects of novel reading, we can see how thoroughly Benthamite Utilitarianism had penetrated the heart of even this most thorough-going Tory. The worst evil of reading novels is that they 'generate an indisposition to read history and useful literature. . . . [Novels] are really a mere elegance, a luxury contrived for the amusement of polished life, and the gratification of that half love of literature which pervades all ranks. . . .' [3]

Bulwer, annoyed by any undervaluing of his craft, was led by Scott's superciliousness to minimize his influence in making the novel respectable. Bulwer conceded grudgingly in *England and the English* of 1833 that Scott 'tended . . . somewhat to elevate with the vulgar a class of composition that, with the educated, required no factitious elevation; for, with the latter, what new dignity could be thrown upon a branch of letters that Cervantes, Fielding, Le Sage, Voltaire, and Fénelon had already made only less than Epic?' [4] But apparently the educated were at least ambivalent in their feelings towards 'this

[1] James T. Hillhouse, *The Waverley Novels and Their Critics* (Minneapolis, 1936), p. 76.
[2] *The Miscellaneous Prose Works of Sir Walter Scott* (Boston, 1829), III, 256.
[3] *Ibid.*, pp. 77–8.   [4] (London, 1874), p. 251.

Branch of letters', if we are to believe the testimony of Coleridge, De Quincey, Jeffrey, Sidney Smith, and Scott.

John Stuart Mill was certainly one of the 'educated', and two years earlier he declared in his famous essay 'Thoughts on Poetry and Its Varieties' that the novel was necessarily an inferior genre because it could *only* depict outward things and not the inner man.[1] It is strange how persistent this critical dictum was—it lasted into the sixties—in spite of the fact that before Mill's essay, Richardson, Sterne, Laclos, Goethe, and Constant had all explored the intricacies of human motive, frustration, and conflict with a psychological acuteness that easily matched that of any other literary period. This *a priori* argument that novels must be concerned with externals such as manners, behaviour divorced from motive, and descriptions of scenery for their own sake, without actually examining whether novels did in fact limit themselves in this way, we find in a curious essay of 1862 by the English Hegelian, T. H. Green, written when he was twenty-six, 'An Estimate of the Value and Influence of Fiction in Modern Times.' His basic thesis is the same as Mill's, and in more extreme form we have seen it in De Quincey. The aspect of reality the novelist 'shows us is merely the outward and natural, as opposed to the inner or ideal'.[2] The novelistic view of the world is opposed to the poetic because the individual in a novel is not seen from within but merely delineated as a function of outward circumstances, and moreover is always happy in these circumstances.[3] Man, as seen in novels, must be presented as self-satisfied, while in the true view of the human situation he is necessarily always 'inadequate to himself; and as such, disturbed and miserable'.[4] After the appearance of the Brontë novels, the early work of George Eliot and Meredith, and the late novels of Dickens, this description of the English novel—not to mention the French, including the work of George Sand, Balzac, Flaubert, and Stendhal—is peculiar. But then it is doubtful if either Mill or Green bothered to read very many novels before condemning the whole genre.

The year after the appearance of *Pickwick Papers* and *Oliver*

[1] Reprinted in *English Critical Essays*, ed. Edmund D. Jones (London, 1947), p. 344.
[2] (Ann Arbor, Michigan, 1911), p. 43.
[3] *Ibid.*, p. 52. [4] *Ibid.*, p. 39.

Twist, 1838, was one of the most decisive years in England for raising the status of the novel and preparing the way for what was later to be called by R. H. Hutton its 'empire' [1] over the whole realm of literature in the second half of the nineteenth century. For it was then that Lockhart published his exhaustive *Life of Scott*, and for sheer detail there had been nothing like it in English literature except Boswell's *Life of Johnson*. Dr. Johnson had been the very incarnation of the dignity of literature (see Miss Deborah Jenkynson on *Rasselas* in *Cranford*), and now a mere writer of fiction was treated to the same honour; and what was more striking, most of literary England and the rest of Europe seemed to acquiesce. There had of course been earlier dissenting voices to Scott's literary eminence. In 1828 and 1829 Frederick Denison Maurice complained in a series of articles in *The Athenaeum*, which he was then editing with John Sterling, that Scott was overrated: he was a superficial writer and had no general ideas. The scenery in his novels was used for its own sake rather than as the 'drapery of the thoughts of the characters', i.e. echoing Coleridge, his master, Maurice held that setting should be symbolic, as it is in all great works of literature. [2]

But Carlyle's review of Lockhart's *Life* in 1838 for the *Westminster* was a much more thoroughgoing attack. 'It seems to us there goes other stuff to the making of great men than can be detected here. One knows not what idea worthy of the name great, what purpose, instinct or tendency, that could be called great, Scott was ever inspired with.' [3] 'If Literature had no task but that of harmlessly amusing indolent languid men, here was the very perfection of Literature. . . .' [4] Carlyle ridiculed the comparison of Scott with Shakespeare, that was being made with more and more frequency, not on the ground that a mere novelist could not be compared with England's greatest dramatist, but on the assumption that the two genres *were* potentially comparable: Scott did not approach Shakespeare in the creation of character. 'Your Shakespeare fashions his character from the heart outwards; your Scott fashions them from the skin inwards, never getting nearer the heart of them!' Shakespeare's 'became living men and women'; Scott's were 'decep-

---

[1] *Spectator*, XLII (January 9, 1869), 43–4.
[2] Hillhouse, *op. cit.*, pp. 98–102.
[3] *Works* (London, 1888), XVII, 177. [4] *Ibid.*, p. 211.

tively painted automatons'.[1] His novels, founded on trivial
interests, could not last; the great passions were out of his
range.[2] Here indeed was a very different view of the novel from
Scott's: far from being considered only a passing amusement,
it was to be judged by the highest canons of literature. Implicit
throughout Carlyle's essay is the view that the novel was potentially a very great form indeed—else why expend so much
earnestness devaluing a mere novelist and complain that 'the
sick heart will find no healing here, the darkly-struggling heart
no guidance. . . .'?[3] Apparently one could find such things in
novels; Carlyle insisted that he found them in *Wilhelm Meister*,
which he gave to the Victorian world in translation. And
though he claimed at times to despise the form for not being
true, as he did in the essay on Diderot, and though he could
call all novelists, and by extension all writers of imaginative
literature, asses for wasting time making up imaginary histories
when they could be writing genuine ones, he was apparently
fascinated by the rapidly developing novel, as his own *Sartor
Resartus* and the unfinished *Wotton Reinfred* testify. Surprisingly
enough, he managed to keep up with most of the important
Victorian novels as they came out. Having enjoyed *Richard
Feverel*, he advised Meredith to switch to history, an almost
automatic response with him by then, and it is a pity that his
reply to Meredith's Aristotelian answer—that his novels were
truer than history—has never been recorded.

For Carlyle, then, the novelist, in order to be called great,
had to be measured against any other great literary artist, and
he had to be more than an artist. The great writer was a hero,
a prophet who would really create the uncreated conscience of
his race. And since Scott had 'no message whatever to deliver
to the world; wished not the world to elevate itself, to amend
itself, to do this or to do that, except simply pay him for the
books he kept writing', the world would soon forget him.[4]

2. BULWER

In the same year as Carlyle's essay, Sir Edward Bulwer, later
Bulwer-Lytton, published in the *Monthly Review* one of the most
important critical documents of the period, 'Art in Fiction', in

---

[1] *Ibid.*, p. 212.   [2] *Ibid.*, p. 213.   [3] *Ibid.*   [4] *Ibid.*, p. 194.

which he came to similar conclusions about Scott. Bulwer's thesis was that the novel must be considered as a work of art, and that as art Scott's novels could not be judged significant. Echoing the great German Romantic critics, he charged that Scott never realized 'that the loftiest merit of a tale rests upon the effect it produces, not on the fancy, but on the intellect and passions'.[1] Scott's novels were of the lowest order, dealing as they did with manners and external descriptions of costumes and postures, rather than the passions, which must be the basis of a great imaginative literature. Great fiction must achieve the same effects as great tragedy or great comedy, and Scott's did neither because he never had a noble conception either of his art or apparently of his subject matter, man. Carlyle's and Bulwer's statements that the novel must be a serious art form and go deep into the delineation of man, as deep as Shakespeare went, were signs of the times and pointed both to the way later novelists conceived of their art and to the demands critics were to make on novels.

Scott's method of hasty improvisation seemed shocking to Bulwer, though he too could toss off novels as quickly as Scott. One's subject must 'lie long in the mind, to be revolved, meditated, brooded over . . . until . . . [the elements of the story] can be reduced to harmony and order'.[2] Unfortunately Bulwer in practice was not nearly so dedicated to his craft as he was in theory, but in his prefaces and critical essays one finds an almost Jamesian or Flaubertian insistence on the need for the novelist to be an intensely dedicated craftsman.

In the Preface of 1843 to *The Last of the Barons*, for example, he anticipates James' favourite analogy for the novelist. 'To my mind, a writer should sit down to compose a fiction as a painter prepares to compose a picture.'[3] He should just as deliberately try to construct a coherent work of art. And just as there are certain rules a painter or a sculptor must learn, so there is a definite art of the novel, and one must master it as he does any other art.

People often say to me, 'I shall write a novel'. If I ask 'On what

---

[1] *The Critical and Miscellaneous Writings of Sir Edward Lytton* (Philadelphia, 1841), I, 70.

[2] *Ibid.*, p. 73.   [3] (London, 1874), p. xiv.

rules?' they stare. They know of no rules. They write History, Epic, the Drama, Criticism, by rules; and for the Novel, which comprises all four, they have no rules. What wonder that there is so much talent *manqué* in half the novels we read? In fact we ought to do as the sculptors do—gaze upon all the great masterpieces of our art till they sink into us, and we are penetrated by the secret of them. Then, and not till then, we write according to rules without being quite aware of it.[1]

His insistence that the novelist consider himself a bona fide historian anticipates James' later criticism of Trollope's 'betrayal of his sacred office' when he admits the events he narrates never happened and the reader is merely reading fiction. In the Preface to *A Strange Story* (1862), Bulwer states, 'Of course, according to the most obvious principles of art, the narrator of a fiction must be as thoroughly in earnest as if he were the narrator of facts. One could not tell the most extravagant fairy-tale so as to rouse and sustain the attention of the most infantine listener, if the tale were told as if the tale-teller did not believe it.'[2]

He lamented to Forster that Goethe's art in *Elective Affinities*, 'so delicate, so noble', was ridiculed in England. 'Our countrymen only understand the broad splosh, the thick brush, lots of outline, and a burly chap in the foreground,'[3] and in writing *The Caxtons*, he deliberately set to work, so he said, to give the English public what it wanted. Instead of intensity, great passions, and great art, he would give them *kitsch*.

The art employed in *The Caxtons* is a very simple one, and within the reach of all. It is just that of creating agreeable emotions. . . . Now to do this, we have only to abandon attempts at many subtle and deep emotions, which produce uneasiness and pain, and see that the smile is without sarcasm and the tears without bitterness. . . . Of course there are many other and much higher branches of art, in the cultivation of which popularity may be very doubtful.[4]

The sad thing about Bulwer is that he thought, or said he thought that he was creating great art in his other novels, when

---

[1] The Earl of Lytton, *The Life of Edward Bulwer, First Lord Lytton* (London, 1913), I, 460.

[2] (Philadelphia, 1879), p. xi.   [3] *Life of Bulwer*, I, 542.

[4] *Ibid.*, II, 105.

in his search for intensity he was merely giving the reader inflated rhetoric and very conventional melodrama. As a matter of fact, *The Caxtons* was not really very different from novels like *Ernest Maltravers* and *Night and Morning*. It was only in his sophisticated scenes that he was successful, and then in an admittedly inferior genre, the copying of manners. As a critic, however, Bulwer's insistence that the novelist respect his art was salutary.

The fault I find chiefly with novelists is their contempt for their craft. A clever and scholar-like man enters into it with a dignified contempt. 'I am not going to write,' he says, 'a mere novel.' What then is he going to write? What fish's tail will he add to the horse's head? A tragic poet might as well say, 'I am not going to write a mere tragedy.' The first essential to success in the art you practise is respect for the art itself.[1]

3. THACKERAY AND CHARLOTTE BRONTË

Thackeray, one of Bulwer's most savage critics during the thirties and forties, was often guilty of this cavalier attitude. 'I don't care a straw for a "triumph". Pooh!—nor for my art enough. It seems to me indecent and despicable to be doing the novelist's business of "On a lovely evening in January . . ." Shall one take pride out of this folly?'[2] While writing *The Newcomes* he confesses, 'I can't but see it is a repetition of past performances, and think that vein is pretty nigh worked out in me. Never mind: this is not written for glory but for quite as good an object, namely money. . . .'[3] And again, 'It seems to me I am too old for story-telling: but I want money. . . .'[4] Apparently these disclaimers were repeated very often in private conversation, and although they were in large measure affectation based on the old idea that novel-writing, and in fact any writing or working for one's living, was beneath the dignity of a gentleman, Thackeray, after *Pendennis*, did feel he had

---

[1] 'Caxtoniana: A Series of Essays on Life, Literature, and Manners', *Blackwood's Edinburgh Magazine*, XLIII (May, 1863), 554.

[2] *The Letters and Private Papers of William Makepeace Thackeray*, ed. Gordon N. Ray (Cambridge, Mass., 1946), III, 13 (hereafter cited as *Thackeray Letters*).

[3] *Ibid.*, p. 287.   [4] *Ibid.*, p. 294.

exhausted what he had to say. 'One of Dickens' immense superiorities over me is the great fecundity of his imagination. He has written 10 books and lo I am worn out after two.'[1] This feeling would go far to explain the gradual swallowing up of his later novels—those written after *The Newcomes*—in a type of extremely repetitive and tedious digression and in commentary only tangentially related to the story.

But such a statement represents only one side of Thackeray's attitude towards his craft. His involvement in his own created world was intense, especially in regard to the lives of his characters. 'I know the people utterly—I know the sound of their voices.'[2] After finishing a book he felt like a deserted inn and missed the people 'who have been boarding and lodging with me for twenty months! They have interrupted my rest; they have plagued me at all sorts of minutes: they have thrust themselves upon me when I was ill, or wished to be idle. . . .'[3] The strangest thing these characters could do was to force their author completely to change his plan half-way through the story:[4] 'They must go a certain way, in spite of themselves.' Often he is surprised at the things they say: 'It seems as if an occult Power was moving the pen,' and sometimes he sounds like a Romantic or a Symbolist poet: the 'writer is like a Pythoness on her oracle tripod. . . .'[5] If Thackeray did think of himself as a jester in cap and bells at one moment, at another he was the rapt recorder of an intensely real imaginative life, so real that he could compare the novelist to a madman.[6]

When Laura Bell, towards the close of *Pendennis*, urged her cousin and husband to write 'good kind books with gentle thoughts',[7] she was not aware of the unconscious irony of her words. Of course she could not be aware that her husband's next effort would be *The Newcomes*, hardly the sort of work she had asked for. Its relentless attack on the English 'marriage market', its portrayal of the sadism of Barnes Newcome, secure

---

[1] *Ibid.*, p. 288.

[2] *The Roundabout Papers*, in *The Works of William Makepeace Thackeray*, Biographical Edition (New York and London, 1899), XII, 370 (hereafter cited as *Thackeray Works*).

[3] *Ibid.*   [4] *Thackeray Letters*, III, 438.

[5] *Roundabout Papers*, in *Thackeray Works*, XII, 374-5.   [6] *Ibid.*, p. 370.

[7] *Pendennis*, in *Thackeray Works*, II, chap. LXVI, p. 663.

behind the English marriage laws, and the consequent elopement of his wife Clare with the man she loved and had been
prevented from marrying because he was not a good match—
these could hardly be 'pleasant' subjects for the domestic Laura.
She certainly would have agreed with one of her husband's
critics who wrote two years later that 'he will not let us be
comfortable. There is a perversity in this, which Mr. Thackeray,
in justice to himself and kindness to his readers should subdue.' [1]
But Thackeray would decidedly demur that his job was to
'cheer', as the critics had said; it was to tell the unpleasant
truths that society tried to cover up with pious phrases and
pleasant euphemisms, and here Thackeray places himself
squarely in the tradition of Dickens and Carlyle. Since English
social arrangements in the middle of the nineteenth century
were, he found, decidedly unsatisfactory, his role was not to
make people comfortable with them, or to try to amuse people
so that they could forget their care. To a complaint about the
ending of *Vanity Fair* he answered: 'I want to leave everybody
dissatisfied and unhappy at the end of the story—we ought all
to be with our own and all other stories.' [2] The Becky Sharps
do end up as the pillars of society and the Dobbins are blind
enough to throw all their love away on silly Amelias. [3]

Thackeray reaffirmed his creed of artistic responsibility and
integrity in the following passage from his lecture 'Charity and
Humour': 'I cannot help telling the truth as I view it, and
describing what I see. To describe it otherwise would be falsehood in that calling which it has pleased Heaven to place me;
treason to that conscience which says men are weak; that truth
must be told; that fault must be owned. . . .' [4] And if the baths
were polluted, he was the Doctor Stockman to tell the people,
even if he were to be labelled cynic.

Charlotte Brontë, although a much less complex literary
personality, deliberately linked herself with the Thackeray of
Vanity Fair at the beginning of her career as a published novelist
through the extravagant dedication to the second edition of

[1] *Westminster Review*, LIX (April, 1853), 377.
[2] *Thackeray Letters*, II, 423.
[3] 'He [Dobbin] is a fool for his pains [in] that he has married a silly little
thing and . . . has found out his error. . . .' *Ibid*.
[4] *Thackeray Works*, VII, 723.

Jane Eyre, comparing him to a Hebrew prophet—one of the views which Thackeray himself held at times about his role as a novelist. That she was a most serious and dedicated artist we know from her letters, and the development of her art from *Jane Eyre* to *Villette* can only confirm this impression. When, in 1853, she was urged by George Smith, her publisher, to finish *Villette* quickly because of the excellent state of the book market, she replied a little didactically: 'I shall get on with it as fast as is consistent with its being done, if not *well*, yet as well as I can do it—*not one whit faster*.'[1] Her stubborn artistic integrity is clear from her refusal to change *Villette* even though Smith found it depressing: 'My heroine *is* both morbid and weak at times.'[2] That was the way she envisaged her material, and when her father wanted a happy ending, the furthest she would go was to throw a slight verbal ambiguity over the sentences describing Paul's death at sea. Although she herself found the ending of Mrs. Gaskell's *Ruth* gratuitously unhappy and questioned the need for the heroine's death, which seemed to her uncalled for by the logic of the situation, she ends her letter to Mrs. Gaskell characteristically: 'And yet you must follow the impulse of your own inspiration.'[3]

An artist could be great only by being faithful to his imagination, and in true Romantic fashion, she connected the imagination with the deepest part of one's being, the unconscious. To Lewes, the first critic unequivocally to hail *Jane Eyre* as a great novel, she wrote in 1848:

If I ever *do* write another book, I think I will have nothing of what you call 'melodrama' [Lewes had cautioned her against her use of conventionally melodramatic situations]; I *think* so, but I cannot be sure. . . . When authors write best, or, at least, when they write most fluently, an influence seems to waken in them, which becomes their master—which will have its own way—putting out of view all behests but its own, dictating certain words, insisting on their being used, whether vehement or measured [she had been condemned by the *Quarterly* for being unlady-like] . . . new-moulding characters, giving unthought-of turns to incidents, rejecting carefully elaborated old ideas and suddenly creating new ones.[4]

---

[1] Clement Shorter, *The Brontës: Life and Letters* (New York, 1908), II, 254 (hereafter cited as *The Brontës*).

[2] *Ibid.*, p. 286.   [3] *Ibid.*, p. 264.   [4] *Ibid.*, I, 386.

In even more Shelleyan terms she conceived that:

> the writer who possesses the creative gift owns something of which he is not always master—something that, at times, strangely wills and works for itself. . . . Be the work grim or glorious, dread or divine, you have little choice but quiescent adoption. As for you— the nominal artist—your share in it has been to work passively under dictates you neither delivered nor could question—that would not be uttered at your prayer, nor suppressed nor chanted at your caprice.[1]

Here certainly is Shelley's fading coal, Coleridge's aeolian harp, or Le Bateau Ivre. When the daemon within every artist which he attempts to chain down by 'rules and principles' finally does break out 'haply without any warning of revolt', it can work for good or evil; once 'it sets to work on statue-hewing . . . you have a Pluto or a Jove, a Tisiphone or a Psyche, a Mermaid or a Madonna, as Fate or Inspiration direct'.[2] The important thing is never to betray one's daemon. 'Not one feeling on any subject, public or private, will I ever affect that I do not really experience.'[3]

This Romantic theory of the imagination, however, could not excuse the vague and windy rhetoric she found among the second-rate Victorian followers of the great Romantics. (And yet she could never find it in her own prose.) 'It seems now very much the custom to admire a certain wordy, intricate, obscure style of poetry, such as Elizabeth Barrett Browning writes.'[4] It was her sister Emily's poetry with its Blake-like clarity and intensity that she admired.

Since her theory of the novel put so great an emphasis on expression, passion and intensity, it was not strange that she demurred to Lewes' praise of Jane Austen as the greatest artist among the novelists, even though, as Lewes admitted, she was no poet. 'Can there be a great artist without poetry?'[5] All literary artists were to be judged by the same canons: one could not be a novelist without being a poet. It was no wonder that she greatly preferred George Sand and Balzac. After finishing *Modeste Mignon* and *Illusions Perdues* she wrote: '. . . I seemed to

---

[1] Preface, *Wuthering Heights* (New York, 1950), pp. xxxi–xxxii.
[2] *Ibid.*, p. xxxi.   [3] *The Brontës*, I, 391.   [4] *Ibid.*, II, 117.
[5] *Ibid.*, I, 388.

enter into the mystery of his craft, and to discover, with delight, where his force lay: is it not . . . in a subtle perception of the most obscure and secret working of the mind?' Even though Balzac's estimate of human nature was too low, and George Sand was too apt to be misled by her feelings, still she infinitely preferred them to Jane Austen, who, to her, seemed cold.[1]

The position of the novelist for Charlotte Brontë was as important as that of the poet for the great Romantics, and indeed, the only difference between novelist and poet was that the medium of one happened to be prose and the other verse. But poetry, in its generic sense as the voice of the imagination, was common to them both, and the novel was certainly not an inferior genre making lesser demands on author and reader, as it seemed to critics like Matthew Arnold, who, in his essay on Tolstoi, made it secondary to the crown of literature, poetry.

4. DICKENS AND CHARLES READE

Dickens' view of the novel was in many ways as Romantic as Charlotte Brontë's. His personal involvement in the world of his novels was always profound, and he wrote because something, almost an instinct, impelled him to. 'I write because I can't help it. . . .' [2] Before starting on *Bleak House* in 1851, he described himself as 'wild to begin a new book', and he speaks of 'the whirling of the story through one's mind . . . the wild necessity of beginning to write. . . .' [3] In the course of his career, however, he became increasingly aware of the need to control and discipline his amazing genius; as a matter of fact, emphasis on careful craftsmanship, method, technique and form became a dominant concern in his theory of the novel, as we shall see in the next chapter. (This kind of development seemed to be inherent in English Romanticism, as the careers of Wordsworth, Keats, Shelley, and Byron show.) In a letter of 1857 to an aspiring novelist, Emily Jolly, Dickens wrote revealingly:

I am inclined to think that you do not discipline yourself enough. When one is impelled to write this or that, one has still to consider:

[1] *Ibid.*, II, 175.
[2] *The Letters of Charles Dickens*, ed. Walter Dexter (London, 1938), I, 546 (hereafter cited as *Dickens Letters*).
[3] *Ibid.*, II, 348–9.

'How much of this will tell for what I mean? How much of it is my own wild emotion and superfluous energy—how much remains that is truly belonging to this ideal character of these ideal circumstances [the world of the novel]?' It is in the laborious struggle to make this distinction, and in the determination to try for it, that the road to the correction of faults lies.

He added in an extremely important parenthesis at the end: 'Perhaps I may remark, in support of the sincerity with which I write this, that I am an impatient and impulsive person myself, but that it has been for many years the constant effort of my life to practise at my desk what I preach to you.' [1]

That he did learn more and more to control the direct and sometimes obsessive expression of his own purely personal emotions and to use them for the illumination of the central theme and organizing principle of a created fictional world, as in the later novels, we have more evidence than the letter to Miss Jolly. One need only compare the death scene of Paul Dombey with that of Jo in *Bleak House*, or David's childhood in relation to the whole of *David Copperfield* with Pip's childhood in relation to the whole of *Great Expectations* to see the direction of Dickens' development.

It follows that in his discussions of the novel he stressed the need for hard work, the effort of wrestling with one's material. He praises one of Collins' stories in a letter of 1855: 'An excellent story, charmingly written, and showing everywhere an amount of pains and study in respect to the art of doing such things that I see mighty seldom,' [2] and in another letter:

It is delightful to find throughout that you have taken great pains with it [Basil] . . . and have 'gone at it' with a perfect knowledge of the jolter-headedness of the conceited idiots who suppose that volumes are to be tossed off like pancakes, and that any writing can be done without the utmost application, the greatest patience, and the steadiest energy of which the writer is capable.[3]

This statement, made during the composition of *Bleak House*, is especially significant of his own attitude towards his craft at this time.

Dickens disliked dilettantes, and his contempt for them is

[1] *Dickens Letters*, II, p. 850.
[2] *Ibid.*, p. 643.   [3] *Ibid.*, p. 436.

made permanent in the figures of Harold Skimpole and Henry Gowan. The reasons he gave to a correspondent to avoid an unpleasant meeting with her are thus much more than an excuse made with tongue in cheek. He was deadly serious when he wrote:

I hold my inventive capacity on the stern condition that it must master my whole life, often have complete possession of me, make its own demands on me, and sometimes for months together put everything else away from me. If I had not known long ago that my place could never be held unless I were at any moment ready to devote myself to it entirely, I should have dropped out of it very soon. . . . Whoever is devoted to an Art must be content to deliver himself wholly up to it, and to find his recompense in it.[1]

It was for this reason that in his otherwise admiring obituary article on Thackeray in *The Cornhill*, he introduced the reservation that Thackeray's work suffered because of his dilettante pose: 'He too much feigned a want of earnestness and . . . he made a pretence of undervaluing his art, which was not good for the art he held in trust. . . .'[2] It was said that Henry Gowan was created with Thackeray in mind.

Dickens insisted again and again on the dignity and seriousness of his calling. 'Every day of my life I feel more and more that to be thoroughly in earnest is everything, and to be anything short of it is nothing.'[3] But if he was a careful and devoted artist, it evidently was not in the later sense of a c aftsman carefully polishing work addressed only to himself or at best the few people who could understand him. He could never have agreed with James's opinion, born out of desperation with his own dwindling audience in the eighties and nineties, in 'Greville Fane' and similar short stories about writers, that the

[1] *Ibid.*, p. 649.

[2] *Cornhill Magazine*, IX (February, 1864), 130.

[3] *Dickens Letters*, II, 712. His sense of his position as an artist forced him to decline the honour of an invitation to the Lord Mayor's dinner as the representative of literature. Since he had already expressed in print in *Household Words* the absurdity of the whole City Corporation as an anachronism, he said, 'I do not think it consistent with my respect for myself, or for the art I profess . . . to laugh at the institution in print, and accept the hospitality of its representative while the ink is staring us all in the face. There is a great deal too much of this among us, and it does not elevate the earnestness or delicacy of literature.' *Ibid.*, p. 637.

greater the writer, necessarily the smaller the audience; or with Pater that the literary artist was a scholar writing to scholars; or with Huysmans, that one writes for a sympathetic audience of ten. Dickens' view was always that the novelist should address the entire literate nation, and the great writer must be a popular writer. As editor, he wrote to one of his contributors, 'I particularly entreat you to consider the catastrophe. You write to be read, of course. The close of the story is unnecessarily painful— will throw off numbers of persons who would otherwise read it, and who (as it stands) will be deterred by hearsay from doing so, and is so tremendous a piece of severity, that it will defeat your purpose.' [1] He complained to Wills, his subeditor, of Mrs. Gaskell's penchant for unhappy endings, 'I wish to Heaven her people would keep a little firmer on their legs!' [2] and to Mrs. Gaskell herself that the death of the wife in the 'Heart of John Middleton' is 'an unnecessary infliction of pain upon the reader, not justified by the necessities of the story'. [3] Mrs. Gaskell agreed. In his own novels, more than once he sacrificed a plan that afterwards seemed too distressing for his readers—the most famous being the 'unhappy' ending of *Great Expectations*.

In the same spirit he disliked novels that lacked humanity, or as he called it, 'tenderness'. When he re-read *Robinson Crusoe* in 1856, he recorded: 'There is not in literature a more surprising instance of the utter want of tenderness and sentiment [sentiment as feeling], than the death of Friday. It is as heartless as *Gil Blas*, in a very different and far more serious way.' [4] Smollett's *Peregrine Pickle* and *Roderick Random* were 'both extraordinarily good in their way, which is a way without tenderness . . .',[5] and for this reason he preferred Cervantes, Fielding, and Goldsmith.

Dickens believed as firmly as Wordsworth that the basis of imaginative power was joy, and 'Joy in Commonalty spread' should be the result of his own work. During the most unhappy period of his life, immediately following the separation from his wife, he wrote to Miss Coutts, 'As to my art, I have as great a delight in it as the most enthusiastic of my readers; and the

---

[1] *Dickens Letters*, II, p. 679.   [2] *Ibid.*, p. 250.
[3] Annette B. Hopkins, 'Dickens and Mrs. Gaskell', *Huntington Library Quarterly*, IX (1946), 361.
[4] *Dickens Letters*, II, 768.   [5] *Ibid.*, p. 560.

sense of my trust and responsibility in that wise, is always upon
me when I take pen in hand. If *I* were soured, I should still
try to sweeten the lives and fancies of others, but I am not—
not at all.' [1]

This is not to say that art should help man escape from
unhappy reality; on the contrary, one of the primary functions
of art is to help transform the world by changing public opinion.
Indeed Dickens was, among other things, one of Shaw's artist-
propagandists. In *David Copperfield*, for example, the Little Emily
episode was included chiefly to illustrate how 'the return to
virtue' was 'cruelly cut off' by England's social mores in respect
to 'fallen women'. He wanted 'to put it before the thoughts of
people in a new and pathetic way, and perhaps to do some
good'. [2] Attacks on specific abuses of the time, such as imprisonment for debt, the Yorkshire schools, the administration of the
New Poor Law, run through his novels from *Pickwick* to *Our
Mutual Friend*, but he came more and more to realize that more
fundamental changes were needed. *Hard Times* is directed at a
whole world outlook: 'My satire is against those who see figures
and averages, and nothing else . . .', [3] against a total failure of
imagination. 'It contains what I do devoutly hope will shake
some people in a terrible mistake of these days. . . .' [4] If we
recall that in Shelley's *Defence of Poetry*, the secret of morals,
on which equitable social arrangements must rest, was the
imagination, and that the key to the imagination was art, we
can easily see Dickens as a direct inheritor of the English
Romantic tradition. It was the great novelists even more than
the poets of the Victorian period who inherited the prophetic
fervour of the poets of the early part of the century.

The importance for Dickens of the theme of *Hard Times* can
be graphically seen in an account of the way he came to write
it: 'I intended to do nothing in that way [novel writing] for a
year, when the idea laid hold of me by the throat in a very
violent manner. . . .' [5] If one considers *Hard Times*, however,
to be a kind of sport among Dickens' works, the only one with
which he had a serious moral involvement, then clearly he fails

[1] Edgar Johnson, ed., *The Heart of Charles Dickens* (New York and
Boston, 1952), p. 370.
[2] *Dickens Letters*, II, 194.
[3] *Ibid.*, p. 620.   [4] *Ibid.*, p. 567.   [5] *Ibid.*, p. 602.

to understand the import of all the novels from *Bleak House* on. Dr. Leavis' statement in *The Great Tradition*, 'But . . . [his] genius was that of a great entertainer, and he had for the most part no profounder responsibility as a creative artist than this description suggests' [1] is absurd in the light of both Dickens' novels and the statements to be found in his letters and *Household Words* and *All the Year Round*.

After the publication of *Little Dorrit* with its satire on the entire English administrative system as the Circumlocution Office, James Fitzjames Stephen attacked the novel in the *Saturday Review* of July 4, 1857, ridiculing Dickens' assumption of the prophetic office. 'We admit that Mr. Dickens has a mission, but it is to make the world grin, not to recreate and rehabilitate society.' [2] He further amplified his arguments in the July issue of the *Edinburgh Review*, vehemently opposing the whole idea that novelists can deal with any serious subjects at all, 'subjects which properly belong to the intellect'. Since the novelist appealed 'almost entirely to the imagination', Dickens in *Little Dorrit* was obviously a charlatan. (For Coleridge the mere understanding—the logical faculty without the imagination—was powerless to arrive at any truth. The reason alone—the whole man thinking and feeling—could attain new knowledge.) Only in a social or political treatise could one treat social or political problems. 'The ordinary domestic relations are the legitimate province of novels.' [3] The *Saturday Review* again attacked Dickens on July 11, this time as a subversive, along with Charles Reade, who had recently treated the system of penal discipline in *It is Never Too Late to Mend*. The two were described as 'writers who are to society what rats and worms are to a ship's bottom'. [4] (But that there was some sort of administrative breakdown during the Crimean War should have been obvious even to the most superficial observer, as the career of Florence Nightingale and the unsuccessful efforts of Sidney Herbert to reform the War Office made clear.) 'The business of professional writers of light literature [apparently all imaginative literature] is to amuse the public, but they seem to shrink from such a conclusion as being unwelcome and degrading,'

---

[1] F. R. Leavis, *The Great Tradition* (New York, 1954), pp. 31–2.
[2] IV, 15.   [3] *Edinburgh Review*, CVI (July, 1857), 125–6.
[4] *Saturday Review*, IV, 34.

like pastry cooks ashamed of their profession and so forced to make preposterous claims for cookery.[1] There were two more slashing attacks that year before the *Saturday Review* considered itself finished with *Little Dorrit*: two articles entitled '*The Edinburgh Review* and the Modern Novelists' and 'Mr. Dickens as a Politician', the latter again written by Stephen.[2] Leslie Stephen, in the biography of his brother, partly explained Fitzjames' anger on the ground that he thought the Tite Barnacles had been intended to stand for their father, Sir James Stephen, and his best friends.[3] But one can also see in these attacks a recrudescence of the old Evangelical hatred of novels, especially when one remembers the connection between the Stephen family and Clapham.

Dickens felt himself forced to answer the *Edinburgh* article—those in the *Saturday Review* he studiously ignored—in his own periodical, *Household Words*, by vindicating his profession and incidentally his patriotism. Stephen had called his *Little Dorrit* un-English ('In "Little Dorrit" Russia is set up as the pattern for England') and saw it tending towards the French kind of 'literature of desperation', which paves the way 'to profligate morals, religious scepticism, and political tyranny, just as surely as drinking produces *delirium tremens*'.[4] In the *Saturday Review*, unconsciously prefiguring Mr. Podsnap, he had said, 'There is not, and there probably never was, a nation in the world which more truly feared and served God, or more nobly ruled man, than the English nation of which Mr. Dickens and his admirers ridicule and revile all the most important members.'[5] Dickens in his answer pointed out that he and Reade were attacked 'for not confining themselves to the mere amusement of their readers, and for testifying in their works that they seriously feel the interest of true Englishmen in the welfare and honour of their country'.[6] The charge had been made that his novel was

---

[1] *Ibid.*, p. 35.

[2] According to Merle Bevington, *The Saturday Review, 1855–1868* (New York, 1941), p. 379.

[3] Leslie Stephen, *The Life of Sir James Fitzjames Stephen* (London, 1895), p. 159.

[4] *Edinburgh Review*, CVI (July, 1857), 152.

[5] *Saturday Review*, IV (July 11, 1857), 35.

[6] 'A Curious Misprint in the *Edinburgh Review*', *Household Words*, XVI (August 1, 1857), 97.

25.

formless and that he thought up the collapse of the Clennam house only after *The Times* had carried the story of a similar occurrence on Tottenham Court Road. His answer vindicated his method of carefully planning his novels before he started writing them; the catastrophe had been thought out from the beginning 'with a painful minuteness and reiterated care of preparation, the necessity of which (in order that the thread may be kept in the reader's mind through nearly two years), is one of the adverse incidents of that [the instalment] form of publication'.[1]

All the Year Round, the successor to *Household Words*, was later to carry a vigorous protest against the attempt to restrict the subject matter of novels to ordinary domestic relations. 'Why is all art to be restricted to the uniform level of quiet domesticity? . . . the actual world contains something more than family life.' The novel is as great an art form as any that has yet appeared, and capable of the greatest effects of tragedy. 'Whenever humanity wrestles with the gods of passion and pain, there, of necessity, is that departure from our diurnal platitudes which the cant of existing criticism denounces. . . .' Like Bulwer-Lytton (Dickens was probably to some extent influenced by his writing), Dickens claimed the greatest subjects for the novelist: 'The mystery of evil is as interesting to us now as it was in the time of SHAKESPEARE; and it is downright affectation or effeminacy to say that we are never to glance into that abyss, but are perpetually to construct our novels out of the amenities of respectable, easy-going men and women.' [2]

---

[1] 'A Curious Misprint in the *Edinburgh Review*', *Household Words*, XVI (August 1, 1857), p. 97.

[2] 'The Sensational Williams', *All the Year Round*, XI (February 13, 1864), 14–15. Although this essay and the succeeding one I quote from, 'The Spirit of Fiction', are not listed in K. G. Kitton, *The Minor Writings of Charles Dickens: A Bibliography* (London, 1900), Dickens claimed direct responsibility for everything printed in his periodicals: 'The statements and opinions of this Journal generally, are, of course, to be received as the statements and opinions of its Conductor.' *All the Year Round*, X (December 26, 1863), 419. He carefully read almost everything he printed in *Household Words* and *All the Year Round* and often rewrote other contributors' essays so that it would be impossible to tell exactly which sentences Dickens wrote and which he did not. The only exceptions to this rule were works of fiction 'first published in these pages as a serial story, with the name of an eminent writer attached to it'. In that case only, Dickens said, 'I do not consider

All the Year Round, three years later, was to rest its defence of the novel and Dickens' own methods as a novelist on new grounds. In 'The Spirit of Fiction' the function of the novel is to make available in concrete form the expression of human ideals and aspirations. The novel was the result of the way the writer perceived and organized his experience, and its chief value was that each author could report his own conception of reality from his point of view, so that there would be as many different kinds of novels as there were novelists. 'Mr. Wilkie Collins and Mr. George MacDonald would vary extremely in the treatment of similar characters and events; George Eliot and Mrs. Gaskell would make the most opposite use of the same material . . . we are all partly creators of the objects we perceive. . . .' [1] As Henry James was later to write, 'The house of fiction has . . . not one window, but a million—a number of possible windows not to be reckoned rather; every one of which has been pierced, or is still pierceable, in its vast front, by the need of the individual vision and by the pressure of the individual will.' [2]

According to *All the Year Round,* because of the great differences that exist between 'the common observer and the writer of genius', the former always 'accuses the latter of intentional exaggeration, substitution, addition, and has never been able in society to see the startling phenomena which he condemns in romance as melodramatic and unnatural. The reason is, that such an individual has never developed the sense required for seeing such things; and, because he is partially blind, he accuses his informant of wilful invention.' [3] (It is a pity this statement is not better known, for it provides the definitive answer to the foolish charges still reiterated that Dickens exaggerates and that his characters are only caricatures.) The artist, here specifically the novelist, is the man whose vision can 'see into the heart of

myself at liberty to exercise that control over his text which I claim as to other contributions.' See Monroe Engels, 'Dickens on Art', *MP,* LIII (1955), 25–36. Dickens always refused to print articles he disagreed with, and in assigning subjects to his staff writers, he often suggested the manner of treatment. Both periodicals very clearly reflect Dickens' own ideas.

[1] *All the Year Round,* XVIII (July 27, 1867), 119.
[2] Preface to *The Portrait of a Lady,* in *The Art of the Novel,* ed. R. K. Blackmuir (New York, 1934), p. 46.
[3] *All the Year Round,* XVIII, 120.

things' and who can communicate his vision of the truth to his readers. The understanding alone cannot deal with reality because it cannot pierce through the surface of things and because only the imagination can unify the many disparate facts of experience to make sense out of them. 'Facts, as they are called, from their very abundance, have to be refunded into the unity of the principle of which they are examples; and this, once declared, has a tendency to impersonation. . . .' [1] The literary artist alone can make the multiplicity of man's environment—all the disparate facts making up the phenomenon called society—meaningful to him. The novelist gives his readers a total vision of the world of the sort Dickens gave to his readers in *Our Mutual Friend, Little Dorrit,* and *Bleak House.* But Dickens never believed he created microcosms of society for their own sake or their own intrinsic beauty. They were given to his reader so that he could understand his world and so change it. Gradgrind and his family were crushed to pieces because they had no such unifying vision, no imagination. Facts for him were hard irreducible things which could never be acted upon, could never 'be refunded into the unity of principle of which they were examples'.

If Dickens' conception of his art came a long way from the reforming of specific abuses, Charles Reade, who thought of himself as a follower of Dickens and a continuer of his work, never did change his rather primitive view of himself as a crusading journalist. His most typical novels all had very specific targets: e.g. *It Is Never Too Late to Mend* aimed to reform the English penal system; *Hard Cash* exposed the abuses of private madhouses; *Put Yourself In His Place* revealed the underhand methods used by labour unions. His criterion for judging his own novels was usually: did they bring about the changes he demanded? and he ended his career as a publicist rather than a novelist, attacking injustices directly in the newspapers. In effect, then, he was a kind of precursor of the American muckrakers and crusaders of the late nineteenth and twentieth centuries.

Whenever Reade was accused of exaggerating the conditions he exposed, he could always point to his tremendous collection of notebooks, consisting of newspaper clippings. Every one of

[1] *All the Year Round,* XVIII, 120.

his novels was severely documented, and so he called them matter-of-fact romances. *Hard Cash* was 'a fiction built on truths; and these truths have been gathered . . . from a multitude of volumes, pamphlets, journals, reports, blue-books, manuscript narratives, letters, and living people. . . .' [1] We are here in a completely different world from that of 'The Spirit of Fiction'. Reade thought of the novel as a vehicle for exposé, and his own novels, aside from the reforming sections, usually consisted of a mélange of the most conventional material from Adelphi melodrama: stagy villains foiled at the last moment, hidden wills suddenly found, exciting encounters with pirate ships, and hairbreadth escapes. His formula was to crowd as much exciting incident as possible into one story so that his reader would be in a perpetual state of suspense. (This part of Reade later became the staple of Grade C movies, especially the old Saturday afternoon serial.) Reade's grandiose claims to be an important critic and artist simply do not hold up: 'I studied the great art of Fiction closely for fifteen years before I presumed to write a line of it. I was a ripe critic long before I became an artist. My critical knowledge has directed my art, but the practice of that has not diminished my studies.' [2] As Malcolm Elwin, his extremely sympathetic biographer, says: 'He had no standards, no detachment, none of the balance and reasoned insight of the critical mind.' [3] As far as his claims to art go, here was one case where a Victorian novelist was no more than a purveyor of entertainment.

5. TROLLOPE

Trollope's concept of the novel is probably the best known of the Victorian period, chiefly because of the relative popularity of his *Autobiography*. As a result, his theories are often taken as representative of those of the period and give it a rather false air of complete 'critical innocence'.[4] Trollope was by no means

---

[1] Preface, *Hard Cash*, Library Edition (London, 1913).

[2] Malcolm Elwin, *Charles Reade* (London, 1934), p. 261.   [3] *Ibid.*

[4] The phrase is Bradford Booth's in 'Trollope on the Novel', *Essays Critical and Historical Dedicated to Lily B. Campbell*, by Members of the English Department of the University of California (Berkeley and Los Angeles, 1950), p. 219.

prepared to make the same sort of claims for his art that Dickens or George Eliot made, though, as he says in his *Autobiography*, he had once intended to write a book 'to vindicate my own profession as a novelist . . .' because of 'a conviction that there still exists among us Englishmen a prejudice in respect of novels . . .' and because there is still wanting to novelists 'a just appreciation of the excellence of their calling. . . .' [1] His defence was based on the ground that the novel presented object lessons in conduct. Girls learned from novels that modesty is the best policy; they learn 'what is expected from them, and what they are to expect when lovers come . . .' and young men learn to be thrifty, industrious and honest so that they can get on in the world. [2] But these unpleasant pills must be sugared, or they would savour too much of sermons, which young people avoid: 'The palpable and overt dose the child rejects; but that which is cunningly insinuated by the aid of jam or honey is accepted unconsciously, and goes upon its curative mission. So it is with the novel' [3]—and so on just like Day of *Sanford and Merton*, or Maria Edgeworth of the *Moral Tales*. Trollope vindicates the major novelists of his day—Dickens, Thackeray, and George Eliot—by asking, 'Can anyone . . . find a scene, a passage, a word [in their works] that would teach a girl to be immodest, or a man to be dishonest?' [4]

The lessons of fiction must 'appertain chiefly to the intercourse between young men and young women'. [5] Hence the need for the one or more pair of young lovers in every novel and the absolute prescription that the centre of any novel be a love story, and that the novel be written 'for the sake of the love story'. Novels 'have other attractions and deal with every phase of life; but the other attractions hang around and depend on the love story, as planets depend upon the sun'. [6] (It would, of course, be very easy to prove that this statement does not hold true—just as the sugared pill theory does not either—of many of Trollope's best novels, e.g. *The Warden, Barchester Towers, The Way We Live Now, The Eustace Diamonds*, and *He Knew He Was Right*.)

[1] (Berkeley and Los Angeles, 1947), pp. 180–1.   [2] *Ibid.*, pp. 183–4.
[3] Anthony Trollope, *Thackeray* (New York, n.d.), p. 199.
[4] *Autobiography*, p. 186.   [5] *Ibid.*
[6] Trollope, *Four Lectures*, ed. Morris L. Parrish (London, 1938), p. 108.

The novel for Trollope is necessarily inferior as a genre because it is written in prose. 'By the common consent of all mankind who have read, poetry takes the highest place in literature.' The novelist does not 'dream that the poet's honour is in his reach. . . .' Apparently Trollope would be forced into saying that *The Faerie Queene* was a greater work than *Don Quixote*, merely because the latter happened to be in prose; apparently he would also agree with De Quincey that all novels were necessarily ephemeral because the novelist had to adapt himself to his age. 'In his own age', Trollope wrote, 'he can have great effect for good or evil; but we know as yet of no prose novelist who has influenced after ages. . . . I fear that the novelist can expect no centuries of popularity. But the poet adapts himself to all ages by the use of language and scenes which are not ephemeral.' [1] Since their works could not last, why spend great pains on them? was the natural question for novelists to ask.

As a matter of fact the novel could not really be considered a work of art at all, but merely a superior kind of amusement. 'We must remember,' Trollope told the audience at his lecture 'On English Prose Fiction as a Rational Amusement', 'that novel reading is an amusement', and like all amusements must not be indulged in too much, [2] and in the essay 'Novel Reading' in the *Nineteenth Century* of January, 1879, he calls the novel 'the recognized amusement of our lighter hours, too often our mainstay in literature. . . .' [3] The ratio between amusement and moral lesson occasionally varies in Trollope's critical writing. Sometimes the emphasis is on the word *instruct*, and *amuse* is in the subordinate clause: 'The object of a novel should be to instruct in morals while it amuses,' [4] but more often the emphasis falls on the word *amuse*: 'A novel, if it fatigues is unpardonable. Its only excuse is to be found in the amusement it affords. It should instruct also, no doubt. . . .' [5]

Trollope may have been doubtful about the real importance of the novel as art, but he disliked Thackeray's frequent affectation that it did not matter at all. 'I am inclined to think that his most besetting sin in style . . . is a certain affected familiarity. He indulges too frequently in little confidences with individual

[1] *Autobiography*, p. 181. [2] *Four Lectures*, p. 111. [3] V, 26.
[4] *Thackeray*, p. 107. [5] *Ibid.*, p. 187.

readers, in which pretended allusions to himself are frequent
. . . they cause an absence of that dignity to which even a novel
may aspire.' He goes on to say that each aside seems like 'a
detached bit' and so robs the book of 'its integrity, by a certain
good-humoured geniality of language, which causes the reader
to be almost too much as home with his author. . . . Familiarity
breeds contempt, and I have been sometimes inclined to think
that our author has failed to stand up for himself. . . .' [1]

By far the most famous of all Trollope's statements on his
own art is related to his own peculiar methods of work: the
daily tasks he set himself, the way he would start a new book
on the day he finished the old one. 'I have allotted myself so
many pages a week. The average number has been about 40.
It has been placed as low as 20, and has risen to 112. And as
page is an ambiguous term, my page has been made to contain 250 words . . . I have had every word counted as I went.' [2]
Insisting on this same point, he wrote to a friend that any man
with good education and good intellect can become a successful
novelist. 'I believe that the profession requires much less of
what is extraordinary either in genius and knowledge than most
outsiders presume to be necessary. But it requires that which all
other professions require . . . much hard grinding industry——
My belief of book writing is much the same as my belief as to
shoemaking.' [3] His undervaluing of genius or what amounts to
the same thing was probably due to his own very sure gift.
Since he could write novels if he forced himself to sit so many
hours at his desk, then anyone could.

But there was another side to the picture which most people
forget, Trollope's tremendous ability to immerse himself in his
imaginative world, to live in it during the time when he was not
actually writing. And when he speaks of this part of his life,
his criticism gains such dignity that the preceding statements
seem almost to come from another pen. 'To think of a story is
much harder than to write it. The author can sit down with the
pen in his hand for a given time, and produce a certain number
of words. That is comparatively easy. . . . But to think it over as
you lie in bed, or walk about, or sit cosily over your fire, to

---

[1] *Thackeray*, pp. 197–8.   [2] *Autobiography*, p. 101.
[3] *The Letters of Anthony Trollope*, ed. Bradford Allen Booth (London, 1951),
p. 57 (hereafter cited as *Trollope Letters*).

turn it all in your thoughts, and make the things fit——' there
is the really difficult job of the novelist. 'The arrangement of
the words is as though you were walking simply along a road.
The arrangement of your story is as though you were carrying a
sack of flour while you walked.' [1]

One becomes a novelist because, in James' phrase, he is 'an
inexhaustible sensibility', or, as Trollope puts it, he has 'been
drawing in matter from all that he has seen and heard'. 'But',
Trollope characteristically asserts, 'this has not been done
without labour, even when the labour has been unconscious.' [2]
He was really very much aware that being a great novelist
required special gifts of imagination and observation—but he
insisted that it also required much hard work.

The aim of the novelist must be

to make his readers so intimately acquainted with his characters
that the creatures of his brain should be to them speaking, moving,
living, human creatures. This he can never do unless he knows those
fictitious personages himself, and he can never know them unless
he can live with them in the full reality of established intimacy. . . .
He must learn to hate and to love them. He must argue with them,
quarrel with them, forgive them, and even submit to them. . . .
The depth and the breadth, the narrowness and the shallowness of
each should be clear to him.

And he goes on to insist he knows 'the tone of the voice, and
the colour of the hair, every flame of the eye, and the clothes
they wear'. [3] The novelist who can not 'give his mind to that
work of observation and reception [sic] from which has come
his power, without which work his power cannot be continued',
who does not write because 'he has a story to tell' rather than
because 'he has to tell a story' can only produce 'one piece of
stiff mechanism' in which 'the characters do not live and move,
but are cut out of blocks and are propped against the wall'. [4]

Though Trollope in many passages would prescribe any real
intensity of emotion, and tragic greatness to novel writers—'for
the sublime we look rather to poetry than to prose . . .'—and
though the best course of the novelist is the middle one, between
the burlesque and the sublime, [5] he was not always consistent.

[1] *Thackeray*, p. 120.　　　　[2] *Autobiography*, pp. 194-5.
[3] *Ibid.*, pp. 192-3.　　　　[4] *Ibid.*, p. 193.
[5] *Thackeray*, pp. 183-4. He defined the sublime as 'an attempt . . . to
soar above the ordinary actions and ordinary language of life'. *Ibid.*, p. 185.

'As in poetry, so in prose, he who can deal adequately with tragic elements is a greater artist, and reaches a higher aim than the writer whose efforts never carry him above the mild walks of every day life.' [1] With this sentence so much of Trollope's theorizing is negated. If novels can give the effect of great tragedy, their defence rests obviously on other grounds than sweetening unpleasant moral lessons, and they are more than mere amusement for 'our lighter hours'.

In practice Trollope certainly does not always keep to ordinary people and ordinary actions, especially in the angry satire of *The Way We Live Now* and *The Eustace Diamonds* and the history of such strange and terrible self-tormentors as the Reverend Josiah Crawley and Louis Trevelyan. But the frightening thing about these characters is that we see how easily we can become like them, for Trollope presents us with 'the men and women among whom we really live,—men and women such as we are ourselves,—in order that we should know what are the exact failings which oppress ourselves. . . .' [2] By immersing us in the story of the breakdown of Trevelyan, we learn more about what Trollope called 'the perversity of the human mind'.[3] Thus, the best part of his work is, in effect, directed towards his own and his reader's self-knowledge, and not amusement in the sense of escape from oneself.

6. GEORGE MEREDITH

With George Meredith the idea of self-knowledge becomes the chief purpose of novel writing. In a much-quoted letter to George Pierce Baker, one of the few letters published in which Meredith discusses his own work, he writes that the end of the novel is to expose and illustrate 'the natural history of man'.[4] This task was especially necessary since in England such

a large body . . . have a sentimental objection to face the study of

---

[1] This passage appears in three places in Trollope's writings: *Autobiography*, p. 190; 'Novel Reading', *Nineteenth Century*, V (January, 1879), 43; *Four Lectures*, p. 123.

[2] From *Ralph the Heir*, quoted in Booth, 'Trollope on the Novel', p. 226.

[3] *He Knew He Was Right*, World's Classics (New York, 1948), p. 364.

[4] George Meredith, *Letters*, ed. William Maxse Meredith (New York, 1912), II, 398 (hereafter cited as *Meredith Letters*).

the actual world. They take up disdain of it, when its truths appear humiliating; when the facts are not immediately forced on them, they take up the pride of incredulity. They live in a hazy atmosphere that they suppose an ideal one. . . . You may distinguish them by a favourite phrase: 'Surely we are not so bad!' and the remark: 'If that is human nature save us from it!'—as if it could be done. . . .[1]

Meredith's novels are directed at these people 'who will not see', and his favourite method was, of course, intellectual comedy, 'finely tempered, showing sunlight of the mind'. Whenever the comic spirit, the spirit informing his most typical novels, sees men

out of proportion, overblown, affected, pretentious, bombastical, hypocritical, pedantic, fantastically delicate; whenever it sees them self-deceived or hoodwinked, given to run riot in idolatries, drifting into vanities . . . planning short-sightedly, plotting dementedly, whenever they are at variance with their professions, and violate the unwritten but perceptible laws binding them in consideration one to another,

it is the use of comedy to unmask them and show them what they truly are by 'thoughtful laughter'.[2]

Science can not help man in this job of knowing himself; all it can show is his relation to the other animals. 'Arts is the specific. We have little to learn of apes. . . . The chief consideration for us is, what particular practise of Art in letters is the best for the perusal of the Book of our common wisdom; so that with clearer minds and livelier manners we may escape, as it were, into daylight and song from a land of fog-horns.'[3] The science of Meredith's day, mechanistic physics and Darwinian biology, in denying man's humanity, also denied his freedom, and any psychology which relied on science would do the same thing. 'Men instructed in the analysis of motives arrive at this dangerous conclusion. . . . It allows them to think they are of such a compound, and must necessarily act in that manner.'[4]

---

[1] George Meredith, 'An Essay on Comedy', in *Comedy*, ed. Wylie Sypher (New York, 1956), pp. 13–14.

[2] *Ibid.*, p. 48.

[3] *The Egoist*, Memorial Edition (New York, 1910), I, 3.

[4] From *The Amazing Marriage*, quoted in Jack Lindsay, *George Meredith, His Life and Work* (London, 1956), p. 322.

But the duty of the poet and novelist is to reaffirm human freedom in the face of scientific determinism and show man that he can control his own actions through knowledge.

If the novelist completely discards the superficial psychology of the mid-nineteenth century, he must formulate his own, which Meredith calls 'Philosophy'. 'If we do not speedily embrace Philosophy in fiction, the Art is doomed to extinction . . .' because the real subject matter of novels is the human mind, 'internal history'.[1]

At key moments in the novel *Sandra Belloni*, a figure called the Philosopher replaces the narrator and explains the motivation of the characters. For instance, when Wilfred Pole flees Emilia because of his fear of life, the Philosopher explains that most novelists would say, ' "None know why." . . . I must own . . . that I do know why. I know why, and, unfortunately for me, I have to tell what I know. If I do not tell, this narrative is so constituted that there will be no moral to it. . . . The springs that moved Wilfred upon the present occasion were simple. We will strip him of his heroic trappings . . . and show them.' [2] In none of his novels would Meredith have considered his task accomplished if he could not have shown the motives for every act, though he rarely resorts to so awkward a device as the intruding Philosopher.

It was for his subtlety in psychological analysis that Meredith particularly admired Stendhal at a time (1861) when he was rarely read in England. 'I think de Stendhal very subtle and observant. He goes over ground that I know.' [3] He called George Eliot 'the greatest of female writers' for the same quality in a letter of advice to a young novelist and further urged her to read Stendhal so that she would learn 'the best fiction is the fruit of a well-trained mind'.[4] Hawthorne, however, he did not like, though he would not deny his power. 'His deliberate analysis, . . . the sentience rather than the drawings which he gives you of his characters, and the luscious, morbid tone, are all effective.' [5] But his subjects were too special:

---

[1] *Diana of the Crossways*, Memorial Edition (New York, 1910), I, 17–19.

[2] *Sandra Belloni*, Memorial Edition (New York, 1910), I, 110–11.

[3] *Meredith Letters*, I, 57. For Stendhal's reputation in England, see Doris Gunnell, *Stendhal et l'Angleterre* (Paris, 1908).

[4] *Meredith Letters*, I, 163. [5] *Ibid.*, p. 168.

As regards Hawthorne, little Meredith admits that your strokes have truth. I strive by study of humanity to represent it, not its morbid action. I have a tendency to do that, which I repress; for, in delineating it, there is no gain. In all my, truly, very faulty works, there is this aim. Much of my strength lies in painting morbid emotion, and exceptional positions; but my conscience will not let me so waste my time. . . . My love is for epical subjects—not for cobwebs in a putrid corner; though I know the fascination of unravelling them.[1]

He thought Hawthorne's novels undramatic; the characters were simply projections of Hawthorne himself and had no independent life. 'Their power lies in the intensity of his egoistical perceptions, and [his delineations] are not the perfect view of men and women.' [2] But the belief that the 'perfect view of men and women' can avoid morbid emotions and putrid cobwebs is a very difficult one to demonstrate. Certainly the greatest English novelists of the period found themselves more and more drawn to characters and subjects Meredith would have labelled morbid (the 'sensation novel' of the sixties was merely a vulgarization of the same tendency). Needless to say, as Jack Lindsay points out, Meredith's criticism of Hawthorne would condemn the entire development of the European novel from Dostoievsky on.[3]

The study of mankind through the novel was not, however, to be made for its own sake. In the letter to Professor Baker (of Harvard) already quoted,[4] Meredith affirms: 'I think that all right use of life, and the one secret of life, is to pave ways for the firmer footing of those who succeed us; as to my works, I know them faulty, think of them worth only when they point and aid to that end. Close knowledge of our fellows, discernment of the laws of existence, these lead to great civilization.' [5] And in the 'Prelude' to The Egoist he calls comedy 'the ultimate civilizer, the polisher' which corrects 'the vestiges of rawness and grossness to be found among us'.[6] It is through his blind selfishness, egoism as Meredith defines and analyses it in his novels, masked by sentimentality, that man is forced back towards the savagery from which he has only half emerged. Meredith points to the condition of women and the injustices of

---

[1] Ibid., p. 171.   [2] Ibid., p. 168.   [3] George Meredith, p. 142.
[4] See above, p. 34.   [5] Meredith Letters, II, 398.   [6] The Egoist, I, 4.

the mid-Victorian class system—the work of men's selfishness—
as signs of the continuing brutishness of English society. Furthermore it is a dull society. It has no life because of the English
tendency towards conformity, and it suffers from 'the malady of
sameness, our modern malady'. 'Why to be alive, to be quick in
the soul, there should be diversity in the companion-throbs of
your pulses. Interrogate them. They lump along like the lob-
legs of Dobbin the horse. . . . Monstrous monotony has en-
folded us as with the arms of Amphitrite.' [1]

Once the evolutionary force has produced creatures capable
of intelligence and self-knowledge, it no longer has to operate
blindly and inhumanly only through 'the survival of the fittest'.
Man controls his own future, and foremost among the means for
controlling and directing it is art, 'the ultimate civilizer'.

Even though for Meredith the novel has a great social mission
and is not autotelic, it must not be didactic in the narrow sense,
as he insisted in his role as reader for Chapman and Hall. The
end of a novel, he reiterated, must arise inevitably and con-
vincingly from the initial situation and the given characters. [2]
The characters determine the action; the plot is not something
imposed on the characters, and in *Sandra Belloni* he pointed
'proudly to the fact that our people . . . move themselves,—are
moved by no outside impulsion,—and that no arbitrary hand
has posted them to bring about any event and heap the catastrophe'. [3] (In Meredith's own practice the catastrophes in
Richard Feveral and *Beauchamp's Career* were indeed quite arbitrary.) In his almost unknown reviews in the *Westminster Review*
of 1857, the year before the composition of *Feverel*, his severest
attacks on the rigidly narrow didactic novel appear. Of *Two
Years Ago*, written to propagate Kingsley's particular gospel of
Christianity, Meredith says, 'The hero is, of course, Kingleyan
— . . . adventurous, muscular, and Saxon—with whom, as with
everyone else in the book, Mr. Kingsley does what he pleases.
He has been equally lordly in the construction of the story. . . .
It will be seen that he has a purpose, and has consequently
given us melodrama instead of life. The characters are in a

---

[1] *The Egoist*, pp. 2–3.
[2] Royal H. Gettmann, 'Meredith as a Publisher's Reader', *JEGP*,
XLVIII (1949), 54.
[3] *Sandra Belloni*, II, 186.

hopeless subjection to purpose.' The hero is

a figure stuffed with reeking straw, and Mr. Kingsley has just as much fellow-feeling for him as we have. . . . He is a chip of purpose, born two years ago to play the fool with a sweet little woman, blight her and everybody dependent on him, stumble up mountains, fire a frantic pistol at his supposed rival, drink laudanum and die, and point a spasmodic moral. No wonder Mr. Kingsley is constantly pummeling him. Compassion for this puny Frankenstein is out of the question.

He sums up his judgment of the book by saying, 'The novel is . . . not artistic, because Mr. Kingsley is always in the pulpit.' [1]

He praises *Madame Bovary* because the author 'does not preach'. Flaubert allows his heroine 'patiently to make her own wickedness manifest, and leaves us to contemplate the picture at our leisure. M. Gustave Flaubert is a singularly powerful writer.' [2] In order to appreciate how remarkable was this first judgment of one of the most important novels of the century we have to follow the critical reception of French Realism in England. [3] Thackeray's reaction was much more typical: 'The book is bad . . . a heartless, cold-blooded study of the downfall and degradation of a woman.' [4]

Meredith also welcomed Trollope's first two important novels, *The Warden* and *Barchester Towers*. 'Unlike most modern satirists who harangue, exhort and scold the world in person, Mr. Trollope entrusts all this to the individual of his story' and so has 'successfully interwoven his satire' into the novel. He found Trollope, however, 'wanting in certain of the higher elements that made a novelist. He does not exhibit much sway over the emotional parts of our nature.' [5] Meredith requires the same qualities of the novel that he finds in great poetry.

That he had very definite formal canons we shall see in a later chapter, and judging his own novels by them he found

---

[1] *Westminster Review*, LXVII (April, 1857), 609–11.

[2] *Ibid.*, LXVIII (October, 1857), 601.

[3] See Clarence Decker, *The Victorian Conscience* (New York, 1952); Desmond Pacey, 'Flaubert and His Victorian Critics', *University of Toronto Quarterly*, XVI (1946), 74–84.

[4] *Thackeray Letters*, IV, 82.

[5] *Westminster Review*, LXVIII (October, 1857), 595.

most of them faulty. As an old man in 1906 looking back at his works, he writes, 'I see many faults in all of them, and though I have not striven for perfection, as that would have cramped my hand in writing, something nearer to it would have pleased me. "The Egoist" comes nearer than the other books to the proper degree of roundness and finish.' [1] One reason he did not attain the kind of formal patterned unity he loved so much in Molière was that he felt it would distort the free life of his characters, and that was always his most important criterion. 'I do not make a plot,' he insisted to an American correspondent in 1887. 'If my characters, as I have them at heart, before I begin, were boxed in a plot, they would soon lose the outlines of their features.' [2]

7. GEORGE ELIOT

Among all the Victorian novelists, George Eliot was perhaps unique in that she formulated her ideas about life and art before she started to write her first novel. In the essays she wrote for the London periodicals from 1851-8, especially the reviews of belles-lettres for the *Westminster Review* from 1855-7, almost all her ideas about art are stated explicitly, and together with her letters, they furnish an invaluable source from which her creed as a novelist may be derived.

In an essay, 'The Natural History of German Life', George Eliot defines the function of the artist. 'The greatest benefit we owe to the artist . . . is the extension of our sympathies. Appeals founded on generalisations and statistics require a sympathy ready-made, a moral sentiment already in activity; but a picture of human life such as a great artist can give, surprises even the trivial and the selfish into that attention to what is apart from themselves, which may be called the raw material of moral sentiment.' [3] Art, in her mind, has a social and moral mission: it helps to destroy our self-absorption and attaches our feelings to other objects. By stimulating the imagination of the reader, art builds up the moral or sympathetic emotions. All men, she

---

[1] *Meredith Letters*, II, 589.

[2] Bertha Coolidge, *A Catalogue of the Altschul Collection of George Meredith in the Yale University Library* (Boston, 1931), p. 27.

[3] *Westminster Review*, LXVI (July, 1856), 54.

believes, are born selfish, i.e. they are interested only in satisfying their own desires. 'We are all of us born in moral stupidity, taking the world as an udder to feed our supreme selves.' [1] But man is morally educable; he can learn to live for a higher object than his own happiness, the good of others. 'If Art does not enlarge men's sympathies, it does nothing morally. . . . The only effect I ardently long to produce by my writings, is that those who read them should be better able to *imagine* and to *feel* the pains and the joys of those who differ from themselves in everything but the broad fact of being struggling erring human creatures.' [2] With Wordsworth she believed that the artist's function was to 'bind together by feeling and passion the vast empire of human society'. She would have agreed with Tolstoi that art is to promote the brotherhood of man, and she felt the same moral repugnance to the French Satanic poets because they created a private world, set apart from the outer world and so isolated from the 'warp and woof of human history, . . . the hard thinking and hard handiwork of life. . . .' [3] Pater's *The Renaissance* seemed to her 'quite poisonous in its false principles of criticism and false conceptions of life',[4] and the whole esthetic movement of the seventies reminded her of Plato's fable of the poets who, 'having heard the song of the Muses could do nothing but sing, and starved themselves so till they died and had a fit resurrection as grasshoppers. . . .' [5] As soon as an artist lost sight of the function of his art, his work would be of no more importance than a grasshopper's singing.

In 1866, after the publication of *Felix Holt*, George Eliot engaged in an extremely interesting exchange of letters on the function of art with Frederic Harrison, one of the leading Comtean Positivists in England. She herself was very sympathetic with the ideals of Comte but always refused to join the Positivist Movement, perhaps because she found parts of the system repellingly authoritarian, as Lewes certainly did. Harrison urged her to write an explicitly Comtean novel: 'There

---

[1] *Middlemarch*, Cabinet Edition (Edinburgh and London, 1878), I, 323.
[2] *The George Eliot Letters*, ed. Gordon S. Haight (New Haven, 1954), III, 111 (hereafter cited as *George Eliot Letters*).
[3] *Theophrastus Such*, Cabinet Edition (Edinburgh and London, 1878), p. 242.
[4] *George Eliot Letters*, V, 455.   [5] *Ibid.*, VI, 99.

is not anyone, there never has been anyone but yourself to whom we could look for this.' He did not want the novel to be directly didactic, but he suggested she might show 'the grand features of Comte's world . . . under the forms of our familiar life'. She should make the society of her novel 'a representation of a new society [that of the *Politique Positive*] without supposing anything but . . . the 19th Century . . .', so that the reader would be able to imagine 'the teacher, the ruler, the capitalist, the labourer, the mother, the child' of the future as set down in the grandiose scheme of Comte, and with 'the social tone of Catholicism . . . as a background for Positivist relations'.[1] In her reply she parried his request (though she was later partly to fulfil it in half of *Daniel Deronda*) by explaining that her novels *were* meant to teach, but not in the way Harrison had envisaged. 'I think aesthetic teaching is the highest of all teaching because it deals with life in its highest complexity. But if it ceases to be purely aesthetic—if it lapses anywhere from the picture to the diagram—it becomes the most offensive of all teaching,' and the advocacy of any theory in a novel would cause such a lapse. Her way, she affirmed, to 'urge the human sanctities', was 'through tragedy—through pity and terror as well as admiration and delight'.[2] That is, she felt she could not write a novel consisting wholly of types for the reader to emulate, as Harrison wanted her to do. After several more letters when Harrison again asked for a work idealizing 'the Positivist vision of society as a whole, especially to typify the great institutions and social functions of the future', she closed the matter by suggesting that he should do it, but not in a novel.[3]

Any separation of form and content in a novel seemed wrong to her, and whereas Harrison would neglect form and treat it as merely a means to present his ideas, the aesthetes would make content negligible in the interests of beautiful form. Her aim was 'to make matter and form an inseparable truthfulness',[4] and she insisted,

I have always exercised a severe watch against anything that could be called preaching, and if I have ever allowed myself in dissertation or dialogue [anything] which is not part of the *structure* of my books, I have sinned against my own laws. I am particularly

[1] *George Eliot Letters*, IV, 286–8. [2] *Ibid.*, pp. 300–1.
[3] *Ibid.*, p. 448. [4] *Ibid.*, V, 374.

susceptible on this point, because it touches deeply my conviction of what art should be, and because a great deal of foolish stuff has been written on this relation.[1]

She disliked the contemptuous dismissal by the aesthetes of the sort of audience that Dickens wrote for. 'It would be narrowness to suppose that an artist can only care for the impressions of those who know the methods of his art as well as feel its effects. Art works for all whom it can touch.' [2] Here again there is a strong parallel between her own and Tolstoy's aesthetics. Moreover the kind of detachment deliberately cultivated by some of her contemporaries as both a defence against and an assault upon the great reading public, seemed utterly antipathetic to her temperament as a novelist.

If I laugh at you, O fellow-men! if I trace with curious interest your labyrinthine self-delusions, note the inconsistencies in your zealous adhesions, and smile at your helpless endeavours in a rashly chosen part, it is not that I feel myself aloof from you: the more intimately I seem to discern your weaknesses, the stronger to me is the proof that I share them. . . . No man can know his brother simply as a spectator. Dear blunderers, I am one of you.[3]

(Compare Baudelaire's 'Hypocrite lecteur,—mon semblable,—mon frère!')

But if art has a moral purpose, that purpose is not to propagate specific doctrines and opinions or to teach a theory of morality. 'I have had heart-cutting experience that opinions are a poor cement between human souls. . . .' [4] Running through all her reviews is a continual condemnation of didacticism and the moral exhortations of her contemporaries. In *Westward Ho!* of Charles Kingsley she saw the possibilities of a good novel, but the book was vitiated by 'his parsonic habit' which prevented him from creating 'truly human characters'. His didactic purpose forced him to 'select one character for unmixed eulogy and another for unmitigated vituperation. . . .' 'If he would confine himself to his true sphere, he might be a teacher in the sense in which every great artist is a teacher—namely, by giving us his higher sensibility as a medium, a delicate acoustic or optical instrument, bringing home to our coarser senses what

[1] *Ibid.*, p. 459.
[2] *Ibid.*, p. 391.
[3] *Theophrastus Such*, pp. 5-6.
[4] *George Eliot Letters*, III, 111.

would otherwise be unperceived by us.' [1] In other words, if he
realized that his task was 'to make you hear, to make you
feel . . . to make you *see*', [2] he would be truly 'a poet and artist'.
But 'his fierce antagonism and his perpetual hortative tendency
. . . enfeeble the effect of all Mr. Kingsley's works. . . .' [3]
Meredith's *The Shaving of Shagpat*, on the other hand, is praised
because there is no 'thrusting forward of moral lesson'.[4] The
spirit of the apologue is 'fatal' to the novel as a form, for 'the
men and women speak and act in order to prove a moral, or to
rouse some sentiment in the reader, and not as a result of any
natural combination of character with circumstances'.[5] This
comment is interesting in the light of modern criticism of
George Eliot's own apologues: the dénouement of *Adam Bede*
and the fate of Dunstan Cass. But she reiterates in her letters
that her novels grow from the 'psychological conception of the
dramatis personae' [6] and not from any preconceived moral
lesson. In over simplifying life, the didactic novel inevitably
falsifies it, for the novel should represent life 'in its highest complexity'.[7]

When a writer's motive is the propagation of ideas or theories,
then, she feels justified as a reviewer in attacking them. Thus
from *Constance Herbert* by Geraldine Jewsbury, a friend of Jane
Carlyle, she extracts the sentence: 'Nothing they [the readers]
renounce for the sake of a higher principle, will prove to have
been worth the keeping,' and destroys the grounds of the ardent
author's morality.

The notion that duty looks stern, but all the while has her hand
full of sugar-plums, with which she will reward us by-and-by, is
the favourite cant of optimists, who try to make out that this tangled
wilderness of life has a plan as easy to trace as that of a Dutch
garden; but it really undermines all true moral development by
perpetually substituting something extrinsic as a motive to action,

---

[1] *Westminster Review*, LXIV (July, 1855), 289–91.

[2] Joseph Conrad, Preface, *The Nigger of the 'Narcissus'*, in *The Portable
Conrad*, ed. M. D. Zabel (New York, 1949), p. 708.

[3] *Westminster Review*, LXIV (July, 1855), 289.

[4] J. G. Hammerton, *George Meredith in Anecdote and Criticism* (New York,
1909), p. 140.

[5] *Westminster Review*, LXIV (October, 1955), 612.

[6] *George Eliot Letters*, II, 299.   [7] *Ibid.*, IV, 300.

instead of the immediate impulse of love or justice, which alone makes an action truly moral.[1]

But even worse than didacticism, for her, was the notion that the novelist was merely an entertainer. Too many of her contemporaries had no realization of the high responsibility involved in publication and lacked 'an appreciation of the sacredness of the writer's art'.[2] She complains to Blackwood in 1861: 'The ordinary tone about art is, that the artist may do what he will, provided he pleases the public.'[3] Such conscientiousness in a mere novelist would have seemed strange to Scott, writing only forty years earlier; he was certain that the novel was an opiate, a mere luxury designed for 'that half love of literature that pervades all ranks'.[4] George Eliot's notion of the novelist's position as a sacred office, however, was much more typical of her period than Scott's was. The truth of this statement will be even more evident when we turn to the critics of the mid-century.

[1] *Westminster Review*, LXIV (July, 1855), 294–5.
[2] *Ibid.* (October, 1856), 460.
[3] *George Eliot Letters*, III, 394.
[4] See above, p. 8.

II

THE SACRED OFFICE
The Critics

I. THE NOVEL COMES OF AGE

WHEN the august *Edinburgh Review*, oldest of the literary quarterlies and very conscious of its authoritative position as the upholder of standards, announced in 1853 that prose fiction was not 'an insignificant or trivial province of literature', the statement could be accepted as definitive for most of the English critics of the 1850's and 1860's. From 1850 on, most quarterlies agreed that the finest works of fiction were 'in a very high rank among the achievements of the human intellect'.[1]

Among the more important critical organs only the ancient rival of the *Edinburgh*, the *Quarterly*, seemed still to hold out against the hundred-year-old upstart. In 1855, when it reviewed a novel for the first time since the notorious attack on *Jane Eyre* by Miss Rigby, later Lady Eastlake, Thackeray's *The Newcomes* was pronounced 'one of the masterpieces of English fiction, if fiction is the proper term' for such a great work.[2] Obviously the word still had unpleasant connotations for this *Quarterly* reviewer. (During the next decade some of the same stigma

---

[1] *Edinburgh Review*, XCVII (April, 1853), 380.
[2] *Quarterly Review*, XCVII (September, 1855), 350.

seemed to be attached to the word *novel*: 'George Eliot's novels are not novels in the ordinary sense of the term—they are really dramas: as the word is understood when applied to "Hamlet", or the "Agamemnon".' [1]) The only other articles on prose fiction that the *Quarterly* published until 1860 were a series of biographical accounts of the major eighteenth century novelists by Whitwell Elwin, the editor, and a review in 1856 of Murger's *Scènes de la vie bohème*; otherwise no novels were reviewed until the appearance of *The Mill on the Floss* occasioned an essay on George Eliot (a very disapproving one because of her coarseness). During the sixties there appeared successively a slashing attack on 'sensation novels', chiefly because of their bad morality, a review praising *Les Misérables*, and an article on Scott when *The Waverley Novels* were reprinted in 1868. The only work of Trollope 'serious' enough to deserve an article, from 1850 to 1870, was his *North America*. Mrs. Gaskell, Dickens, and Meredith were totally ignored; so were all American novelists except Harriet Beecher Stowe and all French novelists except Murger and Hugo. Thackeray, a personal friend of Elwin, had the extreme honour of having two of his works noticed, *The Newcomes* and 'The Lectures on the English Humourists of the Eighteenth Century'.

This editorial policy of the *Quarterly* was probably unique, with the possible exception of some violently partisan religious publications. Although the Saturday Reviewers could, on occasion, label novels 'light literature' and compare their writers to pastry cooks,[2] this position was apparently reserved for novels which attacked the British legal or administrative systems or which subverted popular morality. A more typical attitude is that of an article dated February 28, 1863: 'Novels have become so large a part of our literature . . . that they cannot be dismissed as so much "light literature", nor their character be considered a matter of indifference. In the hands of some writers, they have almost risen to the dignity of the drama and the epic, and have become models of thought and style to all who come after them.' [3] If the works of Dickens and Thackeray hardly 'are, or were intended as works of art' but are more in the nature of entertainments offered to the British public 'and

---

[1] *Westminster Review*, LXXXVI (October, 1866), 200.
[2] See above, pp. 24–5. [3] *Saturday Review*, XV, 280.

adapted, not to their deeper and permanent tastes, but to their immediate wishes', still the reviewer of Taine's *Contemporary English Literature* insisted that Balzac and George Sand were artists in their novels.[1] Moreover, the works of George Eliot and George Meredith were consistently treated as important and reviewed in the same way as works of poetry.

Among the evangelical middle-class public, however, not all the prejudice of the period from 1780 to 1830 had disappeared by the 1850's. But the difference is that evangelical periodicals themselves were apparently now trying to break this feeling down. Hugh Miller, editor of the *Witness*, an organ of the Free Kirk of Scotland, complained in 1855: 'Even yet . . . the novel is thought of rather as a light, though not always laudable toy . . .' and insisted, 'The novel *per se*, the novel regarded simply as a literary form, is *morally* as unexceptionable as any other literary form whatever,—as unexceptionable as the epic poem, for instance, as the allegory, or the parable. . . . We must hold that, on every occasion in which the *form* is made the vehicle of truth . . . it should be received with merited favour, —not frowned upon or rejected.'[2] Miller's idea of truth would not of course be the same as Balzac's or Courbet's. *Essays in Biography and Criticism* (1857), a collection of literary essays by Peter Bayne, Miller's successor on the *Witness*, included favourable criticism of Dickens, Thackeray, Bulwer-Lytton, and the Brontës, and the rather dogmatic statement: 'We cannot but deem it a crude and shallow error to pronounce upon it [the novel] a sentence of indiscriminating condemnation.'[3] And yet, among the more extreme sects, like the Plymouth Brethren, novels were still forbidden delights, as Edmund Gosse tells us.

The *British Quarterly Review*, the most important representative of educated dissenters,[4] holding a position roughly equivalent to the *Evangelical Magazine* of the early part of the century, was much more vigorous in its attack on the lingering religious prejudice against the novel. In an essay of 1867 on George

---

[1] *Saturday Review*, XIX (January 7, 1865), 22.

[2] *Essays Historical, Biographical, Political, Social, Literary and Scientific* (Boston, 1865), pp. 471–6.

[3] (Boston, 1857), p. 392.

[4] See R. V. Osbourne, 'The British Quarterly Review', *RES*, n.s., *I* (1950), 147–52.

Eliot it saw the newest genre as a combination and summary of all the others, virtually the greatest literary form ever contrived, containing all that the epic was in narrative, the drama in 'delineation of character by means of colloquy', and the lyric in 'effusion' of feeling. If Shakespeare were alive he would be writing novels, which are 'adapted in an extraordinary degree to afford play to a versatile, inventive, all-comprehending mind'. In terms almost identical with those of James almost twenty years later, the essayist waxed enthusiastic over the 'limitless freedom' of this great form, which was 'restricted to nothing, capable of adaptation to everything'; the only conditions the novelist must meet were 'that he shall interest his reader' and 'concern [himself] . . . with the serious interests of men'.[1] In this essay we have something very much like Arnold's touchstone of high seriousness, applied to novels rather than to poetry. 'No true work of art can be trivial: the law is universal and inexorable. . . . Every important work of art shall have . . . that gravity which belongs to all worthy and well-considered effort.' Tried by this canon the Scottish novels of Scott, 'the result of perfect knowledge and perfect sympathy worked up by a perfectly veracious genius . . . are works of imperishable art . . .' but the historical romances like *Ivanhoe* and *Quentin Durward* 'must fail, as nonsense sooner or later always fails, to attract the attention of grown men'. A great novelist like George Eliot, who has 'moral earnestness', can never become a mere literary entertainer.[2] (We are here not very far from Leavis' *The Great Tradition*.) The word *fiction* itself should not cause any distrust among the readers of the *British Quarterly Review* because 'in precisely the same sense in which the novel is fictitious, are poetry and the drama fictitious'.[3] So important is the sacred office of the novelist that 'a writer of fiction who neglects his high vocation, and accepts only the low one of paid entertainer,—paid to amuse or excite, careless of the means or the

---

[1] XLV, 141-3. For similar statements, see *National Review*, IV (April, 1857), 240; VIII (October, 1858), 416; *Fraser's Magazine*, XLI (January, 1850), 111; L (November, 1854), 489; LXI (January, 1860), 20; James Cordy Jeaffreson, *Novels and Novelists from Elizabeth to Victoria* (London, 1858), II, 305-6.

[2] *British Quarterly Review*, XLV, 143-4.

[3] *Ibid.*, p. 142.

result,—commits a crime against the age in which he lives, and against all future ages'.[1] The only trouble with this extreme view of the responsibility of the writer is that mediocre authors could assume very great importance merely because their novels advocated positions similar to those held by the reviewer. Thus Dinah Mulock, author of the best-seller *John Halifax, Gentleman,* 'lacks the deep and full insight of George Eliot . . . [and] even the knowledge of the outside look of all ordinary characters, which distinguishes so many novelists of only average ability'; her command of language is defective, 'her views are neither broad nor profound, she has no wide field of vision, and the depths of the spiritual struggle are unknown to her. . . .' Nevertheless she is considered to be a significant writer because she 'points always upwards and onwards'.[2]

Aside from its use as a polemical weapon, the idea that the novel is merely a kind of light escape literature is usually set forth with a consciousness that it is outmoded and unpopular. 'We are almost afraid to say, it is so very old-fashioned, but in our younger days there were novels called "The Waverleys", which were not considered totally devoid of interest. . . . Dare we confess to having been excited by the improbable romances of Cooper the American, and diverted by the *Adventures of Gilbert Gurney*? Must we sink yet lower, and admit that these and similar stories amuse us *now*?'[3] Abandoning his rather heavy irony, directed against the new earnest generation, the author of this essay from *Fraser's* of August, 1860, wants novels to be 'simply read as a relaxation to minds wearied with more important studies, not looked upon as substitutes for such'.[4] He complains that one can no longer 'lie upon a sofa and read novels', because the demands they make on the reader are too great; instead of a sofa, 'it is well if sitting up to your reading desk, with *Lemprière* and the *Encyclopedia Britannica* within reach, you can fathom the depth of your author'.[5] And if the reader can understand his author, 'the frightful revelations of *Yeast*, the dramatic horrors of *Jane Eyre* . . . certainly do not supply the kind of relaxation he is looking for'.[6]

As a critic in the *North British Review* pointed out, Scott's comparison of the critic of a novel to the child who plays with

---

[1] *British Quarterly Review*, LXIV (July, 1866), 34.   [2] *Ibid.*, p. 58.
[3] LXII, 209.   [4] *Ibid.*, p. 217.   [5] *Ibid.*, p. 205.   [6] *Ibid.*, p. 209.

a new toy and finds it still more amusing on the next day to tear it to pieces, certainly would not hold true at this period; 'novels now-a-days are not quite so humble in their pretensions. . . .'[1] Rather, as the majority of critics would insist, the novel was the greatest genre of the times, what the drama was to the Elizabethan and Periclean ages. 'To say that the novel is the modern substitute for the drama is only to repeat one of the commonplaces of criticism.'[2]

2. W. C. ROSCOE, WALTER BAGEHOT, AND R. H. HUTTON: THE SEARCH FOR TRAGEDY

According to W. C. Roscoe, one of the finest and least known of Victorian critics, in an essay on Defoe in the *National Review* in 1856, the rapid growth of the novel into the 'most characteristic literature of modern times' was due to the development of political democracy. With the diminishing power of the state and the growth of personal liberties in nineteenth-century England, the individual became more important and could more and more shape his own future. As a result, he became interested in his own character, and 'an increased interest in the individual characters of others; and the examination and representation of character has been the most universal object of modern imaginative literature, its most special characteristic, and its highest excellence'. Since 'the limits of the drama' were insufficient to portray the development of character, 'an intimate union of the dramatic and narrative modes of delineation has been contrived [i.e. the modern novel] to give scope to the new requirements of art'. But because of this increase in civil liberties, men tended to seem more alike. Like Mill and Tocqueville, Roscoe noted that there were 'fewer sharp diversities in character than there used to be'. 'When men are sharply constrained by an external power, which can grasp only a part of their nature, the very pressure there will make other parts of their nature stand out in strange and abnormal excrescences. The more external restraint is removed, the more rounded and the more alike' will men appear. As 'differences of character become less apparent on the surface, . . . a finer discrimination, a more comprehensive insight, and

[1] XL (May, 1864), 369.
[2] *Westminster Review*, LXXXVIII (October, 1867), 593.

a more delicate expression, are necessary to delineate its diversities'. This characteristically modern demand for more subtlety, a greater penetration into the human psyche, Roscoe found, could certainly not be satisfied by Defoe, who was more interested in a 'particular mode of life' than the life of a particular person, or in adventures told for their own sake, not for 'any light they throw on the supposititious narrator'. [1]

It was for similar reasons that Roscoe found Thackeray's novels marked by 'thinness and superficiality'. [2] Thackeray only gives us 'social man' and paints manners, but he 'never penetrates into the interior, secret, *real* life that every man leads in isolation from his fellows. . . .' [3] His characters are distinct and individual enough, and he has a great power of 'producing the impression of reality'. [4] But verisimilitude is not the test of the highest creative power; rather 'the highest distinguishing prerogative of poetry or fiction, or whatever we choose as the most comprehensive name for the art which has language for its medium . . . [is] that it gives the artist the power of delineating the actual interior life and individual character of a living soul. It is the only art that does so.' [5] Since Thackeray abstained from this task, his genius is of a lower order and he exists 'entirely on the surface of things'. Roscoe shrewdly points out that he is perhaps so excellent an observer and recorder of manners 'because he never cares to penetrate below them'. [6] Meeting characters in Thackeray's books is 'exactly as if you had met the people in actual life, mixed constantly with them, known them as we know our most intimate friends. Of course, this is all we can *know* of a man; but not all we can imagine, not all the artist can, if he chooses, convey to us.' [7]

Related to a failure in imagination is a want of thought in Thackeray's novels. 'He occupies a good deal of space in half-meditative, half-emotional harangues on the phenomena of life,' but in all his books there is a total absence 'of what we usually call ideas'. Fielding on the other hand 'was a reflecting man; you feel that his writings are backed by a body of thought, though it is far from an intrusive element in them'. [8]

Roscoe's essay 'Sir E. B. Lytton, Novelist, Philosopher, and

---

[1] III (October, 1856), 380-2.   [2] *National Review*, II (January, 1856), 186.
[3] *Ibid.*, p. 179.   [4] *Ibid.*, p. 183.   [5] *Ibid.*, p. 180.
[6] *Ibid.*, p. 185.   [7] *Ibid.*, p. 180.   [8] *Ibid.*, pp. 185-6.

Poet', in the *National Review* of April, 1859, is an excellent example of the kind of demands he made on the novel. Bulwer he found 'but indifferently qualified' for being a great novelist. 'Nature has not endowed him with the power to think deeply or justly, or to see with a clear eye and reproduce with a faithful imagination.'[1] To illustrate this point, Roscoe subjects Bulwer's style to a searching analysis. Underneath all his eloquence, of the kind 'which values ideas as a thread on which to string glittering images and gaudy words', are the most threadbare truisms.[2] 'No one who really wished to discover truth could deal with language in the way Sir Bulwer Lytton does.'[3] Throughout his novels 'blurred and incompletely explored ideas are covered up in loose phraseology and indistinct metaphor' so that his style, rather than being polished, is really varnished; it 'does not give the highest effect to the sense which lies under it, but conceals it beneath an opaque glitter. . . . Where one word would express his idea most exactly, he uses another because it is more uncommon, more pretentious, more good-looking,' whereas 'refinement of taste and accuracy of mind' are shown in using words 'as they most exactly express our meaning. . . .'[4]

There is the same inaccuracy in Bulwer's imagination that there is in this use of language, Roscoe contended, and as a result Bulwer cannot perceive or represent things and people truly. His characters all seem manufactured and are monotonously alike. 'He never . . . penetrates into the recesses of another mind or heart. He never paints the complex reality. He has none of the poetic power of flashing a light upon the mysteries of human hidden life, the life within the man's own breast.'[5] Bulwer's preference for what 'he oddly calls types' [and we would call symbolic characters] rather than individuals springs from the same failure of thought and imagination.

Those who are deeply impressed with the richness and infinite variety of created things, who are sensible to the fine links which unite, the subtle and melting distinctions which separate, who feel into what an intermingling and delicate web of existence the lives of men are interwoven—such men are shy of 'types'. . . . If a type

---

[1] *Ibid.*, VIII, 283. [2] *Ibid.*, p. 287. [3] *Ibid.*, p. 283.
[4] *Ibid.*, p. 287. [5] *Ibid.*, p. 290.

is to be true, it must embody in a single individual form the universal and essential characteristics of that of which it is the type. . . .

But Bulwer's types, rather than having this kind of complexity, have the simplicity of papier-mache figures.[1]

Walter Bagehot, a close friend of Roscoe's, and co-editor of the *National Review*, along with Richard Holt Hutton, subjected the Waverley Novels to the same kind of scrutiny that Roscoe had given Defoe, Thackeray, and Bulwer-Lytton. Although Scott gave us 'fresh pictures of practical human society',[2] he omitted the most essential element in a novel. In the Waverley Novels we have merely the 'exterior delineation of character but we know nothing of the inner life of his people. Scott leaves out completely the 'delineation of the soul'. 'We have mind, manners, animation, but it is the stir of this world.' No picture 'of human nature [in a novel] can be considered complete which omits to deal with man in relation to questions which occupy him as man, with his convictions as to the theory of the universe and his own destiny'.[3] Roscoe two years earlier had made the same point about Thackeray: 'He professes to paint human life; and he who does so, and who does not base his conception on that religious substructure which alone makes it other than shreds of flying dreams, is an incomplete artist and a false novelist.'[4]

Besides the superficiality of Scott's characterizations, his other major defect is his style. Bagehot ends his essay with a plea for closer attention to style in imaginative fiction: 'On great occasions . . . there should be passages in which the words seem to cleave to the matter.' But he did not want the kind of purple passages so many novelists were then attempting. A great style is marked by 'exquisite accuracy and inexplicable appropriateness'; and Scott, content with 'the first sufficient words that came uppermost',[5] never found *le mot juste* and remained a second-rate novelist.

For Bagehot, and for all the other writers in the *National*

[1] *National Review*, VIII (April, 1859), pp. 298-9.
[2] *Ibid.*, VI (April, 1858), 463. [3] *Ibid.*, pp. 468-70.
[4] *Ibid.*, II (January, 1856), 20. See also VI (July, 1856), 127-46.
[5] *Ibid.*, VI, 471-2. For similar pronouncements on style, see *George Eliot Letters*, II, 206 and 421; also G. H. Lewes in the *Leader*, VIII (March 7, 1857), 231, and *The Principles of Success in Literature* (London, n.d.), *passim*.

Review, 'the greatest living writer of fiction',[1] after the publication of *Adam Bede* in 1859, was George Eliot, and it was by her standards that all other novelists were henceforth to be measured. Thus Thackeray's characters seemed too superficial and Dickens' were caricatures.[2] The author of 'The Novels of George Eliot' in the *National Review* of July, 1860, who on internal evidence alone would appear to be Bagehot, finally finds what he had been looking for in the English novel. Up to that time the inspiration of fiction in England had been social, with the character 'delineated with great accuracy down to the same very inconsiderable depth, and no farther. . . .' Now for almost the first time there is a novelist who can pierce below 'the social surface' and 'give us more insight into the deeper roots of character'. The Brontës did go much deeper into character than Trollope and Thackeray, and their characters were 'more profoundly imagined', but George Eliot can give us 'more of depth in the deeper characters imagined', along with 'a broader touch, [and] a stronger, directer fashion of delineation'.[3] Too often novels have depended on 'artificial enhancements of interest which do not arise fairly out of the moral constitutions of the characters'. Too often characters are smothered in society or smothered in incident.[4]

Charles Kingsley, who had long been rather leniently treated in the pages of the *National Review* because he had an 'aim beyond amusing' the reader,[5] was subjected to a very severe examination in January, 1860. 'His ordinary style of workmanship is slovenly and slipshod. . . . his ordinary standard is unfixed and low. . . . He has none of the noble, artistic, old Greek thirst for perfection. He "goes in" for quantity rather than quality' and trusts too much to 'inspiration'. No amount of earnestness, purpose or message can excuse the neglect of the art of the novel. 'A genius like Mr. Kingsley's not only deserves

[1] *National Review*, XVIII (April, 1864), 533.
[2] See Bagehot's essays, 'Sterne and Thackeray', *National Review*, XVIII (April, 1864), 523–33; and 'Charles Dickens', *ibid.*, VII (October, 1858), 458–88.
[3] XI, 191–4.
[4] *Ibid.*, p. 206. See also in the same periodical the essays 'Mr. Charles Reade's Novels', XIV (January, 1862), 134–49; and 'Orley Farm', XVI (July, 1862), 27–40.
[5] I (July, 1855), 128.

the most sedulous culture, but demands the most severe control . . . [and] needs to be *employed*, not *indulged*.' Nothing can excuse 'the inconsiderate confusion in which the incidents of [his stories] . . . jostle and stumble over one another and the indistinctness with which many of them are told. . . .' He is destined to remain 'an *improvisatore*', not an artist.[1]

The *National Review*, although it ran only from 1855 to 1864, produced some of the best criticism of the period. Matthew Arnold, in a letter to Bagehot,[2] praised it highly and paid it an even higher compliment when he chose to publish in it three of his *Essays in Criticism*—'The Function of Criticism at the Present Time', 'Joubert', and 'Eugenie de Guerin'—despite its extremely low rate of pay. R. H. Hutton, when he became literary editor of the weekly *Spectator* in 1861, maintained the same standards and critical traditions, although by that time he had lost the brilliant assistance of Roscoe and Bagehot.[3]

Since most of Hutton's important essays still remain uncollected, any real estimate of him as a critic of the novel must rely on his weekly reviews in the *Spectator* during the sixties and seventies, especially the series dealing with the successive books of Trollope as they came out. *Orley Farm* misses greatness because Trollope does not brood over his characters sufficiently. One can find no trace of the 'agony of meditative travail about his mind', as one does throughout the Brontë novels. Trollope is only a spectator of his world, and the book is written in 'an easy sliding manner'. As a matter of fact, he seems always 'narrating, not conceiving, telling you how the figures look as they pass along. . . . [They are] not so much offsprings of his heart, sentiment, and self-knowledge, as results of his alert, observing, and combining eye. No great novelist probably ever drew so little from the resources of his own visionary life. . . .' But although Hutton found Trollope not sufficiently committed to his world in *Orley Farm*, he saw great possibilities for future development. At times the delineation of Lady Mason's criminal experience was 'really powerful and tragic',

[1] X, 18–19.

[2] Mrs. Russell Barrington, *The Life of Walter Bagehot* (London, 1915), p. 247.

[3] Roscoe died July 30, 1859, and Bagehot became editor of the *Economist* in January, 1861.

and he caught 'a straining of the eye into an interior almost beyond the artist's sight'; sometimes Trollope actually gets to 'a deeper passion in the depths in which he sounds'.[1]

The Small House at Allington, The Claverings, and *The Belton Estate* all give evidence of Trollope's amazingly keen eye for 'the moral "hooks and eyes" of life', the way people influence or fail to influence each other.[2] As a painter of social life he was unrivalled among his contemporaries, but Hutton kept looking for something more, and in *Can You Forgive Her?* of 1865, he almost discerned it, but not quite. 'If Mr. Trollope had had the heart (shall we say the nerve?) to ruin Lady Glencora, he might have given (what is rare with him) a genuinely tragic interest to his story. . . .' But by running 'as close as he dare to the edge of tragedy without incurring the responsibility of delineating its darkest features'[3] Trollope failed to give Hutton the novel he seemed to be looking for—something like an English *Anna Karenina* or *Madame Bovary.* Alice Vavasor, ostensibly the main character, Hutton declared a complete failure. She was too 'misty', and not enough of her inner life was rendered to make her behaviour credible.[4]

The Last Chronicle of Barset, coming out two years later, was the best of the novels up to then, 'the richest and completest of Mr. Trollope's works', chiefly because of the tortured figure of the Reverend Josiah Crawley, one of the most complex and fully rendered figures in all the Trollope novels up to that date. 'Mr. Trollope has never before drawn a character either so full of (indicated rather than delineated) intellectual power, or so devoted to the diviner ends of life, or, again, so deeply involved in the strife of morbid personal feelings' and as a result, has given us 'a picture of the highest interest and power'.[5] But it was the publication of *He Knew He Was Right* in 1869 that won Hutton completely over to Trollope. In the tragic story of Louis Trevelyan and his wife, Emily, Trollope 'impresses us with a power of conception he has rarely equalled in any of his novels, and gives us quite his highest style of execution'. 'There

[1] *Spectator,* XXV (October 11, 1862), 1136–7.
[2] *Ibid.,* XXXVII (April 9, 1864), 422.
[3] *Ibid.,* XXXVIII (September 2, 1865), 979.
[4] *Ibid.,* p. 978.
[5] *Ibid.,* XL (July 13, 1867), 778.

has been little in our recent literature so good or so painful
. . . ' as this 'tale of truly tragic jealousy'.[1]

If Hutton followed Trollope's slow development towards real
tragedy with great interest, the unsuccessful attempt by Wilkie
Collins and his prolific followers[2]—Miss Braddon, Mrs. Henry
Wood, Ouida, and a score of others—to rise above the flatness
of the usual domestic novels of Charlotte Yonge, Mrs. Oliphant,
and Dinah Mulock was roundly condemned as melodrama.
At a time when a great deal of moral indignation was indis-
criminately spilled over 'sensation novels'—even the Arch-
bishop of York preached a sermon against them[3]—Hutton insisted their failure was artistic and not ethical, for it lay in 'the
use of illegitimate means to produce an effect upon the reader.
. . . Our sense of the fitness of things is offended by the continual recurrence of what ought to be sparingly employed to
bring out a catastrophe or to disentangle a plot.' When a
reader is drenched in gore, he soon becomes indifferent to the
sight of blood. Furthermore, the claim of Collins and his followers that they were writing tragedy was absurd; all they could
produce was melodrama—'the melodrama of the cheap theatres
is an acted sensation novel. . . .'[4]

In melodrama the plot becomes 'a series of striking surprises'[5] so that an author can contrive 'a position of highly
strung suspense' and its effect is aimed solely at the reader's
'nerves'.[6] The only emotions the reader is meant to feel are
'suspense and horror'.[7] Pity and terror are out of the question
because the characters are reduced to cogs in the machinery,
always subservient to the plot. In true drama, as opposed to
melodrama, 'the conception of the characters and that of the

---

[1] *Spectator*, XLII (June 12, 1869), 707.

[2] The best study of the sensational novels of this period is Walter C.
Phillips, *Dickens, Reade, and Collins, Sensation Novelists* (New York, 1919).

[3] An account of this sermon appeared in *The Times* (London) for November 2, 1864. See also *Blackwood's Edinburgh Magazine*, XCI (May, 1862),
564–79; *Quarterly Review*, CXIII (April, 1863), 482–514; *North British
Review*, XLIII (September, 1865), 180–205, for typical examples of this
kind of treatment.

[4] *Spectator*, XLI (August 8, 1868), 931–2.

[5] *Ibid.*, XXXVI (January 10, 1863), 1501.

[6] *Ibid.* (January 31, 1863), pp. 1586–7.

[7] *Ibid.*, XXXVII (December 24, 1864), 1475.

framework of events . . . [should be] simultaneous', or the latter 'rather subordinated to the former'. There should be no stroke put in without 'some definite bearing on the delineation of character as well as on the evolution of the plot'.[1] In Mrs. Wood's *Verner's Pride,* instead of characters, we have 'colourless, flavourless dummies', so that although her story may seem pleasant 'to habitual novel readers . . . it is not an addition to literature' (the standard by which Hutton judged novels) but mere melodrama.[2] He found Collins as unsatisfying as his epigone, and for the same reason. The characters of *Armadale* were 'shadowy beings put in to answer the requirements of Mr. Wilkie Collins' plot',[3] and *The Moonstone* reduced the novel to the level of a puzzle. It has 'no person who can in any way be described as a character, no one who interests us. . . .' Franklin Blake, on whom Collins evidently expended great pains, was 'a person to whom all manner of fascinating qualities are attributed' but he is 'clumsily worked out'.[4] *The Woman in White* was the only one of Collins' novels Hutton liked, and that was because Count Fosco interested him as a character.[5] Since Collins insisted in the prefaces to most of his novels that he was concerned with the delineation of character, Hutton's criticisms are extremely relevant.

Hawthorne, on an entirely different literary level, also failed as a writer of tragedy, though for other reasons. 'It was one great cause of his comparative sterility as a novelist that he had real difficulty in rising to any tragic crisis, and could scarcely do so without placing himself in a position of external observation, and writing of the passion and the suffering he introduced as a striking phenomenon to be analysed, instead of throwing himself and his reader's heart and soul into them.'[6] Hawthorne as described by Hutton would have fulfilled Zola's ideal of the novelist—clinician-scientist. He did picture true anguish, 'but more as an anatomist would lay bare a convulsive movement of the nerves, than as a poet would express passion',

---

[1] *Ibid.,* XXXVI (January 31, 1863), 1587.
[2] *Ibid.* (February 14, 1863), p. 1644.
[3] *Ibid.,* XXXIX (June 9, 1866), 639.
[4] *Ibid.,* XLI (July 25, 1868), 881.
[5] *Ibid.,* XXXVI (January 10, 1863), 1501.
[6] *Ibid.,* XLII (January 2, 1869), 15.

and his novels, in French naturalist fashion, are more often studies of human nature rather than tales. In Hawthorne's works there is 'little of that imaginative *sympathy* with pain which is at the heart of all true tragedy'.[1]

The two greatest contemporary novelists for Hutton were George Eliot and Dickens. George Eliot exhibited triumphantly just that quality Hawthorne lacked. It was her imaginative sympathy that gave her best characterizations their scope and depth, though she too had great limitations. 'Her strenuousness was too self-conscious to reach the point of positive strength,' [2] and her novels tended to become too diffuse because of 'their too wide reflectiveness'. But this limitation was related to her 'largeness of mind, largeness of conception', a major source of her strength.[3]

Writing of Dickens at a time when his reputation with the critics was at its nadir, Hutton noted his 'swift, sudden and keen vision, and . . . his large sense of humour, which brings an indefinite range of analogy and contrast within the field of view at any one moment' and 'the presence of mind (which is the soul of wit) displayed in his satire [which makes] . . . him such a humourist as many centuries are not likely to reproduce'. Although Hutton repeats Bagehot's criticisms of Dickens almost verbatim, namely that Dickens 'hardly ever goes beneath' 'the superficial stratum of real life', two pages later this limitation is completely denied; here he discovers in Dickens qualities that were later to be called Dostoievskian by Gissing. 'No author indeed could draw more powerfully than he the mood of a man haunted by a fixed idea, a shadowy apprehension, a fear, a dream, a remorse. . . .' No one could better portray 'the restlessness of a murderer' or 'knew better the sort of supremacy which a given idea gets over the mind in a dream, and in those waking states of nervous apprehension akin to dreams'.[4] The ability to appreciate such widely differing kinds of genius makes Hutton one of the most catholic critics of the period.

[1] *Spectator*, XLII (January 2, 1869), 15.
[2] *Essays on Some of the Modern Guides in English Thought in Matters of Faith* (London, 1887), p. 263.
[3] *Brief Literary Criticisms* (London, 1906), pp. 175–6.
[4] *Criticisms on Contemporary Thought and Thinkers* (London, 1894), I, 89–92.

3. SENTIMENTALITY

But one aspect of Dickens Hutton disliked very much—his sentimentality. Referring to the ripple of sunlight that Paul Dombey watches so intently on his death-bed, he remarks that Dickens 'spoils his best touches by his heavy hand in harping on them . . . Dickens is so obviously delighted with himself for this picturesque piece of sentiment, that he quite fondles his own conception', and the whole scene, with its reiterated question, 'What are the wild waves saying?' makes upon him 'the most painful impression of pathos feasting on itself'.[1] In an earlier article called 'Unctuous Sentiment' (1862), he used similar imagery to describe Dickens' handling of Ruth Pinch and Little Nell: 'It almost gives us the sensation of absolute gluttony to enter into the appetizing spirit with which he spoons and stirs the subject of grief and death.'[2] This criticism was not restricted to Dickens. George Macdonald's *Alec Forbes of Howglen* was guilty of the same 'sentimentalism', that is, 'a wish to dwell on the sweetness of certain forms of emotion as an epicure dwells on the delicacy of certain forms of food'.[3] Besides describing sentimentality as one of the seven deadly sins, Hutton diagnosed it as a disease: 'There is in the moral sentiments and emotions, as well as in the physical system, a certain *litheness* and *spareness* which implies both health and strength, and the absence of which denotes some inferiority and degeneration like that the physiologists call "fatty degeneration of the tissues".'[4]

This strong condemnation of sentimentality was fairly widespread among the critics of the fifties and sixties. Fitzjames Stephen defines it as 'habitual indulgence in feelings of tenderness' and notes that the 'word is seldom used without implying disapprobation'.[5] According to the *OED*, it was in the beginning of the nineteenth century that the word *sentimental* lost its use as a term of approval, meaning capable of feeling, and came

[1] *Brief Literary Criticisms*, pp. 56–7.
[2] *Spectator*, XXXV (April 2, 1862), 406.
[3] *Ibid.*, XXXVIII (July 1, 1865), 723.
[4] *Ibid.*, XXXV (April 12, 1862), 406.
[5] 'The Relation of Novels to Life', *Cambridge Essays* (London, 1855), p. 173.

to be used in the pejorative sense of showing excessive emotion or falsifying the expression of emotion. Thackeray in a letter of 1849 still has the eighteenth century meaning in mind when he writes 'under the mask satirical there walks about a sentimental gentleman who means not unkindly to any mortal person'.[1]

The principal illustration of this vice for Stephen is Dickens' treatment of death, 'apparently for no one reason but that of showing his skill in arranging affecting details so as to give them this horrible pungency'. Dickens 'gloats over' little Nell's death-bed, 'the scene over which so many foolish tears have been shed'. He 'touches, tastes, smells and handles it as if it were some savoury dainty which could not be too fully appreciated'.[2] Ironically, Stephen compared this scene with the death of Friday in *Robinson Crusoe* and praised Defoe's restraint, whereas Dickens, in a letter which Stephen could not possibly have seen, had been repelled by Defoe's lack of feeling.[3]

For *Fraser's*, Thackeray's treatment of death is much superior to that of most of his contemporaries: 'His pathos is introduced in the most perfectly natural way, and ever forced into artificial prominence. Death-bed scenes—which some writers would dwell upon as if they could not be content without actually rubbing the onions into their readers' eyes—are by him almost always left in the background, and rather indicated than described.'[4] In the same way Charles Lever is praised in *Blackwood's* for his 'hearty abhorrence of all sentimentality and false writing. The most tempting occasion never betrays him into this—he is always manly, simple, and sincere in his treatment of sentiment and passion. This is no small virtue in modern novelist—many of our modern writers, like our modern singers, are always in *falsetto*; and the public is in both cases always entrapped into applause.'[5]

Thackeray's tone as omniscient author of *Pendennis* was sub-

---

[1] *Thackeray Letters*, II, 539.   [2] *Cambridge Essays*, p. 174.
[3] See above, p. 22.   [4] LXIX (April, 1864), 406.
[5] XCI (April, 1862), 459. This essay is probably by Bulwer-Lytton's son, Robert Lytton, who wrote poetry under the pseudonym of 'Owen Meredith'. See *The Life of Edward Bulwer, First Lord Lytton* by his grandson the Earl of Lytton (London, 1913), II, 394. In the letter quoted on that page Bulwer-Lytton advises his son about an essay the latter is writing on Lever for *Blackwood's*.

jected to an interesting analysis in the *Prospective Review* of April, 1851. 'Mr. Thackeray . . . seems apt to look at life from the point of view of an effeminate sentimentalist of two-and-twenty.' His mask of cynicism, which this critic found Thackeray assuming too often, serves to gloss over 'moral problems which he is not clear-sighted enough to solve', especially those connected with Pendennis' weak attempt to seduce Fanny Bolton. Thackeray's uncertainty of tone, which assumes the form of cynicism or lachrymose sentimentality, is most evident in his treatment of Amelia Sedley and Helen Pendennis, 'pretty, soft-hearted women, with very little intellect, living wholly on their affections, and generally bestowing those affections on rather unworthy objects'. On one page Thackeray exalts them 'as the most angelic types of womanhood . . . in the next they are sneered at as silly slaves. Throughout we find a sort of contemptuous fondness for them displayed by the author, which unpleasantly recalls the caresses of the harem.' [1]

According to *Bentley's Quarterly Review* of March, 1859, in an article on the novels of Bulwer-Lytton, sentimentalism is 'a word invented to define a loose, unreasoning, weak condition of feeling, dwelling not in heart or brain, but in the debatable land of nerves, fancies, tastes, propensities . . . and without any settled basis in reason, morals or fact'. In sentimental writing all is 'show and seeming, which it accepts for reality; sentimentalism does not discern between shadow and substance. . . . Wherever there is fair show, high pretension, assumption of any sort, there sentimentalism gives its allegiance, gets up its little fervours, expends its wordy enthusiasm, falls into raptures.' The sentimentalist forgets that 'feelings are genuine things and can only deal with genuine things'. This 'spurious state of emotion' is the chief fault of Bulwer's novels, and its root lies in their author's vanity, which is betrayed by 'a perpetual self-consciousness', never allowing the author 'to forget himself or to wish the reader to forget him in the interest of the story'.[2]

As a result, Bulwer's characters lose their identity since 'every character is the author, every person in the piece uses his language . . . illustrates his views'. The chief sufferer in the world of his novels is the heroine, to whom he always marries his hero; she is 'some gentle creature, who does not . . . understand

[1] VII, 175–9. [2] I, 80–4.

one word in ten that he utters, but who looks up to him all the more with docile, undoubting worship'. This kind of ideal, more like a fawning dog than a woman, makes the novelist's job impossible; 'it is too great a demand on a writer's genius to invent varieties of incapacity and fatuity. . . .' Love, the ostensible core of the Bulwerian novel, can not exist in such a world where the 'woman's being is to be merged into her lover's without any reciprocal fusion. . . .' [1]

This anonymous essay, besides being remarkable for its searching criticism, anticipated by about three years Meredith's very similar analysis of sentimentality worked out in novelistic terms in *Sandra Belloni* and later developed in *The Egoist* and most of his later novels. In all of them we find the same connection made between vanity, sentimentalism and egoism (misnamed love), i.e. the attempt by man to absorb rather than marry his mate. Wilfred Pole, Willoughby Patterne, Alvan, Fleetwood and the rest are very like the picture the author of this essay draws of Sir Edward Bulwer-Lytton.

4. THE USES OF FICTION

Whereas this critic, in common with all the best critics of the period, thought the novelist's 'crowning gift' was to delineate 'the passions and the deeper emotions of human nature in action',[2] some reviewers called any real treatment of passion painful or unpleasant. According to the *North British Review*, George Eliot's stories were too 'uniformly of a painful nature'. Although pain and horror should not be totally excluded from fiction, they should 'not occupy a too prominent place'.[3] Another article in the same magazine found Trollope's *The Mac-Dermots of Ballycloran* too 'painful' and 'sad'. Since we read novels for amusement, we feel 'we are playing with human miseries'. Trollope's story of the decline of an old Irish family is too disquieting. The reviewer ends by asking, 'Are there not heartaches enough in the world?' [4]

The *British Quarterly* asked for works that were 'restful'.[5] 'Our own preference inclines us to the sunshiny view of life in fiction, though we do not object to tragedy now and then. . . .'

[1] I, pp. 90–3.   [2] *Ibid.*, p. 89.   [3] XLV (September, 1866), 205.
[4] XL (May, 1864), 394.   [5] XLIV (July, 1866), 33.

But it must be a qualified kind of tragedy: 'heartache' is permissible, but not 'heartbreak'.[1] The *Quarterly* in its 1860 article on George Eliot even went so far as to count the number of deaths in her novels up to that date and found she allowed six principal characters to die in three books. 'Surely this is an exaggerated representation of the proportion which sorrow bears to happiness in human life. . . .'[2] The *Saturday Review*, employing a patently false analogy to painting, thought a novel ought to 'contain a balance of light and shade', and so condemned a novel entitled *George Geith of Fen Court* because of the 'extreme and untempered gloom which pervades the whole story'.[3]

The use of novels as an escape from unpleasant reality is dealt with competently in the *North British Review* of May, 1853. 'This feeling, that novels ought to be *pleasant*, is one so often met with, that really it seems to deserve a critic's attention.' After listing most of the standard objections to novels that have unhappy endings ('The world is sad enough . . . why make it sadder? . . . I do grieve every day over real miseries; why must I weep afresh over imaginary ones? If I have ever time to spend over a novel, let me at least escape to some better and brighter world than the gloomy one of every day. . . . Of course there must be very wretched people in the world, but why should I be told of it?'), the writer of the article gives what he thinks should be the 'novelist's true answer'. 'I have to paint God's world as I find it. . . . The sadder you say the world is, the sadder I must paint it.'[4]

The question of why we read fiction, what is its use, was widely canvassed in all the periodicals of the period. According to the *Prospective Review* of April, 1853, 'all genuine fiction' shows us 'that we have all of us one human heart' (the same echo of Wordsworth we have already found in George Eliot). Fiction 'conjures up an ideal world in the midst of our prosaic realities, and men, absorbed in selfish interests, are awakened to more generous sympathies, and their hearts, severed in the

[1] LXIX (April, 1869), 305–8.

[2] CVIII (October, 1860), 474. Ruskin, in what is probably his worst critical essay, 'Fiction Fair and Foul', written in 1881, counted the number of murders in *Bleak House* and also found them excessive.

[3] XIX (March 11, 1865), 290–1. For the same criticism applied to Thackeray, see the *Westminster Review*, LIX (April, 1853), 363–88.

[4] XIX, 160–1.

turmoil of the world, find a bond of fellowship by the creation of the poet'.[1] For George Brimley, reviewing *Westward Ho!*, novels can 'conduct us through a wider range of experience than the actual life of each generally permits'. By making us live in the lives of others, fiction enables us 'to pass by sympathy into other minds and other circumstances'. It is in this way that art can affect morality and make us 'wiser and larger-hearted'. (There is the same relationship between art and morality in Shelley's *Defence of Poetry*.) Because of the high aims of fiction, the powers necessary to write it 'rank supreme among the gifts of the human race'.[2]

In a similar vein, for the author of 'Charles Dickens and *David Copperfield*' in *Fraser's*, December, 1850, 'Boz, and men like Boz, are the true humanizers, and therefore the true pacificators of the world. They sweep away the prejudices of class and caste, and disclose the common ground of humanity which lies beneath factitious, social and national systems.'[3] For E. S. Dallas, in *The Gay Science*, one of the major works on critical theory in the Victorian period, no one 'is better employed than he . . . who widens through fiction the range of our sympathies and teaches us not less to care for the narrow aims of small people than for the vast schemes of the great and mighty'. Through fiction 'the private individual' has been 'invested with a new importance'.[4] Dallas, like most mid-Victorian critics, believed that the importance of art is in its ability to affect life. 'After all, the question of supreme interest in art, the question upon which depends our whole interest in art is, what are its relations to life.'[5] In the July, 1859, issue of *Bentley's Quarterly*, the novel is even more closely related to the ideals of the French Revolution and liberal faith of the century. 'It is the aim of the loftier race of novelists to show us the universal brotherhood of humankind, that there are common sympathies which unite us all . . .',[6] and the author of this review of *Adam Bede* finds it 'a steady protest against exclusiveness'.[7]

[1] IX, 222–3.   [2] George Brimley, *Essays* (London, 1868), pp. 294–5.
[3] XLII, 700.
[4] Eneas Sweetland Dallas, *The Gay Science* (London, 1866), II, 287.
[5] *Ibid.*, p. 144.   [6] I, 456.
[7] *Ibid.*, p. 434. For this same idea see also *Spectator*, XXIX (August 6, 1856), 877; *Macmillan's*, XIV (August, 1866), 279; *North British Review*, XXVI (November, 1856), 210.

Novels also, for the same writer, give us 'a clearer insight' into our own experience[1] and help 'us to read more clearly and to see further into the mysteries of our complete being. . . .' [2] According to the *North British Review* of August, 1851, we can learn much more about human nature from fiction than from history or biography. Novels 'help to unriddle the *mystery* of life', for in 'the peculiar province of the novel, the study of character, the creation of a truthful imagination, will give a longer, fuller, more complete truth, than any fragmentary specimens of humanity can, however carefully extracted from the world of fact'.[3]

'What do we look for in fiction?' asks the author of the essay on Bulwer-Lytton in *Bentley's Quarterly* of March, 1859, and he answers that besides having our interest held, 'we expect to have our feelings roused, our fancy kindled, our knowledge of life enlarged, our taste cultivated, our social conscience refined and quickened. . . .' To do all this the novelist needs 'rare gifts and faculties', 'thought at once intense and varied, an eye to embrace the range of nature and art, unwearying observation, an ever-watchful ready intelligence, a capacious memory, a keen wit, a universal sympathy. . . .' [4] In other words, the novelist must be, in James' phrase, a man on whom nothing is lost.

5. DIDACTICISM

Among mid-Victorian critics there was also a much simpler account of the relation that should exist between novels and morality. In its most elementary form, all novels should conceal 'moral or doctrinal instruction under the veil of an apologue or parable' to advocate 'the common cause of morality and truth' and to make 'virtue attractive and to render vice odious and repulsive in the same degree'. Furthermore, all moral teaching must be uniform, since it is to be 'founded on the immutable principles of Christian morality'.[5] For the *Dublin Review*, these are the only standards by which novels are to be judged, and as a result, Lady Georgina Fullerton is much

---

[1] *Bentley's Quarterly Review*, I, 433.   [2] *Ibid.*, p. 471.
[3] XV, 420–1. See also *National*, II (January, 1856), 180; *North British Review*, XLV (September, 1866), 198.
[4] (March, 1859), 73.   [5] XXIV (March, 1853), 176–9.

preferred by the author of 'Novel-Morality' to Charlotte Brontë and Thackeray, whose books are clearly immoral.[1] Although this position—the novel as an apologue or moral fable—was very close to Trollope's and, to a lesser degree, to Thackeray's, for neither of them was the idea of morality so rigid and circumscribed, and morality was by no means their only canon of judgment.

The comparison between the functions of clergymen and novelist was very frequently made and often it seemed as if there was really little difference between the two, except that the novelist could wield a greater influence—a difference in degree not in kind. A critic for the *National Review* observed: 'The novel-writer's desk is used as a second pulpit, to attract a larger and more awakened audience for the author than . . . the preacher.' [2] There is a 'law, that the writer of fiction now-a-days must be the teacher and preacher, as well as the amuser'.[3] But *Fraser's Magazine* would make a distinction between the way novels and sermons affect their audience. The novel 'ought to exemplify, not to preach'.[4] But the ultimate purpose of both is the same: 'The novel, however charlatans may degrade it, and the lazy would love to have it degraded, is, in idea, next to the drama, the highest organ of moral teaching, and in practise just now, a far more powerful one.' [5] It should do for the nineteenth century what the Homeric epics did for Greece —fill the mind 'with an admiring reverential love of virtue, and . . . impel the soul to aspire after goodness'. The novelist cannot perform his highest function or produce works of genius 'unless he presents us with [a character having] the sum total of the noblest characteristics of the spiritual as well as material life'. Poor Jane Austen, when looked at in this light, seems to fail completely: 'We receive but little improvement' from *her* characters, and yet the reviewer admits to a kind of illicit fascination for her art. 'We almost wonder how we could ever have been so strongly interested in characters which have nothing high or ideal about them.' [6]

The direct effect that novels were supposed to produce on the conduct of adult readers was almost of the same sort that comic

[1] XXIV (March, 1853), 183–98. [2] I (July, 1855), 153.
[3] *Ibid.*, p. 128. [4] XLIV (October, 1851), 386.
[5] XLI (January, 1850), 111. [6] L (November, 1854), 489–90.

books and television programmes are supposed to have on children today. *Macmillan's* in 1861 warned all novelists that fiction 'is at the core of all the truths of this world, for it is the truth of life itself. He who dares reproduce it is a Prometheus who has stolen the celestial fire: let him beware that he uses it for the benefit of his fellow-mortals.' *The Mill on the Floss* is perfect so far as art and literary skill go, but has it reproduced life for the benefit of mankind? 'Ask what good it will do?—whether it will lighten any burdened heart, help any perplexed spirit, comfort the sorrowful, succour the tempted, . . . What is the answer? Silence.' [1] Since the poet and novelist rival the preacher in influence, according to the *North British Review*, 'the responsibility of the poet and novelist, for the wholesomeness of their instructions, is scarcely inferior to that of the preacher'. In the same article, 'American Novels', Hawthorne is condemned for making 'the moral subserve the art, instead of the art the moral'. [2] There are almost no critics of this period who would deny the moral purpose of art, but the best of them would rather make the art and the moral coincide with each other than have either one subserve the other.

By far the majority of critics were against direct moral exhortation, even though the practice was very widespread. The novelist should never write 'with a definite didactic aim; there may be little moralising and no formal exhortations—the less of either [*sic*] the better'. Novels can only teach by example, and the example ought to carry its force without precepts. [3] According to one writer in *Fraser's*, October, 1851, the English novel was being ruined by its 'exuberance of religious and moral sentiment', and the French novel had achieved a very definite superiority in art, if not in morality. 'We are too didactic, thinking too much of the moral, and too little of the story through which it is enforced, we suffer the end to overwhelm the means.' [4] This essay anticipates Taine's famous chapter on Thackeray which appeared in the following decade.

The *Prospective Review*, edited by a Unitarian divine, the Reverend James Martineau, considered a specific didactic intention enough to kill any novel. In Bulwer-Lytton's *My Novel* 'the characters . . . lose their spontaneity, and want the breath

---

[1] III (April, 1861), 442–4.   [2] XX (November, 1853), 81–6.
[3] *Edinburgh Review*, XCVII (April, 1853), 381.   [4] XLIV, 380–6.

of life; they seem not so much to have sprung into being from the fervent depths of a creative imagination . . . as to have been called into being for the purpose of embodying certain moral ideas. The moral tone should be felt through a work . . . never obtruding itself into notice. . . .' [1] George Eliot and George Meredith as critics in the *Westminster Review* expressed almost the same ideas,[2] and their criticism of Kingsley, that he fails to distinguish between his two occupations of clergyman and novelist, is repeated in *The Athenaeum*: the story of *Westward Ho!* is 'straggling, tumultuous, incoherent' but 'the capital error in the book—the error that swallows up its success—is, that Mr. Kingsley . . . is all along in a pulpit preaching at his readers, expounding the meaning of his mystery, and making the virtues of his different characters the themes for so much scolding. . . .' [3] G. H. Lewes in the *Leader* used even stronger terms for *The Mildmays*, 1857: 'Another novel with an earnest purpose. How long is our patience to be abused by these insults to our taste and understanding? . . . Every monomaniac who wishes to force his one idea upon his neighbour now writes a tale. . . .' [4]

It would be a mistake, however, to say that this thorough campaign against didactic fiction extended to all novels with a 'purpose'. Many reviewers did distinguish between those in which the writer's thesis was well worked out in wholly novelistic terms. 'Let writers with a purpose not forget that when they make use of fiction to develop their views, these, not to appear contemptible, require the display of narrative and dramatic power. . . .' [5] Novels like *Uncle Tom's Cabin*, for instance, were, on the whole, well received in the same periodicals which led the fight against didacticism, and G. H. Lewes wrote in the *Leader* that Mrs. Gaskell's *Ruth* was a 'moral problem worked out in fiction'; her lesson was suggested, not preached or formally inculcated, but 'carried straight to the soul by the simple vehicle of the story'. Her novel succeeded because it dealt with 'human nature, not with ideal abstractions'.[6] But when the characters were straw men to be knocked down at will by the author, when they had no independent life, a book

---

[1] IX (April, 1853), 228. [2] See above, pp. 38–40 and 43–5.
[3] (March 31, 1855), p. 376. [4] VIII (January 3, 1857), 18.
[5] *Westminster Review*, LXVIII (July, 1857), 307.
[6] IV (January 23, 1853), 89–90.

was condemned, and the novelist who was merely a pamphleteer bore the brunt of a rather fierce attack: 'Every season we are bored to death with a host of wretched and wearisome *pamphlets*, broken into chapters and interspersed with dialogue.' [1] Apparently, for the *Westminster Review* of July, 1857, the novel was in danger of being overwhelmed by its use as a slightly dramatized argument. 'Why relinquish the pamphlet, the ancient, approved, and honourable weapon of controversy, in order to overfreight fiction with a load that sinks it. . . . We have a race of writers who now imagine they would be disgraced by simply telling a story.' [2]

Much of this kind of criticism was of course directed against purposes the reviewer specifically disapproved of. Dickens' *Hard Times*, for *Blackwood's*, a very conservative periodical, was a failure because it was 'a story made on the didactic principle, with all its events forced into proofs of an untenable theory'.[3] Here the emphasis falls not on the fact that the book illustrates a theory, but that this theory is untenable according to the reviewer. W. R. Gregg, a Manchester manufacturer, roundly attacked Mrs. Gaskell's *Mary Barton* for the same reasons,[4] and we have already seen how Fitzjames Stephen treated Dickens and Reade.[5] But, of course, this kind of criticism—in which political commitment gets in the way of disinterested evaluation—is still very much with us, as some of the recent attacks in this country on Greene's *The Quiet American* prove only too conclusively.

The *North British Review* of November, 1856, towards the end of a thorough discussion of a group of religious novels, tried to show why these books were failures. The purpose of the novelist, according to this critic, should be 'to present, in artistic shape, and yet in one which is felt in the main to be true to nature and experience, those aspects of life, and phases of character that lay hold on the general sympathies of men'. The novelist openly advocating some particular doctrine, especially a religious one, thus narrows down his appeal to those who hold his specific beliefs. Furthermore, the novelist should show the

[1] *North British Review*, XXXI (November, 1859), 388.
[2] LXVIII, 306.   [3] LXXVII (April, 1855), 454.
[4] *National Review*, VIII (January, 1859), 144–67.
[5] See above, pp. 24–5.

71

destinies of the characters, 'influenced by one another and by circumstances in accordance with the natural course of events, as presented to us by experience'. When the didactic writer makes his 'characters, plot, conversation, and circumstances' fit the theories of the author our sense of the way things happen in life is necessarily outraged. The representation of life, which should be the primary aim, is thus forced into a position that is secondary to the advocacy of a particular point of view, so that, 'by aiming at two incompatible objects, the author does not succeed in either'. In addition—and here we have a repetition of the argument in the *Prospective Review* of 1853 and in Roscoe's essay on Bulwer-Lytton[1]—the characters in such a novel tend to lack vitality because they become 'impersonations of abstractions'. When a novel would deal with social or religious questions, it should begin 'in living sympathy', not in a 'theory'.[2] Nassau Senior, reviewing a collected edition of Bulwer-Lytton in the August, 1855, edition of the *North British Review*, also thought the object of a novel was not to give lessons in conduct, but to represent life. A true picture of life is always instructive, 'but the instruction is incidental'. 'Whenever a poet labours to be a teacher, whenever he suffers his attention to be withdrawn from its principal object, his work . . . attains each of its purposes imperfectly.'[3]

One of the most thorough discussions of this whole question was a series of two articles in *Bentley's Miscellany* of 1859, 'Of Novels, Historical and Didactic.' The author piled up an impressive list of authorities to prove fiction should not be written for a specific moral purpose, but that did not mean a novel should be purposeless. Following De Quincey, the author says the moral should be immanent throughout the work, never appearing explicitly. The novel belongs to the literature of power, not of knowledge, so that its purpose is to move, not teach. Any attempt, moreover, to use fiction as an exemplum to prove a specific case could never have the force of logical argument, because the author makes up his own events to prove his point.[4]

---

[1] See above, pp. 53–4 and 69–70.

[2] XXVI, 210–14. See also G. H. Lewes, *Life of Goethe* (Leipzig, 1864), II, 273.

[3] XXIII, 366. See also *Westminster Review*, LVII (January, 1852), 284.

[4] XLVI, 42–51, 135–47.

6. POETIC JUSTICE

One of the chief means didactic novelists used in enforcing their moral was the use of poetic justice—rewarding the 'good' characters and punishing the 'bad' at the end of the book. In a rather full discussion of Scott's invariable use of this device for ending his novels, Bagehot pointed out that novels in which the good suffer and the evil prosper leave the 'impression of an uncared-for world', a world where there is no overruling providence. Bagehot affirmed that he himself believed that on the whole, in the real world, the good prosper and the wicked suffer. 'Most people who ought to succeed, do succeed; most people who do fail, ought to fail.' Since in Scott's world all violations of the moral law were subject to stern retribution, his novels satisfied the moral sense. The extreme form of poetic justice, however, which apportioned pain and pleasure in proportion to the moral qualities of the characters was as wrong as that which completely denied any sort of punishment for evil.[1] In the essay on George Eliot in the *National Review* of July, 1860, the whole question of punishment and reward is dismissed as wholly unimportant. All that is necessary is that authors clearly discriminate 'the relative nobility of the characters they do conceive'. We must sympathize with the good and not the evil ones.[2]

It was on this ground that Thackeray mercilessly attacked the morality of Bulwer's novels in the thirties and forties as critic for *Fraser's*; he disliked Bulwer's sympathetic criminals like Paul Clifford and Eugene Aram. But the convention of poetic justice Thackeray deliberately spoofed in his own work, as in the ending of *Vanity Fair*, where Becky lives happily, comfortably and respectably ever after on Jos Sedley's insurance money after poisoning him; and in *Pendennis*, where Blanche Amory, we are led to believe, lives a very pleasant life on the Foker millions. His classic treatment of this subject is the burlesque continuation of *Ivanhoe*, *Rebecca and Rowena*, where poor Ivanhoe lives on to be the henpecked husband of his 'good' wife. The *Westminster Review* saw these deliberate satires of an outworn convention as basic to Thackeray's method as a novelist. He knew

[1] *National Review*, VI (April, 1858), 458-9.   [2] XI, 213.

that the old and easy manner of the novelist in distributing what is called poetical justice, and lodging his favourites in a haven of common-place comfort at the close of some improbable game of cross-purposes, had little in common with the natural course of things in the world, and could convey little either to instruct the understanding, to school the affections, or to strengthen the will.

The endings of his novels were, for this reviewer, an integral part of his determination to call things 'by their right names' and rid the novel of the 'sham sentiment, sham morality, sham heroism' of Bulwer, Ainsworth, Mrs. Gore, and G. P. R. James.[1] For another *Westminster* reviewer, it was Balzac who did away with last judgments in novels, 'the terrible last chapter, when the good used to be gathered together and be respectably married, while the bad were cast out into single-lived perdition'.[2]

For the *Saturday Review*, in an essay exclusively concerned with poetic justice, the function of rewards and punishments at the end of a novel is to excite 'a soothing emotion' in readers, but the novelist's task is a far higher one than that of pleasing his reader; it is to give him insight into the nature of the world. Conventional poetic justice, therefore, is seen as an evasion of the writer's responsibility, and nothing can ever be at stake in a novel that we are sure will always turn out well at the end.[3] Using much stronger terms, Fitzjames Stephen, in his most important literary essay, 'The Relation of Novels to Life', which appeared in *Cambridge Essays*, 1855, called poetic justice a 'taint from which few authors have escaped', and like the *Westminster* reviewer of 1853, he praised the ending of Thackeray's novels. 'In this, as in almost every department of novel literature, Mr. Thackeray appears to us to have conferred immense benefit on novel readers.' Bulwer-Lytton, on the other hand, was one of the worst offenders. Of a character in one of his novels, Stephen writes: 'He utterly ruins himself, taking some trouble to do it, and takes to drinking, merely from a sense of duty to Sir E. Lytton; and because he feels that if a wicked man in a novel were to become rich, all the foundations of morality would be out of course.'[4] (Meredith made a very similar comment on the hero of Kingsley's *Two Years Ago*.[5])

[1] LIX (April, 1853), 372–3.   [2] LX (July, 1853), 209.
[3] XVII (April 2, 1864), 407–8.   [4] Pp. 179–80.   [5] See above, pp. 38–9.

7. LESLIE STEPHEN: THE MORALITY OF ART

Leslie Stephen, in his essay 'Art and Morality', has given us what will probably remain the classic attack on didactic fiction and the convention of poetic justice.

Novels with a purpose are proverbially detestable, for a novel with a purpose means a book setting forth that a villain is hanged and a good man presented with a thousand pounds—that is silly and really immoral; for in the first place the imaginary event is no guarantee for the real event; secondly, a particular case does not prove a rule; thirdly, it is not true that virtue is always rewarded and vice punished; and fourthly, virtue should not be inculcated with a simple view to money or the gallows.[1]

'The highest morality of a great work of art', Stephen asserts in his essay on Fielding, depends not on the way an author rewards and punishes his characters but 'on the power with which the essential beauty and ugliness of virtue and vice are exhibited by an impartial observer'. Iago is an ugly character and does not have to come to a bad end to repel the reader.[2] When Fielding, who is a great writer by virtue of his 'seriousness of purpose',[3] loses this impartiality and becomes angry with Blifil, 'he simply reviles' and ceases to understand. The resulting character is a blur, rather than a consistent portrait. With the consequent loss of insight, due to the overpowering of his judgment by his moral sense, he ceases to be an artist at all.[4]

But Stephen's cool and logical demolition of the simple-minded novel with a moral purpose does not mean that literary art can ever be divorced from morality, 'a system of rules for regulating our passions'. It was folly to underestimate the danger to society of such 'brutalizing and anti-social instincts' and habits of mind as 'cynicism, prurience and voluptuous delight in cruelty'. These, for Stephen, were 'simply abominable', and 'he who keeps them alive is doing harm, and more harm if he has the talent of a Shakespeare, a Mozart, or a Raphael. . . . Nobody should compose poems for human

[1] *Cornhill Magazine*, **XXXII** (July, 1875), 101.
[2] *Hours in a Library* (New York, 1904), III, 35–6.
[3] *Ibid.*, p. 4.
[4] *Ibid.*, p. 20.

75

beasts.' [1] A novel or poem, Stephen writes, should not attempt like a Chinese vase to exist for no purpose except to please the aesthetic sense, but must have 'a ruling thought, though it should not degenerate into a tract; and the thought should be one which will help to purify and sustain the mind by which it is assimilated; and therefore tend to make society so far healthier and happier.' [2] Like all the major Victorian novelists and critics, Stephen demanded of fiction a definite social and moral function, not to be realized by direct preaching. Instead, the reader should be 'affected by the morality which permeated the whole structure and substance' of the book. [3] Bulwer-Lytton, a favourite whipping boy of the Victorian critics, was thus condemned because 'his moral is not embodied in his works, but exhibited with all the emphasis of sententious aphorism'. His works could have no real effect on their readers, moral or otherwise, because they lacked 'spontaneity and vigour', because he had 'no firm grasp of real life . . . no imaginative intensity'. And all the serious purpose in the world could not make one a first-rate novelist if he lacked these gifts. [4]

Stephen evidently felt that he had somewhat oversimplified the whole problem in his 'Art and Morality', for his ideas appear in a more fully developed form in 'The Moral Element in Literature', which was also published in the *Cornhill Magazine*. Here the morality of a work has nothing to do with anything specific that the author says; rather the influence of a work 'depends upon a man's total power, upon his intellectual and emotional vigour, upon the strength of his passions, the clearness of his reason, the delicacy of his perceptions, the general harmony of his faculties. . . .' In short, there could be no divorce between literary standards and moral standards; they were one and the same thing, so that the idea of 'a Shakespeare, a Mozart, or a Raphael' creating immoral works was impossible. The very qualities which were responsible for their genius—strength, clarity, harmony—were *ipso facto* moral. Morality Stephen now sees as health, 'the whole organisation working soundly', and this quality, if it is in the man, must be

---

[1] *Cornhill Magazine*, XXXII (July, 1875), 92–4.
[2] *Ibid.*, p. 101.   [3] *Ibid.*, p. 96.
[4] *Ibid.*, XXVII (March, 1873), 348–54.

in his work. Any moral degradation would be immediately perceptible by the literary critic as a literary fault. 'The literary equivalent of moral degradation is blunted feeling, the loss of delicate perception which enables a man to distinguish between exalted passion and brutish appetite, and disqualifies him from dealing with the highest problems of human nature. . . .' [1]

Morality for Stephen could never be merely passive, a 'spontaneous obedience to a certain code of rules—a dislike to lying, stealing, drunkenness and so forth'. Such an idea he found 'an utterly inadequate measure of a man's total excellence', rather it is something active, 'the amount of energy he represents and . . . the vigour of his impact on the world of thought'. As a result, the ultimate value of any book was dependent on the nature of its author. 'I measure the worth of any book by the worth of the friend whom it reveals to me. . . . The worth of an author is in proportion to his whole intellectual force.' [2] George Eliot had come to a very similar conclusion about the relationship between a novel and its novelist. 'Don't you agree with me that much superfluous stuff is written on all sides about purpose in art? A nasty mind makes nasty art, whether for art or any other sake. And a meagre mind will bring forth what is meagre. And some effect in determining other minds there must be according to the degree of nobleness or meanness in the selection made by the artist's soul.' [3]

It was in his penetrating analysis of Charlotte Brontë that Stephen showed how he would apply the ideas he worked out in his more theoretical essays. *Jane Eyre* was a result of two wholly conflicting aims: one, stated in the preface, was a 'protest against conventionality', and the other was a most 'unflinching adherence to the proper conventions of society'. 'At one moment . . . we seem to be drifting towards the solution that strong passion is the one really good thing in the world . . .', and at another that 'Duty is supreme', duty to the moral conventions of society. If one asked the rather awkward question: 'What would Jane Eyre have done, and what would our sympathies have been, had she found that Mrs. Rochester had

---

[1] *Ibid.*, XLIII (January, 1881), 41–7.   [2] *Ibid.*, pp. 41–2.
[3] *George Eliot Letters*, V, 391 (letter to Edward Burne-Jones, March 20, 1873).

not been burnt at Thornfield?' it becomes apparent that Charlotte Brontë has left 'an unsolved discord' in her book and 'an inharmonious representation of life'. Stephen finds the same symptoms in her style, 'a certain feverish disquiet' marked by strong mannerisms. 'At its best, we have admirable flashes of vivid expression, where the material of language is the incarnation of keen intuitive thought. At its worst, it is strangely contorted, crowded by rather awkward personifications, and degenerates towards a rather unpleasant Ossianesque. More severity of taste would increase the power by restraining the abuse.' [1]

In *Villette* Stephen finds the same qualities that he found in *Jane Eyre*. 'She is between the opposite poles of duty and happiness, and cannot see how to reconcile their claims, or even . . . to state the question at issue. She pursues one path energetically, till she feels herself to be in danger, and then shrinks with a kind of instinctive dread. . . .' [2] Stephen here, in Charlotte Brontë, is, of course, giving the classic description of neurosis, a conflict engendered by alternate attraction and withdrawal without any possibility of a resolution. 'Undoubtedly such a position speaks of a mind diseased, and a more powerful intellect would even under her conditions have worked out some more comprehensible and harmonious solution.' Her only possible position is the one she is left with at the end of her novel: 'that life is a mystery, but that happiness must be sought by courting misery.' As a result, any claims made for Charlotte Brontë as a novelist of 'the highest rank' must be denied, because she is not 'amongst those who have fought their way to a clearer atmosphere, and can help us to clearer conceptions. . . .' [3]

In the same essay Stephen tries to define precisely the ideal critical approach to novels: 'to feel strongly, and yet to analyse coolly'. Even though our reactions are necessarily at first strongly emotional, 'the product of instinctive sympathy [or antipathy], instead of deliberate reason', 'when we are seeking to justify our emotions', we must become as objective as we can, 'applying with rigid impartiality such methods as are best calculated to free us from the influence of personal bias'. His notion of a kind of scientific objectivity in criticism, like

[1] *Hours in a Library*, III, 306-7.　　[2] *Ibid.*, p. 310.　　[3] *Ibid.*, p. 311.

Arnold's, has very strong affinities with the main stream of French criticism in the nineteenth century, especially Taine and Saint-Beuve.

Though criticism cannot boast of being a science, it ought to aim at something like a scientific basis, or at least proceed in a scientific spirit. The critic, therefore, before abandoning himself to the oratorical impulse, should endeavor to classify the phenomena with which he is dealing as calmly as if he were ticketing a fossil in a museum. The most glowing eulogy, the most bitter denunciation have their proper place; but they belong to the art of persuasion, and form no part of the scientific method.[1]

And one can search in vain through all Stephen's critical writings for the purple passages of impressionistic critics like Swinburne and Pater. It is important, though, to remember that Stephen never treated a piece of literature as purely a historical artifact, a fossil, that has no power to influence our lives. The value of any novel lay in the fact that it was an extension of the reader's world, and as such, should have a very definite influence on him. To read a novel in the true sense 'is to lay aside for a moment one's own personality, and to become a part of the author. It is to enter the world in which he habitually lives—for each of us lives in a separate world of his own—to breathe his air. . . .' [2] It was Stephen's ability to project himself into a novel, identify himself with its author, and, at the same time, to maintain his objectivity that gives his best criticism its special quality. 'To be an adequate critic is almost to be a contradiction in terms; to be susceptible to a force, and yet free from its influence; to be moving with the stream, and yet to be standing on the bank.' [3]

8. G. H. LEWES AND DAVID MASSON: THE NOVEL AS A WORK OF ART

Like Stephen, George Henry Lewes formulated a distinct critical programme, but Lewes considered the novel primarily as a work of art, and in discussing any art one must always refer to the absolute standards which govern it. 'The art of novel-writing, like the art of painting, is founded on general

[1] *Ibid.*, pp. 272–3.   [2] *Ibid.*, IV, 53–4.   [3] *Ibid.*, III, 273.

principles, which, because they have their psychological justification, because they are derived from tendencies of the human mind, and not, as absurdly supposed, derived from "models of composition", are of universal application.' [1] The discussion of Lewes' very definite formal criteria for the criticism of novels will be reserved for a later chapter, as well as his interesting theory of realism, but it is important to notice in this context that he believed novel criticism, if it was to have any value, must confine itself chiefly to questions of form. Too much contemporary criticism seemed irrelevant to him because it resolved itself into matters of taste. One can say that he likes a book because it is amusing, but that kind of statement admits of no discussion; 'those whom it amuses *are* amused' and there is an end to the matter. [2] In the same way there is the reader who can not become interested in Wordsworth's potters and waggoners just because potters and waggoners cannot excite his imagination. For Lewes these judgments cannot be considered criticism and admit of no rejoinder. But he does insist that 'when a question of Art comes to be discussed, it must not be confounded with a matter of individual feeling; and it requires a distinct reference to absolute standards'. [3] Thackeray's statement, which had become a critical cliché by this time, that *Tom Jones* 'as a work of art . . . is absolutely perfect', can thus be very easily refuted by showing that Fielding violates the all-important law of artistic economy. Lewes would admit that *Tom Jones* shows humour, 'a real talent for story-telling— for presenting the various elements of a story in an animated succession of illustrative scenes—an eye for characteristics in person, manner, and speech, and a style easy, idiomatic and vigorous'. But none of these merits makes a masterpiece. 'They are none of them high or rare merits.' [4]

It was only Jane Austen, among English novelists, whom Lewes would call a perfect artist: 'if the *truest* representation, effected by the *least expenditure* of means, constitutes the highest claim of art, then we may say that Miss Austen has carried the art to a point of excellence surpassing that reached by any of

---

[1] *Blackwood's Edinburgh Magazine*, LXXXVI (July, 1859), 108.
[2] *Ibid.*, LXXXVII (March, 1860), 331.
[3] *Ibid.*, LXXXVI (July, 1859), 108.
[4] *Ibid.*, LXXXVII (March, 1860), 331–3.

her rivals.' George Eliot, who was at the beginning of her career as a novelist at the date of this essay (July, 1859), Lewes found superior to Jane Austen in 'culture, reach of mind, and depth of emotional sensibility', but Jane Austen's superiority in 'the art of telling a story; and generally . . . the "economy of art",' makes her the more perfect artist, simply *qua* artist.[1]

But there are other criteria one can use for works of art. Even though Jane Austen may be a perfect artist, greatness is dependent on other qualities as well. When it is admitted that Jane Austen has limited herself to 'quiet scenes of everyday life, with no power over the more stormy and energetic activities which find vent even in everyday life . . . [and that] she never stirs the deeper emotions, . . . never fills the soul with a noble aspiration, or brightens it with a fine idea . . . , we have admitted an objection to rank her among the great benefactors of the race. . . .' [2]

Lewes firmly believed that a novelist's choice of subject matter was extremely important in deciding his ultimate rank. 'It is obvious that the nature of the thing represented will determine degrees in art. Raphael will always rank higher than Teniers. . . . It is a greater effort of genius to produce a fine epic, than a fine pastoral; a great drama, than a perfect lyric . . . the higher the aims, the greater is the strain, and the nobler the success.' But he also believed that 'no art can be high that is not good. A great subject ceases to be grand when its treatment is feeble.' [3] His belief in the importance of subject matter in a work of art is clearly opposed to most modern aesthetic speculation: 'A well-painted table-cover is better than an ill-painted face; but a well-painted face, with a noble expression is the highest reach of art, as the human soul is the highest thing we know.' [4]

As an extremely prolific critic of novels,[5] it is surprising how wide was the range of Lewes' tastes, and how many of his judgments have been verified by posterity, especially when we remember that most of his essays were written as reviews of novels as they came out. The only demands he made on the

---

[1] *Ibid.*, LXXXVI (July, 1859), 101–4.   [2] *Ibid.*, pp. 112–13.
[3] *Ibid.*, pp. 102–3.   [4] *Westminster Review*, LXX (October, 1858), 499.
[5] Lewes was weekly reviewer for the *Leader* from 1850 to 1857. He was also a contributor to most of the important periodicals of the period.

book under consideration were that it be original and that it have imaginative power, and so he was especially severe on the writer of tame domestic novels who thought they were in the tradition of Jane Austen. 'It is only plenitude of power that restrains her from the perils of the form she has chosen—the perils, namely of tedium and commonplace. . . . She makes her people speak and act as they speak and act in everyday life; and she is the only artist who has done this with success. . . .' Furthermore the imitators of Jane Austen invariably fail because 'they cannot keep to the severe level of prose; they rise above it and the result is incongruity; or they fall below it, and the result is tediousness'.[1] Of *Kathie Brand*, by Holme Lee, a popular novelist usually placed in the 'school of Miss Austen', he wrote, 'None of the characters impresses us with any vivid sense of their reality; they are pale water-colour sketches, when not conventional novel types.' Miss Lee lacks a 'keen sense of reality, or the power of vivid representation of reality, which alone can make quiet everyday life interesting. . . .'[2] Mrs. Gaskell was one of the few English writers who had this power for Lewes, especially in *Cranford*, and that was why he predicted it would be 'more permanent than the others [of Mrs. Gaskell's novels up to 1853], though less noisy in reputation'. Because of the way her material was rendered, it 'stands out in the memory like an experience. . . . Provincial life in its ineffable dullness moves before us; we enjoy every detail of the pageant as heartily as we should detest the reality!'[3]

When *Moby Dick* was published in England in 1851 under the title of *The Whale*, it passed almost unnoticed or was damned as rant. But Lewes in the *Leader* cited it, along with the prose of Poe and Hawthorne, as the real beginning of a genuine American literature. For him it was 'a strange, wild, weird book, full of poetry, and full of interest. . . . The daring imagery often grows riotous and extravagant. . . . Criticism may pick holes in this work, but no criticism will thwart its fascination.'[4]

---

[1] Anna Theresa Kitchell, *George Lewes and George Eliot, A Review of Records* (New York, 1933), pp. 103–4.

[2] *Leader*, VII (November 15, 1856), p. 1097.

[3] *Ibid.*, IV (July 2, 1853), 644.

[4] Kitchell, *op. cit.*, p. 106. Compare the review in *The Athenaeum*, October 25, 1851, pp. 1112–13.

When Lewes received a review copy of *Jane Eyre* by the un-known writer Currer Bell from Smith, Elder and Company in 1847, he became so enthusiastic that he wanted to write a long article on it in *Fraser's Magazine*. The editor, however, objected that it might seem foolish to devote so much space to a book no one had ever heard of and whose reception was far from cer-tain.[1] As a result Lewes had to include several other novels in the same essay under the heading of 'Recent Novels: French and English'; but the other books were huddled into two pages, and nine were spent praising *Jane Eyre*. He pointed out that though the author was obviously addicted to 'melodrama and improbability which smack of the circulating library', she was 'unquestionably setting forth her own experience' by means of 'the machinery of the story'. 'Unless a novel be built out of real experience, it can have no real success.' Currer Bell had almost all he required of a novelist: 'perception of character, and power of delineating it; picturesqueness; passion; and know-ledge of life'. But the quality he prized most in this new book was the sense that an individual wrote it. 'It has the capital point of all great styles in being *personal*,—the written speech of an individual, not the artificial language made from all sorts of books.' [2] *Shirley*, which Lewes reviewed in the *Edinburgh* in 1850, he found a falling off in power compared to *Jane Eyre*. Currer Bell had no real involvement in her social theme, the struggle between mill owners and their employees at the be-ginning of the nineteenth century.[3] *Villette*, however, he ad-mired very much indeed. 'Here . . . is an *original* book. Every page, every paragraph, is sharp with *individuality*. It is Currer Bell speaking to you, not the Circulating Library reverberating echos, [*sic*] how *she* has looked at life . . . what she has thought, and felt, not what she thinks others will expect her to have thought and felt. . . .' And even though the book was lacking in unity and progression, Charlotte Brontë still had no living rival in passion and power.[4]

Cousin Pons was one of the French novels reviewed in the

[1] Franklin Gary, 'Charlotte Brontë and George Henry Lewes', *PMLA*, LI (1936), 518–42.

[2] *Fraser's Magazine*, XXXVI (December, 1847), 691–3.

[3] CLXXXIII (January, 1850), 159.

[4] *Leader*, IV (February 12, 1853), 163.

Fraser's article that acclaimed *Jane Eyre*, and Lewes could find no evidence of any decline in Balzac's amazing energy. 'Wonderful it is to see how with what marvellous power such a simple subject is wrought into a story of deep, unceasing interest. To those who prate about Balzac's having written himself out [Balzac was almost at the end of his career], we would oppose the first volume of *Le Cousin Pons* as a triumphant answer.' [1] In order to appreciate Lewes' critical acumen, we should read this criticism in the context of the kind of moralistic interpretation Balzac received in the English press during the forties. [2]

Lewes praised *Barchester Towers* too for its 'astonishing energy', [3] and nine years earlier he had noted the change in Thackeray with *Vanity Fair*, from a minor writer of travel books, *nouvelles*, and burlesques, to a major novelist. But characteristically in this review in *The Athenaeum* he disliked Thackeray's cavalier attitude towards his craft. [4]

As a result of Lewes' almost uncanny ability as a critic to pick out the important novels from the chaff, John Blackwood, with whom Lewes had had no previous dealings, immediately became very much interested when Lewes announced that he had discovered a new genius who had written the first story in a projected series, 'Scenes from Clerical Life'. And undoubtedly it was Lewes' encouragement and her faith in his critical ability that finally broke through the ice of George Eliot's doubts about her powers as a novelist.

It was unfortunate for Lewes' reputation as a critic of novels that probably his best known essay today is 'Dickens in Relation to Criticism', originally written in 1872 for the *Fortnightly Review*. Hutton was certainly right in calling it 'a mere blunder', [5] for Dickens was one of the few writers with whom Lewes was totally out of sympathy. He attributed Dickens' enormous popularity to 'overflowing fun' rather than humour, and to Dickens' 'marvellous vividness' of imagination, which he recognized as almost akin to the hallucinations of madness. But here Lewes was merely echoing Taine's famous essay on Dickens.

---

[1] *Fraser's Magazine*, XXXVI (December, 1847), 694.
[2] See Clarence Decker, *The Victorian Conscience* (New York, 1952).
[3] *Leader*, VIII (May 23, 1857), 497.
[4] (August 12, 1848), 794–7.
[5] *Contemporary Thought and Thinkers*, I, 89.

Dickens' work was sure to be ephemeral because of his terrible limitation: 'the pervading commonness' and the lack of any thought or passion in his novels. In Dickens 'sensations never passed into ideas', and, as a result, compared with Thackeray's or Fielding's, his is 'a mere *animal* intelligence'. Lewes' insufferable condescension at the end of his essay—'He gave us his best. If the efforts were sometimes too strained, and the desire for effect too obtrusive, there was no lazy indulgence' [1]—almost maddened John Forster, who attacked Lewes as a traitor in the second edition of his *Life of Dickens*. Lewes' very broad and catholic view of the novel had evidently, by 1872, become very restricted, probably because of the influence of George Eliot, who was now a universal yardstick for him. 'I do not suppose a single thoughtful remark on life and character can be found throughout the twenty volumes [of Dickens' collected works].' It was not only the 'marked absence of a reflective tendency' that bothered Lewes, but he could find no evidence that 'the past life of humanity . . . ever occupied him; keenly as he observes the objects before him, he never connects his observations into a general expression, never seems interested in the general relations of things'. Dickens was completely 'outside philosophy, science or higher literature' (this implication that novels were mere 'light literature' was very far from the Lewes who was a major critic of fiction in the forties and fifties), and he was shocked to see the state of Dickens' library—only novels, books of travel and presentation copies. [2] It must be remembered that for more than ten years Lewes had been an important writer on science and philosophy and had completely lost his interest in current imaginative literature. In 1858 James Cordy Jeaffreson's statement, in his *Novels and Novelists from Elizabeth to Victoria*, that G. H. Lewes was 'perhaps the best philosophical and critical essayist now living' [3] would not have found much disagreement among readers of Victorian periodicals, and Trollope was probably referring to the same period when he called Lewes 'the acutest critic' he knew. [4] Lewes' great critical reputation was also responsible for his being asked in 1862 to become the editor of the *Cornhill Magazine* after Thackeray's

[1] *Fortnightly Review*, XVII (1872), 144–52.
[2] *Ibid.*, pp. 151–2.   [3] (London, 1858), II, 368.
[4] *Autobiography* (Berkeley and Los Angeles, 1947), p. 128.

resignation. Although he refused because of the pressure of his new scientific interests, he was retained as a consulting editor for several years at a high salary, and upon the formation of the *Fortnightly Review*, he became the first editor.

David Masson, the author of the monumental *Life of Milton*, had, like Lewes and Stephen, definite critical ideas on what the novel should be and in which direction its development should move. First of all the novelist must realize that he is an artist working in a form that is as dignified and important as any other art form. All art, of course, he concedes, in '*Pendennis* and *Copperfield*, Thackeray *and* Dickens', an essay appearing in the *North British Review* of May, 1851, must interest its audience, and

in a certain deep sense, it may be maintained that no kind of literary composition whatever is valuable that is not interesting, [yet] it would seem as if recently the determination to achieve that special kind of interest which consists in mere amusement, had prevailed too largely among our writers of tales and novels. We do not often see now that effort at artistic perfection, that calm resolution to infuse into a performance the concentrated thought and observation of the writer, and to give it the final roundness and finish, which did exist in old times, and which supreme authorities have always recommended.[1]

He was able to develop and amplify this point in a series of four lectures he delivered to the members of the Philosophic Institution of Edinburgh in 1858, and the following year he expanded and published the lectures as a book entitled *The British Novelists and Their Styles*. Dividing all imaginative literature into the classical genres of lyric, dramatic and epic, he followed Fielding in classifying the novel with the epic, which includes all narrative poetry, though he would not have agreed with him in deriving the novel from the comic epic. To do so unduly limits its potentialities, and Masson believed the novelist may treat his material in the way any of the great narrative poets did. 'The Novel, at its highest, is a prose Epic; and the capabilities of the Novel, as a form of literature, are the capabilities of Narrative Poetry universally, excepting in as far as the use of prose, instead of verse, may involve necessary differences.'[2] But these differences are only that 'Prose can

[1] XV, 88.   [2] (Cambridge, 1859), p. 2.

concern itself more intimately than Verse with what is variable in time and place'—that is, with the particulars of social reality.[1]

The decision made by the literary artist whether to employ verse or prose as his medium can not be used as a value judgment. Even though it may be difficult to recall more than one or two novels that could be seriously compared to *The Iliad* or *The Odyssey*, there are 'hundreds of performances, ranking in the same general class of poetry as these epics, which we should as little dare to compare, in respect of genius, with some of our best novels'. Comparing Cervantes with Dryden and La Fontaine, he finds *Don Quixote* to be 'a work of far higher, and even of more truly poetic genius', than the fables of the other two authors. The fact that one wrote in prose and the other in verse had nothing to do with the matter. He quotes Baron Bunsen approvingly: 'Every romance [a term used interchangeably with *novel*] is intended or ought to be a new *Iliad* or Odyssey.'[2]

Masson disliked any attempt to limit the novel. Richardson, although a genius because of his 'subtle imagination of the progressive states of feeling rather than of changing external scenes' and his 'minute inquisition into the human heart . . . especially the female heart', concerned himself almost entirely with one passion, love, and powerfully influenced all succeeding novelists. But since the love story only deals with a 'limited portion . . . of human circumstances . . . the novel is thereby contracted in its capabilities as a form of literature'.[3]

In order to widen their scope novelists 'must at least be abreast of the best speculation of their time'. Not that they were to be speculative thinkers, 'but the imagination of a well furnished mind is one thing, and that of a vacuum is another'. Besides, 'every artist, poet or novelist is also a thinker whether he chooses or not. . . . The imagination is not a faculty working apart; it is the whole mind thrown into the act of imagining; and the value of any act of imagination, therefore, . . . will depend on the total strength and total furnishing of the mind. . . .' It is for that reason that he demanded, as Arnold was later to demand in 'The Function of Criticism at the Present Time', that the literary artist be 'acquainted with the best thoughts that may be current on subjects of greatest general interest and

[1] *Ibid.*, p. 16. [2] *Ibid.*, pp. 2–4. [3] *Ibid.*, pp. 113–19.

importance'. Masson found appalling the ignorance of human nature displayed in 'the ordinary run of novels', 'a Psychology, if the truth must be spoken, such as would not hold good in a world of imaginary cats, not to speak of men—impossible conformations of character; actions determined by motives that could never have determined the like; sudden conversions brought about by logical means of such astounding simplicity that wonder itself is paralyzed in contemplating them. . . .'[1]

One of the most important parts of Masson's critical theory was his attack on realism, which will be examined in a later chapter. As a result of this theory he saw English prose fiction being reduced to a grey sameness, faithful studies of contemporary English society or certain very limited portions of English society. To continue along the same path meant for him the death of the novel as an art form. What English fiction needed was boundless imagination, and he called for more 'prose-poets' like Richter, Cervantes, and Rabelais: 'men avoiding nothing as too fantastic for their element, but free and daring in it as the verse-poet is in his'.[2]

At the end of *The British Novelists*, Masson makes a plea for more novels dealing with 'the grand, the elemental, the ideal' or subjects that are 'large, comprehensive, primitive, impressive, enduring', like 'Birth, Life, Death; Labour, Sorrow, Love, Revenge; the thought of whence, the thought of why, the thought of whither. . . .'[3] These are the subjects that he called 'elemental' rather than those concerned with giving a faithful surface representation of contemporary life. It is surprising that he mentions neither *Wuthering Heights* nor *Moby Dick* anywhere in his book, for these novels more than any others that he could have read best exemplify his programme. Yet Masson predicted what remained perhaps the most fruitful line of development for the European novel in the late nineteenth and twentieth centuries: Dostoievsky, Conrad, Kafka, Lawrence, and Faulkner.

[1] (Cambridge, 1859), pp. 296–301.
[2] *Wordsworth, Shelley, Keats, and Other Essays* (London, 1874), p. 214.
[3] *British Novelists*, pp. 302–5.

PART TWO

III

THE CRAFT OF FICTION

Aᴄᴄᴏʀᴅɪɴɢ to Joseph Warren Beach, the most impressive fact in the history of the English novel is the disappearance of the author.

In Fielding and Scott, in Thackeray and George Eliot, the author is everywhere present in person to see that you are properly informed on all the circumstances of the action, to explain the characters to you and to insure your forming the right opinion of them, to scatter nuggets of wisdom . . . and to point out, how from the failures and successes of the characters, you may form a sane and right philosophy of conduct.

In the modern novel, however, the author 'does not appear at all. The story tells itself; the story speaks for itself. The author does not apologize for his characters; he does not give an account of them; he does not describe them; he does not even tell us what they do. . . .' [1]

The idea that the novelist should completely efface himself from his creation and give his readers a direct rendering of the thoughts, words and actions of his characters, as if the action were being presented on a stage (except that in a novel thoughts can become audible without the use of soliloquy), was not new in English critical theory in the late nineteenth century, nor did it originate with the famous statement in Flaubert's correspondence: 'It is one of my principles that a writer should

[1] Joseph Warren Beach, *The Twentieth Century Novel* (New York, 1932), pp. 14–15.

not be his own theme. An artist must be in his work like God in creation, invisible and all-powerful; he should be everywhere felt, but nowhere seen.' [1]

At least as early as 1785 the question of the impersonality of the novelist comes up. Clara Reeve, in her very charming dialogue, *The Progress of Romance*, makes Euphrasia, her mouthpiece, say: 'Perhaps there is not a better criterion of the merit of a book, than our losing sight of the author,' [2] and Dr. John Moore, writing some time before 1797, distinguishes between presenting a character dramatically and merely describing him. About Richardson's Lovelace he says: 'It is easy for an author to declare, that his hero is possessed of an infinite deal of wit and pleasantry, invention and eloquence: To make him display those qualities through a great variety of scenes, is very difficult, yet it has been executed by this author in the most successful manner.' [3]

For Scott, reviewing Maria Edgeworth's *Patronage* in the *Quarterly* of January, 1814, the comic characters in that novel are successfully drawn because the hand of the author is never perceived (as it almost always is in our modern comedies, to the entire disgust of all persons of tolerable taste), but they are led in the most natural manner . . . 'to cover themselves with ridicule';[4] and in October, 1815, Scott singles out the dialogue of *Emma* for special praise because of the skill with which Jane Austen 'makes the characters of the speakers evolve themselves with dramatic effect'.[5]

But aside from a few passing remarks on this subject, such as Moore's and Scott's and Lamb's complaint to Wordsworth in a letter of 1801, meant chiefly as an indirect rebuke to Wordsworth himself, about 'many novelists' who 'continually put a sign post up to show where you are to feel',[6] there was no extensive discussion of the position of the novelist in his books

---

[1] Gustave Flaubert, *Selected Letters*, trans. Francis Steegmuller (New York, 1953), p. 195.

[2] Clara Reeve, *The Progress of Romance* (Colchester, 1785), reprinted by the Facsimile Text Society (New York, 1930), II, 25.

[3] Dr. John Moore, 'A View of the Commencement and Progress of Romance', *Works*, V (Edinburgh, 1820), 58.

[4] X, 307.   [5] *Quarterly Review*, XIV, 199.

[6] Quoted in Frederic T. Blanchard, *Fielding the Novelist* (New Haven, 1926), p. 312.

until the 1850's when the subject became one of the most important points in the criticism of fiction. As a result, Harriet Martineau, looking back in 1855 on her novel *Deerbrook*, published in 1838, finds herself dissatisfied with her earlier work. 'I should now require more of myself, if I were to attempt a novel . . . more simplicity, and a far more objective character. . . . The laborious portions of meditation, obtruded at intervals, are wholly objectionable in my eyes. Neither morally nor artistically can they be justified.' [1]

The use of the word *objective* in this context of course comes from German romantic speculation, especially that of Friedrich Schlegel, Schiller and Goethe, on the relation between the poet and his work. After the second decade of the nineteenth century the subjective-objective antithesis was brought into English aesthetic speculation chiefly by Coleridge, Carlyle and Henry Crabb Robinson, and as M. H. Abrams has shown, these terms were 'multiple and variable in their meaning'. They could be used to describe certain periods of literature (Greek literature was objective and modern literature subjective), differences between the various genres (the epic was objective, the lyric subjective), or qualities in the character of any work of art, regardless of period or genre. Professor Abrams quotes from Robinson's attempt to clarify the use of these terms:

The epic is marked by this character of style,—that the poet presents his *object* immediately and directly, with a total disregard of his own personality. He is, as it were, an indifferent and unimpassioned narrator and chronicler. . . . The opposite class of poetry is the *lyric*, in which the poet gives mainly objects as they are reflected in the mirror of his own individuality. . . . These same classes, designated generally, as the *objective* and *subjective*, were called by Schiller the naive and the sentimental and they have also been named the real and the ideal. [2]

But for many critics of the novel the 'dialectical variability' [3] of the two terms was unimportant. Since the novel was not a lyric poem, the author's own comments on his story or characters were as out of place as they would be in the drama. *Fraser's*

[1] Harriet Martineau, *Autobiography* (Boston, 1877), I, 415.
[2] Meyer H. Abrams, *The Mirror and the Lamp* (New York, 1953), pp. 241–3.
[3] *Ibid.*, p. 243.

of November, 1854, praised a novelist for avoiding the error 'of giving running commentaries upon . . . [his characters], rightly considering that their words and actions ought to be the best interpreters of the motives that guide them'.[1] The same periodical in January, 1860, declared that Jane Austen achieved 'a perfection in the exhibition . . . of characters which no one else has approached' because of the way 'her people are made to develope themselves in the progress of the story . . .; the machinery of representation is almost wholly concealed from observation.' As a result of the author's complete self-efface-ment, she has been able to create a perfectly autonomous whole. 'The whole thoughts of the reader are abstracted from the world of outer life, and are confined to the mimic world con-tained within the covers of the book. . . . The figures never step out of the frame, and the frame itself is unseen.' [2]

A year earlier, G. H. Lewes, in his essay on Jane Austen, had also singled out the dramatic quality of her genius and the resulting objective and impersonal character of her novels as the mark of their greatness.

> The real secret of Miss Austen's success lies in her having the exquisite and rare gift of dramatic creation of character. . . . She seldom describes anything, and is not felicitous when she attempts it. . . . But instead of *description*, the common and easy resource of novelists, she has the rare and difficult of art of *dramatic presentation*: instead of telling us what her characters are, and what they feel, she presents the people, and they reveal themselves.

It is here that Lewes finds the essence of the novelist's art, which he defines as 'the representation of human life by means of a story'.[3] When he examined *Hide and Seek* in the *Leader* in 1854 in the light of this criterion, he found Wilkie Collins had not succeeded as a creator of character because he substituted 'portrait painting for development. The characters in this book are well conceived, well drawn, but they are *described*; they do not move through the story, revealing themselves in it.' Too much of the book is 'simply narrated' instead of presented in 'fully worked out' scenes.[4]

An anonymous reviewer in the *North British Review* of Novem-

[1] L, 491. [2] LXI, 30-1.
[3] *Blackwood's Edinburgh Magazine*, LXXXVI (July, 1859), 101-5.
[4] V (June 24, 1854), 591-2.

ber, 1858, noticed that there was decidedly less commentary in novels written by women and offered as an explanation the fact that women 'believe so much more intensely in their own stories' than men do. As a result 'you have more sense of the present reality of the circumstances detailed. You are more identified with the story. . . .' He therefore declared flatly: 'There can be no doubt that the interest is more intense, where the tale does not in any way introduce the writer's thoughts or comments upon it.' [1]

Trollope's presence in his own novels was felt by the same periodical in May, 1864, to be an 'inartistic obtrusion of the author himself and his opinions'.[2] Earlier another critic in the *National Review* thought *Barchester Towers* a good novel, but 'it might have been better, if he would have refrained [*sic*] from frequently and somewhat offensively coming forward as author to remind us that we are reading a fiction. Such intrusions are as objectionable in a novel as on the stage: the actor who indulges in extempore and extra-professional hints and winks to the audience, and the author who interprets his characters to introduce himself to our notice, are alike guilty of a violation of good taste.' [3] In *Partial Portraits* James was later to characterize this mannerism of Trollope as 'a pernicious trick', a 'suicidal satisfaction in reminding the reader that the story he was telling was only, after all, make-believe';[4] and in 'The Art of Fiction' he called this trait 'a terrible crime'.[5] (It is a coincidence that the *National Review* anticipated yet another of James' criticisms of Trollope: his rather clumsy use of names from moral allegory or comedy of manners, like Dr. Fillgrave, lawyer Chaffanbrass, Messrs. Hardlines, Minusex, and Golightly. They remind us 'at every moment that we are reading a purely fictitious story. . . . In this species of nicknaming there is neither grace, sense nor cleverness. . . .' [6]) But when Trollope is compared to Thackeray in an article on *Orley Farm* in January, 1863, he is found to be a much lesser offender against 'the wholesome rule of impersonality'; 'the author is for the most part kept well out of sight . . .', while Thackeray's 'curious taste' for always talking directly to the reader is severely censured. He does not 'scruple to stop at

---

[1] XXIX, 469–70. [2] XL, 371. [3] VII, 425.
[4] (London, 1905), p. 116. [5] *Ibid.*, p. 379. [6] VII, 431.

every convenient point of . . . [his] narration to indulge in a few personal confidences, and enunciate . . . [his] views about . . . [his] story, . . . [himself], or the world in general'.[1]

The Saturday Reviewer of *Artist and Craftsman*, a forgotten novel of 1860, was also annoyed by any appearance of the novelist in his book, and for the same reasons we have seen reiterated by so many other critics. 'We are forced by these comments of the author on his own performance to remember we are only reading fiction. . . . We do not want the author to come in, like Bottom, with his prologue, and tell us that the lion is only Snug the Joiner . . .',[2] and in 1861 in the same weekly, Thackeray's favourite metaphor for himself as a novelist is attacked in a review of another ephemeral novel, *Who Breaks —Pays*: 'The author has continually to speak for his characters, and perform the part of showman to each in succession, instead of allowing them to speak for themselves and cast their own shadows on the wall.'[3] The two other important literary weeklies of the period made the same demand for the elimination of all commentary and for the dramatic presentation of character through speech and action rather than exposition and formal description. *The Athenaeum*, for example, objected to *The Newcomes* because of the long essays interpolated into the text of the novel so that it tended to become 'a handful of characters for Mr. Thackeray to lecture upon . . .';[4] and the *Spectator* declared all description of characters to be wrong: the author should make 'his *dramatis personae* develop their own characters in a legitimate and effective manner in the course of the story'.[5]

Probably very few critics of the period would have disagreed with Nassau Senior's strictures on Thackeray, which appeared in the *Edinburgh Review* of January, 1854. 'Mr. Thackeray indulges in the bad practice of commenting on the conduct of his *dramatis personae*. He is perpetually pointing out to us the generosity of Dobbin, the brutality of the Osbornes, the vanity of Joseph Sedley, and so on, instead of leaving us to find out their qualities from their actions.'[6] Two years earlier an article in the same review had announced definitively to all novelists: 'The first rule is—stick to your story; whatever you add that is

[1] XVI, 37.
[2] X (July 7, 1860), 23–4.
[3] XII (September 7, 1861), 251.
[4] (August 3, 1855), p. 895.
[5] XXXV (December 27, 1862), 1447.
[6] XCIX, 202.

not part of it, though ever so valuable in itself, will be an incumbrance. . . .' [1]

Occasionally, however, an author's comments were defended, but the critic's tone makes us aware that he is upholding an unpopular belief or making an exception for a single writer to the widespread demand for objectivity and impersonality. For example, the author of an article in the *National Review* of July, 1860, objected to 'the miscellaneous observations in which George Eliot so often indulges us' because they 'break the spell' of her novels, but in the case of Thackeray, on the other hand, the commentary is in keeping with the very nature of his books. [2] The *Quarterly* of 1855 also refused to balk at Thackeray's many reflections and observations: 'These disquisitions would be blemishes if they were not signal beauties . . . were they less perfect, [they] would incumber the tale.' [3] In 1866 the *North British Review* coupled George Eliot with Thackeray as an author privileged to break the rule of severe impersonality.

She acts herself the part of chorus, showing us how and why things go wrong. . . . In the hands of most writers this would become tedious; it is not so in her hands. On the contrary, as in the case with Thackeray, though these comments may detract from the animation of the story, they give breadth and power to the whole work. [4]

John Morley, in an early essay in *Macmillan's*, thought George Eliot's reflections and comments some of the best things in her novels. For him they promoted 'the active circulation of ideas' and were literally 'a criticism of life'. [5]

But the strongest defence of this widespread practice came from Leslie Stephen in his essay on George Eliot. 'We are indeed told dogmatically that a novelist should never indulge in little asides to the reader. Why not? One main advantage of a novel is precisely that it leaves room for a freedom in such matters

---

[1] XCVI (October, 1852), 385. The reviewer objected to William Carleton's comments that broke into his story. The following are some of the periodicals which also objected to the practice of an author's commenting on his own story: *British Quarterly Review*, XLVII (April, 1868), 332; *Blackwood's Edinburgh Magazine*, XCI (April, 1862), 467; *National Review*, VIII (April, 1859), 291; *Westminster Review*, XVII (April, 1857), 310; *The Athenaeum* (February 19, 1855), 217.

[2] XI, 198.   [3] XCVII (September, 1855), 356.

[4] XLV (September, 1866), 214.   [5] XIV (August, 1866), 273-4.

. . .', and he goes on to deal with the most serious objection to comments made directly to the reader.

A child . . . dislikes to have the illusion broken. . . . But the attempt to produce such illusions is really unworthy of work intended for full-grown readers. . . . But till [the critic] gives me some better reason for obedience than his *ipse dixit*, I shall refuse to respect what would destroy many charming passages and obliterate touches which clearly contribute to the general effect of George Eliot's work.[1]

For Stephen, only the substance and style of an author's commentary are open to criticism; the mere fact that a novelist indulges in asides to the reader is not grounds for condemning him.

Charles Kingsley was one of the few Victorian novelists who attempted to defend his practice of including long explanatory sections in his novels, avowedly directed by the author to the reader. (Thackeray generally dodged the issue by saying that he could not help the long asides in his novel; he was forced into them by his wayward muse, which he could not control.[2]) In a letter to George Brimley, who had attacked his *Two Years Ago* in the *Spectator* for just this reason, Kingsley wrote,

People are too stupid and in too great a hurry, to interpret the most puzzling facts for themselves, and the author must act as showman and do it for them. Whether it's according to 'Art' or not, I don't care a fig. . . . Art ought to mean the art of pleasing and instructing, and, believe me, the passages in which the author speaks in his own person do so. . . . Women like them better than any part of a book. They like to be taught a little now and then. . . .[3]

The commentary of Thackeray and George Eliot, however, could not stem from distrust of their reader's intelligence. If one examines their asides and explanatory sections, one finds always the assumption that reader and writer are intellectual equals, but Kingsley's condescension may be the reason for the

[1] *Hours in a Library* (New York, 1904), IV, 150–2.
[2] See Biographical Edition, XII, 374.
[3] Charles Kingsley, *His Letters and Memories of His Life*, ed. by his wife, III, 41.

prolixity of many minor novelists. Kingsley, however, in the same letter felt he had to modify his original statement:

> Of course it is very easy for a reviewer who disagrees with this doctrine to call it an obtrusion of the author's self; but the author's business is to see that it is just not that—to speak, if he can, the thoughts of many hearts, to put into words for his readers what they would have said for themselves if they could. . . .[1]

When Trollope in *Framley Parsonage* called himself the 'leader of the chorus', he probably had a similar idea in mind. His own comments on the action become in some sense impersonal because they are not merely his own individual opinions; they belong to all right-thinking readers, just as the comments of the Greek chorus were not merely personal opinions of the play-wright. According to Howard Baker, in the *Southern Review*, commentary seems natural in a novel by Fielding or George Eliot because they 'drew upon settled and universally recognized standards; they could point the moral and put a price on values because their readers shared in their attitudes towards morals and values. . . .' But the modern novelist writing in a period of unsettled values can no longer use this device; he is forced to become impersonal, to refine himself out of existence.[2]

Dickens' attitude towards his audience was markedly different from the one Kingsley revealed to Brimley. He always insisted to the contributors of *Household Words* and *All the Year Round* that, though their essays must be clear, they should not write down to their audience, and to Collins in 1860 he wrote concerning the *Woman in White*: 'You know that I always contest your disposition to give an audience credit for nothing, which necessarily involves the forcing of points on their attention. . . .'[3] For Dickens, Collins' lack of subtlety was an insult that his reader was bound to resent. Perhaps this attitude was related to Dickens' insistence throughout his correspondence on the need for impersonality in novel writing. For example, when he refused a novel of Mrs. Brookfield's (Thackeray's friend) for *All the Year Round*, he wrote to her in explanation, 'It strikes me that you constantly hurry your narrative (and yet without getting on)

---

[1] *Ibid.*
[2] 'An Essay on Fiction with Examples', *Southern Review*, VII (1941), 395.
[3] *Dickens Letters*, III, 145.

by telling it, in a sort of impetuous breathless way, in your own person, when the people should tell it and act it for themselves. My notion always is, that when I have made the people play out the play, it is, as it were, their business to do it and not mine.' [1] To a certain Miss King he wrote in 1855: 'The people do not sufficiently work out their own purposes in dialogue and dramatic action. You are too much their exponent; what you do for them, they ought to do for themselves.' [2] Another aspiring novelist had his story rejected with this comment: 'There is too much of the narrator in it—the narrator not being an actor. The result is, that I can *not* see the people, or the place, or believe in the fiction.' [3] To yet another author he wrote enthusiastically, 'You had not existence, as to me when I read it. The actions and sufferings of the characters affected me by their own force and truth. . . .' [4] Dickens' dislike for all comments by the author was so great that he even disapproved of prefaces 'on the ground that a book (of all things) should speak for and explain itself'.[5]

Dickens' canon of dramatic presentation of his story did not stop with action and dialogue but extended to the revelation of the inner life of his characters. Formal psychological analyses of the states of mind of his people were out of the question in a novel that was meant to be dramatic, to have the same impact on a reader as a swiftly moving play. Such analyses he called dissection, and though he admired the technique of *The Woman in White*, he felt that the characters in their respective accounts of the action tended to analyse their own minds too much; they had a 'DISSECTIVE property in common, which is essentially not theirs but yours; . . . my own effort would be to strike more of what is to be got *that way* out of them by collision with one another, and by the working of the story'.[6] He disliked *The Scarlet Letter*, which he thought fell off after a fine opening scene (fine because it was objectively and dramatically presented); 'the psychological part of the story is very much overdone, and not truly done, I think'. (It is interesting that Dickens objected to Pearl on the grounds that she is 'out of nature altogether'.[7] The fact that some of his own children like Little Nell and Paul

---

[1] *Dickens Letters*, III, 461. [2] *Ibid.*, II, 624. [3] *Ibid.*, III, 138.
[4] *Ibid.*, II, 685. [5] *Ibid.*, p. 436. [6] *Ibid.*, III, 145.
[7] *Ibid.*, II, 335.

Dombey were very strange indeed never seems to have struck him.)

Dickens by no means shared Reade's belief that the novel should be strictly objective in the sense that the author should never concern himself with trying to communicate anything of the inner life of his characters; in *Griffith Gaunt* Reade writes of his heroine:

> Her mind was in a whirl; and, were I to imitate those writers who undertake to dissect and analyse the heart of such moments, and put the exact result on paper, I should be apt to sacrifice truth to precision; I must stick to my old plan, and tell you what she did: that will surely be some index to her mind. . . .[1]

At times Dickens, in his belief that 'every writer of fiction . . . writes, in effect, for the stage',[2] resorts to the device of the formal soliloquy. This convention, still very much alive in the theatre of his day, is bound to seem awkward in the novel because there was no real need for it. In *Our Mutual Friend*, for example, when John Rokesmith finally reveals himself to the reader as the missing John Harmon, he does so in a long address to the reader that seems to come right from the stage of his own day, explaining his motives for pretending to be dead and impersonating another man:

> Dead, I have found the true friends of my lifetime still as true, as tender, and as faithful as when I was alive. . . . Dead, I have heard from the woman who would have been my wife if I had lived, the revolting truth that I should have purchased her, caring nothing for me, as a Sultan buys a slave. . . . What course for me then? This, to live the same quiet Secretary life . . . until the swarm of swindlers under many names shall have found newer prey.[3]

A more effective device is the one Dickens used to show us the inner life of Miss Wade in *Little Dorrit*. Here he resorted to the inserted autobiographical narrative, in this case 'The History of a Self-Tormentor'. Although this convention is as old as story-telling itself, Dickens was interested in using it in a new way. Unlike Fielding's story of the Man of the Hill or Smollett's

---

[1] Library edition, p. 164.
[2] J. W. T. Ley, *The Dickens Circle* (London, 1919), p. 75.
[3] (London, 1953), Book II, chap. XIII, p. 353.

Confessions of a Lady of Quality, or Cervantes' Curious Imper-
tinent, he wanted to make Miss Wade's narrative an organic
part of *Little Dorrit*, even though it interrupted the regular
chronological development of the novel: 'I had an idea, which
I thought a new one, of making the introduced story so fit into
surroundings impossible of separation from the main story, as
to make the blood of the book circulate through both.' [1] The
relationship between the inserted narrative and the main body
of the work must have presented itself in a similar fashion to
Dostoievsky in writing the story of the Grand Inquisitor and
to Proust in 'Swann in Love'.

Besides the formal soliloquy and the inserted narrative,
Dickens sometimes tells us explicitly what his characters are
thinking. Edmund Wilson has shown that with characters about
to die, like Fagan and James Chuzzlewit, their thoughts are
often presented directly. [2] Dr. Boege has observed in a recent
essay on Dickens that at times, as with Carker in *Dombey and
Son*, the rendering of thought 'approaches so closely to stream-
of-consciousness . . . that the application of that term is not
unjustified'. [3]

In a novel written in the first person, like *David Copperfield* or
Great Expectations, of course the author has no difficulty in giving
us the inner life of his central character, since the narrator and
central character are identical. But as Dr. Boege has shown,
Dickens in several places very consciously manipulated the
point of view in his novels written in the third person, so as
to get the reader into his character's mind. For example in
Book I, Chapter XIV of *Little Dorrit* Dickens wrote: 'Arthur
Clennam rose hastily, and saw her standing at the door. This
history must sometimes see with little Dorrit's eyes, and shall
begin that course by seeing him.' (Up to this point the point of
view had been fairly consistently limited to Clennam.) In a
letter Dickens refused a suggestion from Collins as to the treatment of Dr. Manette: 'This is quite apart from the peculiarity
of the Doctor's character, as affected by his imprisonment;
which of itself would, to my thinking, render it quite out of the

[1] *Dickens Letters*, II, 776.
[2] 'Dickens: The Two Scrooges', *The Wound and the Bow* (New York, 1941),
pp. 15–17.
[3] 'Point of View in Dickens', *PMLA*, LXV (1950), 102.

question to put the reader inside of him before the proper time, in respect to matters that were dim to him,' since his mind was diseased. 'I think the business of art is to lay all that ground carefully.' The notes in which Dickens thought out the structure of *Our Mutual Friend* contain the following significant passage: 'Book III, Chapter IV: Work up to *Bella's account* of the change in Mr. Boffin—*Broken to the reader through her*—Mercenary Bella, Money, Money, Money *Lay the ground very carefully all through* Book III, Chapter XI: Bradley's state of mind Book IV, Chapter VII: *Pursue Bradley and unrepentant state of mind.*' [1] From the evidence Dr. Boege presents, it is clear that Dickens was very much aware of the device of a limited point of view and saw it as a valuable means of rendering the inner life of his characters, although obviously he never used it as elaborately as Henry James.

Thackeray's theories about the relationship between the novelist and his work were of course as different as possible from Dickens'. Thackeray was not aiming at the immediacy of drama, as if the action were taking place before the reader's eyes; he wanted to convey the sense that he was writing of events long past. As he says of *The Newcomes*: 'This narrative . . . is written maturely and at ease, long after the voyage is over whereof it recounts the adventures and perils . . .', and he takes the position of Arthur Pendennis, friend of Clive Newcome, his central character. Pendennis is piecing Clive's life together from stray papers, conversations reported to him, and his knowledge, right or wrong, of the characters of the persons engaged. [2] Thackeray realizes that this relation to his material forces him to explain his powers of omniscience, and he is very much aware of the problems of the point of view he has adopted in this novel. (In *Henry Esmond*, of course, such a problem could not come up because of the autobiographic form.) 'That a biographer should profess to know everything which passes, even in a confidential talk in a first-class carriage between two lovers, seems perfectly absurd. . . .' [3] As a result he has to be careful to give authority for his facts: 'All this story is told by one, who, if he was not actually present at the circumstances

---

[1] These examples are taken from Dr. Boege's article, pp. 92–3.

[2] *Thackeray Works*, VIII, chap. XXIV, p. 236.

[3] *Ibid.*, chap. XLI, p. 436.

here narrated, yet had information concerning them, and could supply such a narrative of facts and conversations as is, indeed, not less authentic than the details of other histories.' [1]

With George Eliot we can clearly see from the following passage at the opening of Chapter 29 of *Middlemarch* why she writes all her novels as an omniscient author, why such a point of view is characteristic of her method and vision:

> One morning, some weeks after her arrival at Lowick, Dorothea —but why always Dorothea? Was her point of view the only possible one with regard to this marriage? I protest against all our interest, all our effort at understanding being given to [Dorothea]. . . . Mr. Casaubon had an intense consciousness within him, and was spiritually a-hungered like the rest of us.[2]

It is this awareness of the fact of Casaubon's consciousness which leads to the pathos of his character and position. Every consciousness in a scene is important to her. Any attempt to limit the representation of a scene to a single point of view would fatally simplify it, and art for George Eliot should represent life 'in its highest complexity'.[3] As a result the point of view in her novels must be multiple and shifting; otherwise her material would be falsified. For this reason she was pained when she learned that the public read *The Mill on the Floss* exclusively from Maggie's viewpoint and that all the characters were seen merely with her eyes. In a letter of 1860 she writes:

> So far as my own feeling and intention are concerned, no one class of persons or form of character is held up to reprobation or to exclusive admiration. Tom is painted with as much love and pity as Maggie, and I am so far from hating the Dodson's myself, that I am rather aghast to find them ticketed with such very ugly adjectives.[4]

One would hardly expect George Eliot, even from a cursory reading of only one of her novels, to object to commentary by the author. But as a critic for the *Westminster Review*, she did insist as strongly as Dickens or Lewes that the novelist must make his scenes act themselves out dramatically. She found fault with *Perversion*, a High Church novel, because the 'home

---

[1] *Thackeray Works*, VIII, chap. XLVII, p. 492.
[2] Cabinet edition (London and Edinburgh, 1878), p. 281.
[3] *George Eliot Letters*, IV, 300. [4] *Ibid.*, III, 299.

life of the brother and sister, are merely described, not *presented*; and these, as well as many other parts of the book, read rather like an account or sketch of a novel than like the novel itself'.[1] She made the same point about *Kathie Brand*, which Lewes also reviewed. 'Instead of vividly realizing to herself the terrible scenes, and vividly representing them . . . the author *writes about* them, does not *paint* them. . . . An analogous want of truth— or vivid realization—in the presentation of her characters and incidents, gives a blurred indistinctness to most parts of this novel. . . .'[2] In her criticism of fiction we find an emphasis similar to Henry James' on the scenic method, the constituted scene. One of the worst things she could say of a novel was that 'its scenes and characters are vague and shadowy'.[3] Hence the greatness of Stendhal, from whom English novelists had much to learn in respect to economy and dramatic power. She singles out his tale of *Ernestine* in the Appendix of *De l'Amour* as the model to which all writers of fiction should go. It is 'no more than thirty pages long, but in that short space . . . we have the story of a naive girlish passion, given with far more finish, that is, with more significant detail, than most of our writers can achieve by the elaboration of three volumes'.[4]

Meredith also was concerned as a critic and publisher's reader with the distinction between merely describing a scene and fully rendering it. The novel as Meredith envisaged it consisted of two elements, narrative and dramatic, and the art of fiction was largely a matter of learning to use both of them properly and in their place. 'After a satisfactory construction of plot, when to dramatize and when to narrate, is the novelist's lesson.'[5] Scene can as easily be overused as narrative summary,

---

[1] *Westminster Review*, LXVI (July, 1856), 260.

[2] *Ibid.*, LXVII (January, 1857), 321.

[3] *Ibid.*, LXIV (July, 1855), 296.

[4] *Ibid.*, LXV (April, 1856), 642. Ironically, she was to be given the same advice by a French critic in 1863. In a review of *Romola* appearing in *La Revue des deux mondes*, 'E. D. Forgues regretted that George Eliot had not better appreciated, or perhaps known . . . Stendhal. From him she would have learnt to condense her action, and not to burden it with useless details and insignificant characters. . . . His vigorous sketches are worth more than any patiently elaborated descriptions' (M. G. Devonshire, *The English Novel in France, 1830–1890* [London, 1929], pp. 374–5).

[5] *Westminster Review*, LXVII (April, 1857), 616.

as he notes in a review of a current novel that he found 'burdened with dialogue'.[1] But as Mr. Gettmann has pointed out in his article, 'Meredith as a Publisher's Reader', one of Meredith's most common complaints about the manuscripts he was given to consider was that the authors could not use dramatic scenes effectively and consequently summarized their material in narrative; a typical comment was, 'Scenes are narrated by a cleverish quick [illegible word] on the spot, but they are not presented.'[2]

He himself, as we have seen, felt free to break in on his own narrative when he felt it was necessary, in order to analyse his characters and explain their motivation;[3] he did it by the device of his alter ego, the Philosopher, or else by the narrator himself, who can arbitrarily stop the action at any point, or by one of the many choric characters he strews his novels with—Adrian Harley, Merthyr Powys, or Lady Mountstuart Jenkinson. At one point in *Sandra Belloni*, during one of these analytic interruptions by the Philosopher, Meredith as narrator notices ironically the usual objection to direct addresses to the reader. 'In vain I tell him [the Philosopher] that he is mean-time making tatters of the puppet's golden robe—illusion: that he is sucking the blood of their warm humanity out of them.'[4] Meredith as a *Westminster* reviewer, however, was all for imper-sonality and disliked authors who 'obtrude their own full lengths on the picture a great deal too much'.[5]

But the insertion of his own remarks was restricted to the narrative portions of his novels which were always considered as leading up to a big scene, and the scene itself was presented in a severely objective manner. Then all of the author's ideas had to be presented dramatically through the characters. As he wrote to Professor Baker of Harvard when the latter noted the sparsity of scenes in a typically Meredithian novel: 'My method has been to prepare my readers for a crucial exhibition of the personae, and then to give the scene in the fullest of their blood and brain under stress of a fiery situation.'[6] Scenes would

---

[1] *Westminster Review*, LXVII, (April, 1857), p. 615.
[2] *JEGP*, XLVIII (1949), 54.   [3] See above, p. 36.
[4] Memorial Edition (New York, 1910), chap. XLIV, p. 186.
[5] *Westminster Review*, LXVII (April, 1857), 614.
[6] *Meredith Letters*, II, 398.

tell more effectively in the whole novel, Meredith believed, if they were saved for the really big moments.

2. POINT OF VIEW

With the fairly widespread demand for dramatic presentation of scene and character and the disappearance of the author from his novel, it was only natural that critics should concern themselves with the allied question of point of view, or the relation between the narrator and his subject matter. The only use of the actual term *point of view*, as it is found in modern criticism, that I have been able to locate during the period under discussion is in an essay from the *British Quarterly Review* of July, 1866. The critic noted that the author of *John Halifax, Gentleman* happened upon the most effective method she could find of telling her story. The use of Phineas Fletcher, an invalid, as observer of the hero's actions, solved Miss Mulock's narrative problem because he

looks at his hero and his friend as a woman would—simply believes in him and loves him. . . . It is essential to the truth and unity of the story that it should be told in this manner, and the author could not have told it from another *point of view*. At the same time the reader knows that he sees . . . John Halifax through the mind of Phineas Fletcher. . . .[1]

Much earlier, Nassau Senior, in his essay on Scott, tried to differentiate between the way a novelist and historian would treat the same event. Scott, he pointed out, in his account of the storming of Front-de-Bœuf's castle, deliberately limited himself to what one person could have seen, and, moreover, presented it through the consciousness of Rebecca, while an historian would try to give us the entire battle, made up from as many different accounts as he could. Scott, in thus limiting the point of view (Senior did not use the phrase) from which the event is seen and presenting it through one of his characters, forced us to imagine ourselves in Rebecca's situation and so gained a concentration and vividness which would be lacking in the historian's account of the same event. It is in this manner of narration that Senior sees the essence of the novelist's art.[2]

[1] XLIV, 43–4 (italics mine).
[2] *Essays on Fiction* (London, 1864), 49–53.

From the vantage point of modern critical theory, there is an interesting treatment in the *Saturday Review* of March 8, 1862, of the attempt made by an omniscient author to 'go behind' (in James' phrase) the characters of his book. The reviewer notes the increasing tendency towards the subjective rather than the objective novel; the modern authors 'prefer to "get inside" their subject, to throw themselves into the inner consciousness of the character represented, and show the motive springs of passion at work'. But, the critic insists, this plan is 'obviously absurd. For who can enter into, and as it were personate, three or four different subjects of consciousness?' The solution to the problem is not James', but it is very close. The psychological novelist, according to this reviewer, can only work in the auto-biographic form, by 'keeping to the consciousness of one character made to assume the first person, and allowing everything else to be seen objectively and as from without'.[1] James, of course, preferred not to use the first person in his longer works, but he did insist in his later period on limiting the point of view in either the whole novel or in a section of it to one character and presenting all the other figures from the outside.

A writer in the *North British Review* of November, 1858, tried to account for the popularity of the autobiographical form at that time. The reason is that so many novelists lack imagination; they can not divine 'the whole *unseen interior*' of their people. As a result, they imitate Charlotte Brontë, who could

paint with considerable depth and detail the interior of *one* character—usually the centre-character of the novel—which is obviously taken from the artist's own experience. But while this central character is deep and vivid, those which come into connection with it are . . . mere sketches. . . . The result is, a certain disproportion of effect that is somewhat distressing in a work of art, and which can only be justified by the autobiographic form, . . . so common in fiction, since it alone seems to suggest good reason for the elaboration of a central figure, and an external treatment of all the others.

Applying these generalizations to Dinah Mulock, this critic finds that in *John Halifax* 'she unwisely takes up her *point of sight* in the mind of a man'. Since she has no understanding of how a man's mind works, the novel fails, for the author has not solved her problem of point of view.[2]

[1] XIII, 276.   [2] XXIX, 473-5 (italics mine).

Discussing the same question in the *Quarterly*, the reviewer of *The Newcomes* thinks that the advantage of using the auto-biographic form is that 'an appearance of reality can be given to events . . . which amounts to a perfect illusion'. This, how-ever, is only true in those novels where the hero is the narrator, so that Thackeray, by using Arthur Pendennis as his pretended editor, 'thrusting himself from time to time upon the notice of the reader', resorted to a clumsy method of telling the story and gained nothing through the device.[1]

In *David Copperfield*, of course, the hero and historian are one, and the *Prospective Review* of 1851 praised Dickens' consummate handling of the point of view through most of that novel:

. . . by the adoption of this difficult form of writing [the auto-biographical novel] the author has secured a unity and complete-ness which we have never seen equalled in a serial tale. It is in truth a very fine specimen of constructive skill. Complicated as the story is, and numerous as are the characters, all flows naturally from the mouth of the narrator, never leaving us to wonder how he got his information [a problem that seemed to bother Thackeray very much in *The Newcomes*], and scarcely ever encumbered with devices to supply the gaps in his personal knowledge. Wonderfully well has the author succeeded in identifying himself with his principal per-sonage. Every line is coloured with the hues of memory, and the subdued tone of a distant view is given to the whole. . . .[2]

The problem of point of view and its relation to verisimilitude is also closely scrutinized by the *Spectator* in a review of James Payn's *Lost Sir Massingberd*:

We confess ourselves at a loss . . . to quite comprehend the actual relation which the author wishes his reader to suppose he occupies towards his *dramatis personae*. He apparently wishes to convey the impression that his story is true, but he has certainly not succeeded in doing so, and his attempt to identify himself with one of the characters is equally ineffectual.[3]

A critic of unusual acuteness, writing on a group of novels set in ancient Greece and Rome, found that the *Faun of Sertorius* by Robert Eyres Landor (brother of W. S. Landor) was the best of the lot, for he alone satisfactorily solved the narrative

---

[1] XCVII (September, 1855), 360.   [2] VII, 180–1.
[3] XXXVII (June 18, 1864), 715.

problems involved in that kind of novel. In writing of such a distant period the presence of the author 'becomes questionable, and possibly inconvenient' because his own modern feelings would get in the way. Instead of attempting the impossible, to 'throw off his modern feelings altogether' while narrating his story, Landor in *The Faun of Sertorius*

is not only anonymous, but, for the purposes of the tale, character-less. He appears only as the English editor of a manuscript. That manuscript is assumed to be the substance of a Roman narrative, reconstructed by an Italian who had not the opportunity of copying it entire. Thus by a sufficiently probable fiction, we are prepared for a story classical in its general spirit, but not destitute of later touches.

This reviewer also discussed in general terms the use of the framing story, or a narrative within a narrative. This device, which had been used in *The Canterbury Tales* and *The Taming of the Shrew*, among many other works, was evidently an artificial contrivance designed to secure an effect that could not be managed without it, 'to apologize, as it were, for something in the character of the work which follows. . . .' It could only be justified by 'necessity or utility'; otherwise, even though the framing story is beautiful in itself, its use is a fault in art and should be condemned by the critic. Examining the same device in Tennyson's poetry, the anonymous author of 'Recent Classical Romances' finds it a violation of the universal law in art, recently enunciated by Pugin in architecture, namely that 'the artist cannot be absolved from the duty of regarding utility, . . . the purpose and imperative requirements of the work which he is contemplating'.

What is there in the *Morte d'Arthur* [this critic asks] to make it come more properly from 'the poet Everard Hall' than from Alfred Tennyson? Where, indeed, do the respective positions of the two poets differ? Or, again, . . . is there anything in the 'Princess' which requires to be understood as the product of an idle interval during a *fete champetre*? Or, if the poet himself was not to be supposed competent to produce a 'Medley' under ordinary circumstances . . . where was the need of imagining a plurality of authors. . . .

This discussion ends with the enunciation of the very modern-sounding principle: 'A writer stands in a certain relation to his subject, and that relation must be accounted for and disposed of.' [1]

In the same periodical, two issues earlier, George Henry Lewes explained to his readers why he found *Shirley* inferior to *Jane Eyre*, by comparing the relationship Charlotte Brontë assumed to her subject in both books.

> In 'Jane Eyre' life was viewed from the standing point [another early term for point of view] of individual experience; in 'Shirley' that standing point is frequently abandoned, and the artist paints only a panorama of which she, as well as you, are but spectators. Hence the unity of 'Jane Eyre' in spite of its clumsy and improbable contrivances, was great and effective. . . . But in 'Shirley' all unity, in consequence of defective art, is wanting.

Using Henry James' favourite metaphor for the novel, and one of the favourite metaphors of mid-Victorian criticism, Lewes states that as a result ' "Shirley" . . . is not a picture; but a portfolio of random sketches for one or more pictures'.[2]

Another interesting anticipation of Percy Lubbock's important critical concept, the distinction between the panoramic and dramatic methods, appears in an essay from *The Times* of 1856 by Samuel Lucas, who noted that Thackeray, especially in *Vanity Fair*, 'spreads his canvas to represent it [society] as a whole. The *panoramic* plan of Mr. Thackeray's workmanship is his primary distinction from other novelists, who adhere more closely to the *dramatic* element. . . .' [3] It is an interesting coincidence that Lubbock also makes this point in an analysis of *Vanity Fair. Blackwood's* of April, 1862, used the same terms only this time in connection with the novels of Charles Lever, which are called 'panoramic rather than dramatic'.[4]

3. UNITY AND STRUCTURE

Allied to the interest in narrative technique was a greatly increased concern, during this period, with the structure of the

---

[1] *Edinburgh Review*, XCII (October, 1850), 488–9.

[2] *Ibid.*, XCI (January, 1850), 159–60.

[3] Reprinted in *Eminent Men and Popular Books* (London, 1859), p. 150. *Panoramic* is italicized by the author and *dramatic* by me.

[4] LXXXVII (April, 1862), 454.

novel as a whole. The subject was not new in the criticism of the fifties and sixties, but at that time it assumed an importance it had never had before. One can find the idea of formal unity brought up at the very beginning of the criticism of prose fiction, in the Abbé Huet's *History of Romances*, where it is evidently derived from Renaissance and French neo-classic theories of the epic. According to Huet, Longus began *Daphnis and Chloe* 'grossly', because instead of plunging into it *in medias res*, he opened with the birth of his hero and heroine.[1] A prose romance should be 'composed after the Rules of an *Heroic* poem', and all romances that are written in ignorance of the rules are condemned as 'irregular'.[2] The regularity of form which Huet wanted in the novel was analogous to that of the state and the human body—both a reflection of the cosmic order.

A Romance should resemble a Perfect Body, and consist of many different Parts and Proportions all under one head; it follows, that the Principal Action of a Romance should be Simple and Illustrious above the rest, that the Subordinate ones, which are as it were the Members, ought to have relation to this Head, yield to it in Dignity and Beauty [just like Louis XIV's courtiers], adorn, sustain, and attend it with Dependence; otherwise it would be a body with many Heads, Monstrous and Deformed.[3]

James Beattie, one hundred years after Huet's treatise, still thought of the novel in terms of neo-classic epic theory, and, like Huet, distinguished between two kinds of structure in prose fiction: the historical and the poetical. The first follows the method of history, in that it attempts a continuous narrative of the life of its central character from birth to marriage, like *Roderick Random*, or else follow a series of adventures from beginning to end, like *Robinson Crusoe*.[4] Beattie, however, much preferred the poetical arrangement, which begins like Homer and Virgil in the middle of its subject. Richardson's novels are poetical since, 'in order to shorten the time of the action', they begin *in medias res*, although his use of the epistolary method makes his compositions 'partly Epick, and partly Dramatick'.[5] Fielding's *Amelia* is 'entirely poetical, and of the true epick

---

[1] *The History of Romances*, trans. Stephen Lewis (London, 1715), p. 78.
[2] *Ibid.*, p. 81.   [3] *Ibid.*, p. 65.
[4] *Dissertations Moral and Critical* (Dublin, 1783), II, 309–15.
[5] *Ibid.*, p. 312.

species; beginning in the middle of the action, or rather as near the end as possible, and introducing the previous occurrences in the form of narrative episode'. But it was for the plot of *Tom Jones* even though it did not begin in the middle of the action that Beattie reserved his most enthusiastic admiration.

> Since the days of Homer, the world has not seen a more artful Epick fable. The characters and adventures are wonderfully diversified: yet the circumstances are all so natural, and rise so easily from one another, and co-operate with so much regularity in bringing on, even while they seem to retard, the catastrophe, that the curiosity of the reader is kept always awake, and . . . grows more and more impatient as the story advances, till at last it becomes downright anxiety. And when we get to the end, and look back on the whole contrivance, we are amazed to find, that of so many incidents there should be so few superfluous . . . that so complex a tale should be so perspicuously conducted, and with such perfect unity of design.[1]

For Beattie's classical taste, the novel had reached perfection with Fielding and had been declining ever since. What Leavis peevishly calls 'the conventional talk about "the perfect construction" of *Tom Jones*', which can be heard 'in almost any course of lectures on "The English Novel"',[2] had already become a critical cliché when Scott in his 'Life of Fielding' said, 'The felicitous contrivance, and happy extrication of the story, where every incident tells upon and advances the catastrophe, while, at the same time, it illustrates the characters of those interested in its approach, cannot too often be mentioned with the highest approbation.'[3]

Fielding himself mentioned structure only in passing, although obviously he was very much concerned with the problem of unity in working out his novels. In the preface to his sister's novel, *David Simple*, he pointed out that 'every episode bears a manifest impression of the principle [*sic*] design'.[4] Fielding's idea of unity came chiefly from critical speculation

---

[1] *Ibid.*, pp. 319–20.   [2] *The Great Tradition* (New York, 1954), p. 12.
[3] *Prose Works*, III, 75. G. H. Lewes, as we shall see, attacked this judgment in his essay on *Tom Jones* in *Blackwood's*, LXXVII (March, 1860), 331–41; and R. S. Crane has recently given a very interesting redefinition of the idea of the perfect plot on *Tom Jones* in 'The Concept of Plot and the Plot of *Tom Jones*', *Critics and Criticism, Ancient and Modern* (Chicago, 1952), pp. 616–47.
[4] R. Brimley Johnson, *Novelists on Novels* (London, n.d.), p. 125.

about the epic; although the epic consisted of separate episodes, each was to be so linked to the others that it formed part of an inseparable whole.

But there was another and much tighter conception of literary structure which derived from neo-classical theories of the drama. Here there were to be no episodes at all; the entire plot was to concern one action. Congreve in his preface to *Incognita* says explicitly that he took the drama as his model of construction 'in the Design, Contexture, and Result of the Plot'.[1] Richardson in the original preface to *Clarissa* uses the same dramatic analogy for his novels. 'Long as the Work is, there is not one Digression, not one Episode, not one Reflection, but what arises naturally from the Subject, and makes for it, and to carry it on.' [2] Thomas Holcroft, a novelist who was also a dramatist, writing at the end of the eighteenth century, asserted in the preface to *Alwyn* that he kept to a severe unity of design and avoided all 'unnecessary circumstances'. As in the drama, everything must 'tend to the illustration, or forwarding the main story. . . .' He rigidly avoided any independent adventure of the kind one usually found in romances.[3]

Bulwer, however, writing in 1838, felt it necessary to distinguish between the unity of the drama and that of prose fiction. A play must unroll progressively in time and every incident must grow logically out of the preceding one, but this was not so of a novel. Here the author could legitimately 'go back instead of forward' in time—and transfer the interest from one character to another; time shifts were impossible in the drama as Bulwer conceived it. The novel also allowed the use of accident, though Bulwer pointed out later that where it affects a *dénouement* accident should be very sparingly employed. Inconvenient characters should not be got rid of by a railway accident or stroke of apoplexy. But in the serious drama accident is rigidly excluded, and any tragic close must be the inevitable consequence of the hero's own acts.[4]

[1] R. Brimley Johnson, *Novelists on Novels* (London, n.d.), p. 20.

[2] Quoted from Alan Dugald McKillop, *The Early Masters of English Fiction* (Lawrence, Kansas, 1956), p. 69.

[3] Quoted from A. A. Mendilow, *Time and the Novel* (London, 1952), pp. 76–7.

[4] *The Critical and Miscellaneous Writings of Sir Edward Lytton Bulwer* (Philadelphia, 1841), I, 79–80; *Blackwood's*, XCIII (May, 1863), 557.

The whole question of unity in the novel was much debated in the 1850's and 1860's. One group of critics called for works with an extremely tight structure, a limited, simple plot, and a small cast of characters, all to be patterned on French classic drama or the kind of novel many French writers were then turning out. According to an anonymous writer in *Fraser's* of June, 1856, author of 'The Art of Story-Telling', the English novel is, first of all, too long—'The novel, in our sense of its weight and dimensions, is nearly unknown in Europe'—and, as a result, it tends to become overlaid with detail, chiefly in the form of descriptions of locale and narration of unimportant incident, or to be overplotted. The French novelist, on the other hand, because he can write 'a single volume, of modest pretensions as to size', simplifies his story and concentrates on what is important. 'Nothing can be more slender than the plots of most popular French stories. Stripped of their finesse, their delicate strokes of character, and the intimate knowledge they disclose of society . . . they become reduced to a mere speck of action. Yet their fascination . . . is irresistible' because, unlike the English novelist,

by a few subtle touches, . . . [the French novelist] reveals to you the secret emotions of the actors, lifts the veil from their hearts and drops it again; puts you, as it were, in direct electric communication with their very thoughts, and, without interrupting the progress of the passing movement, which never flags, he lets you see into the whole machinery of hidden motives, designs, speculations, and cross-purposes in full play.

Far from the enormous cast of supernumerary characters in so many English novels,

none of the actors ever come upon the stage without having something indispensable to do. You never find a walking character introduced for the sake of typifying a particular class, or an eccentric hanging loose upon the story.

As a result in French novels 'the texture is so close, that there is not a single superfluous thread in it'.[1]

In October, 1851, another critic of *Fraser's* admired the supreme art of French novels, especially their economy and rapid movement.

[1] LIII, 727–31.

Everything seems to flow obviously and easily; every line contributes to the onward and accumulating interest; there is nothing *de trop*; no waste in the way of descriptions or ruminations; all is essential, natural, fresh. . . . Expectation is never excited, and then disappointed; on the contrary, you are continually surprised at the ability of the writer, who, with means apparently slight and unimportant, produces the most striking results. Assuredly the art in these books may be studied with advantage. . . .[1]

At the end of the decade *Fraser's* ran another plea for tighter construction in the English novel, only this time a native model was proposed—Jane Austen, who through her 'finely-disciplined genius' was able to create perfect works of art. The advantage that her deliberate simplification of her plots and her subject matter gives her is described by an apt metaphor: 'the field of view may be in some sense a small one; but like that of a good microscope in able hands, there is abundance of light, and the minutest markings of character are beautifully shown in it'.[2] So impressed is this critic with the importance of formal unity that he denies the name of novel to Defoe's books, since they are merely a succession of adventures without any fixed sequence; 'there is no necessary connexion between the beginning, the middle, and the end. . . . Incident is added to incident, as beads may be strung upon a thread, but the filament of adventures is single. There is no contexted fabric of composition—no web and no woof. . . .' Hence his novels lack any real pattern; they 'have no threads which lie concealed under others, and only emerge to the surface when their appearance is wanted to complete the intended design'.[3]

Severe unity resulting from concentration and economy were as important for the *Saturday Review* as for *Fraser's*. Too many characters or scenes produce 'the same result on the mind as the blending together of inharmonious colours upon the eye'. (The pictorial metaphor seems omnipresent in Victorian criticism of fiction.) Moreover, too many persons placed in 'temporary juxtaposition and with no connexion' cause the powers of the novelist to be dissipated over a number of characters instead of being concentrated on a few.[4] In *Verner's Pride*, a

---

[1] XLIV, 378–9.
[3] *Ibid.*, p. 24.
[2] LXI (January, 1860), 31.
[4] XII (September 7, 1861), 252.

novel by Mrs. Wood, the reviewer noted that there was enough material for half a dozen plots:

. . . parsimony is as truly an attribute of genius as wealth; art and ingenuity are as worthily spent and as fully proved in making the most of a conception as in producing it originally.[1]

Another reviewer notes that too often the English novelist is content with merely exhibiting a series of characters. 'He is not wanted to draw portraits so much as to design a composition.' [2]

One convention that almost all critics condemned and yet seemed powerless to do anything about was the publishing of novels in three volumes.[3] For a number of observers throughout the period, this very mechanical demand for a certain fixed length seemed to be on the verge of disappearing. In 1847 Bulwer wrote to John Blackwood, 'I am more and more inclined to think that for sales the usual three volume form is wearing out',[4] and two decades later Blackwood himself thought 'the days of the three volume novels are over for profit. . . .' [5] But the system was still very much alive in the eighties when the novelist, Reardon, in George Gissing's *New Grub Street* thinks of the triple decker as a 'triple-headed monster, sucking the blood of English novelists'.[6] The action of this novel took place in 1882, and by 1885 Gissing observed that 'the old three volume tradition is being broken through. One volume is becoming commonest of all.' [7]

The objection to this custom was, of course, based on the fact that so many novels did not have enough material to fill the required length. As a result, books were often filled out with irrelevancies in the form of extra plots, little essays, and purposeless scenes. The reviewer for the *Westminster Review* of July, 1852, noted the 'inconsiderate attempt' by the author of *Adam Graeme* 'to spin out the material of a short and simple tale into

---

[1] XV (February 28, 1863), 279.   [2] XVI (October 31, 1863), 587.

[3] See Michael Sadleir, *XIX Century Fiction* (London, 1951); Amy Cruse, *The Victorians and Their Reading* (London, 1935); and Kathleen Tillotson, *Novels of the Eighteen-Forties* (Oxford, 1956).

[4] Margaret Oliphant, *Annals of a Publishing House* (Edinburgh, 1897), II, 420.   [5] *Ibid.*, III, 175.

[6] Modern Library edition (New York, 1926), p. 215.

[7] *Letters of George Gissing to Members of His Family*, ed. Algernon and Ellen Gissing (London, 1927), p. 166.

the length, breadth, and thickness of the conventional three-volume novel. . . .'[1] The *Saturday Review* of May 24, 1856, called 'the stupid notion that a novel must have three volumes' 'a very great nuisance' for leading the author to dilute the first two volumes 'to eke out the last'.[2] It was no wonder that compression often became, in the eyes of critics, a virtue in itself —no matter what sort of material was being compressed. 'In these days of literary gold-beating,' the *Spectator* observed on September 3, 1853, 'when an ingot of matter is generally hammered out into that acreage of flimsy leaf, which subsequently figures in a three-volume form on the shelves of the circulating library, it is refreshing to take up a novel in one volume. . . .'[3] Fitzjames Stephen in the *Saturday Review* of September, 1857, set up *Guy Livingstone* as a model of economy:

> In addition to other merits of the book, it is *in one volume*—a consequence and an indication of unusually careful writing and an artistic power of compression, partly derived from a high classical education. We wish some popular novelists would take the lesson— they would live the longer, though they would not sell so well.[4]

But, to give the Victorian book-buying public credit, *Guy Livingstone* easily sold as well as its more prolix rivals. Sometimes even cutting a novel down to one volume was not enough; a book with the foolish title *Labour and Love* had for Meredith in the *Westminster Review* of October, 1857, 'the merit of being in one volume' but could 'bear cutting down by half'.[5]

There was wide agreement among the Victorian critics that the publication of novels in instalments either in magazines or by themselves seriously impaired the integrity of the novel.[6] Harriet Martineau resolutely refused to allow any of her novels to come out in this form because it was 'a method so unprincipled in an artistic sense'.[7] The *Prospective Review* thought it 'probably the lowest artistic form yet invented; that, namely, which affords the greatest excuse for unlimited departures from dignity, propriety, consistency, completeness, and proportion. In it, wealth is often wasted in reckless and riotous profusion,

---

[1] LVIII, 268.   [2] II, 85.   [3] XXVI, 851.   [4] IV, 247.
[5] LXVIII, 597.
[6] Dickens and Thackeray, however, liked this method of publication. See Tillotson, *op. cit.*, pp. 33-9.   [7] *Autobiography*, I, 416.

and poverty is concealed by mere superficial variety, caricature, violence, and confused bustle.' No matter how great a genius undertakes this form, he cannot make it 'a high form of art'. *David Copperfield* will therefore not achieve the rank of a classic, even though Dickens did triumph over some of the disadvantages of his method of publication.[1] For the *Saturday Review*, a novel which is 'the aggregate of twenty-four monthly pamphlets must always be disjointed and languid. . . .' Such a method makes impossible the unity of a well-constructed plot.[2] An essay on Dickens in *Fraser's* noted the gradual change in *Pickwick* as the various numbers came out. As a result the novel, when completed, was not a whole because there was no unity of tone pervading it. 'The fault lies with the mode of publication—fractional and periodical; for thus the author has no opportunity of revising his work as a whole, of correcting mistakes, and producing uniformity of tone.'[3] David Masson thought 'the fashion of publishing novels in serial numbers' enough to prevent any author from achieving 'his ideal of excellence' by compelling him 'to supply the parts of his story before he has thoroughly conceived the whole, and also by compelling him to spice each separate part, so that it may please alone'.[4] For all these critics serial publication was not compatible with unity, just as the tradition of three volumes was not conducive to sound proportion.

For George Brimley unity was the central critical question. 'We estimate works of art . . . more by their unity and completeness than by their richness and profusion of raw material. It is coherence, order, purpose, which makes the difference between Nature and Chaos.'[5] Scrutinizing *Bleak House* in the *Spectator* of September 24, 1853, he failed to find any form at all.

Bleak House is, even more than any of its predecessors, chargeable with not simply faults, but absolute want of construction. A novelist may invent an extravagant or an uninteresting plot—may fail to balance his masses, to distribute his light and shade—may prevent his story from marching, by episode and discursion: but Mr. Dickens discards plot, while he persists in adopting a form for his thoughts

[1] VII (1851), 158. [2] VIII (November 19, 1859), 610.
[3] XLII (December, 1850), 701.
[4] *North British Review*, XV (May, 1851), 89.
[5] *Essays* (London, 1868), 308.

to which plot is essential, and where the absence of a coherent story
is fatal to continual interest.

Brimley found no necessary connection between the incidents
or characters and even went so far as to say that the chancery
suit 'has positively not the smallest influence on the character
of any one person concerned. . . .' [1] This strange judgment on
Bleak House, substantially repeated by both Joseph Warren
Beach and Lord David Cecil in the twentieth century,[2] seems
to me to show how wrong a critic can go if he approaches one
kind of novel with criteria drawn from a very different sort.
Just because Dickens' construction is not that of Flaubert or
Jane Austen, his work is not necessarily amorphous. Such judgments sound very much like those delivered by the Restoration
on Elizabethan plays.

For Nassau Senior, the search for unity in a contemporary
novel was all but a lost cause. In Bulwer's *Lucretia*, he noted,
'the plot is deficient in unity; it cannot be said to have any main
action. . . . This, however, is rather the absence of a rare merit
than a positive fault. Many of our best novels are equally defective.' [3] That Senior's view of unity in novels was derived from
dramatic literature is evident in his judgment of his brother's
novel, *Charles Vernon*. 'The story is amusing and natural, but
wants unity and cohesion. The incidents are very numerous,
but the greater part of them have no influence on the ultimate
catastrophe.' [4]

The importance of unity and construction in the criticism
of G. H. Lewes places him squarely in the tradition of mid-
nineteenth-century classicism along with Matthew Arnold (in
his 1853 preface), Walter Bagehot, Henry Taylor, and George
Brimley. For Lewes, 'the object of construction is to free the
story from all superfluity. Whatever is superfluous—whatever
lies *outside* the real feeling and purpose of the work, either in
incident, dialogue, description, or character—whatever may
be omitted without in any degree lessening the effect—is a
defect in construction.' Unity in a novel is no different in kind
from unity in the drama, according to Lewes. 'The drama is

---

[1] *Essays*, pp. 282–3 (reprinted from the *Spectator*).
[2] Beach, *op. cit.*, pp. 127–8; *Early Victorian Novelists* (Harmondsworth,
Middlesex, 1948), p. 127.
[3] *Essays on Fiction*, p. 285. [4] *Ibid.*, pp. 204–5.

more rigid in its requirements than the novel, simply because in the drama there is less time to tell the story in . . .; moreover spectators are necessarily less patient than readers.' But, Lewes insists, 'the requirements as to construction . . . are the same in principle' for both forms. In the drama, any scene is purposeless if it does not 'directly tend to forward or elucidate the action'; if it can be 'cut out without rendering the story less intelligible, less effective, [such a scene] is an absolute defect, let it be never so splendidly written'. A purposeless scene is a serious mistake' not only because it occupies some of the dramatist's precious time allotment and causes him to skimp other scenes, but also because 'it helps to weary the spectator, by calling his attention away from the action, and by starting new expectations, which will not be fulfilled'.

That which is true of whole scenes, is also true of parts of scenes, and of speeches. . . . Remarks *away* from the immediate business of the scene . . . are faults: they may be beautiful, they may be witty, they may be wise, but they are out of place; and the art of the dramatist consists in having everything in its proper place.

For Lewes even words and clauses that are superfluous are to be excised according to this same principle of economy.

But, according to Lewes, although 'the laws of economy are rigid, . . . the public must never feel the rigidity', hence the need for art which conceals art. All ' "coincidences" and situations . . . introduced . . . for the sake of helping the author out of a difficulty' makes the machinery of the plot painfully evident and 'our illusion vanishes'. The construction of a play or a novel, even though it is in reality mechanical and artificial, must always seem 'natural' and 'organical', and this feat can only be accomplished by having 'all *secretly* and inevitably tending towards it. The artist must be careful in his selection, yet never suffer us to feel there has been a selection. . . .' [1]

The difference in the way these principles will be followed in plays and novels stems from the fact that 'in the novel the persons are *described* instead of being seen. . . .' Lewes realized that when he spoke about presentation as opposed to description, he was only using a metaphor; strictly speaking it is impossible literally to present a character in a novel. This condition

---

[1] *Blackwood's*, LXXXVII (March, 1860), 333-4.

renders it necessary that the author should supplement as far a
possible this inferior vividness of presentation, by a more minut
detail, both physical and moral. He must describe the tones an
looks of his characters; on the stage these could be represented. H
must make up for this inferiority of presentation by telling us mor
accurately the mental condition of his characters. Hence it is tha
the comments and reflections of the novelist are real aids to hi
effect, and become part of construction. Where, however, . . . h
wanders into mere reflection and digression, suggested by, but no
elucidating his characters and situations, he is guilty of a fault i
construction. . . .

To illustrate his theories, Lewes examines the plot of *Tor
Jones* and finds that 'far from being a masterpiece of construc
tion', it is 'a very ill-constructed novel'. In the first place
Fielding relies too much on coincidence, and in the second—
and this would condemn all picaresque novels—his plot is reall
made up of separate episodes and so lacks unity of action. It i
true that this method gives variety to the story; but variet
must be achieved in other ways. 'If Fielding is episodical, it i
simply because he wanted to produce the effect of variety, an
was not artist enough to make the variety spring from and ten
to unity.' *Pride and Prejudice*, on the other hand, 'is a finely
constructed work' because 'the characters, scenes, and dialogue
in relation to each other and to the story' contain nothing super
fluous. 'All this variety is secretly tending to one centre. . . .'

Charles Kingsley, who agreed with Lewes that the dram
should provide the standard of construction for the novel, com
plained that critics looked to the well-made French play rathe
than to Shakespeare for their ideas of unity. In Shakespeare, h
pointed out to George Brimley,[2] there are characters and whol
scenes which could be cut out without any damage to the plo

Now in the modern novel you ought to have all this, if it is
be a picture of actual life. You must have people coming in, infl
encing your principal characters for a while—as people do influen
you and me, and then go on their way, and you see them no mor
. . . You must . . . have people talk, as people do in real life, abo
all manner of irrelevant things, only taking care that each man
speech shall show more of his character, and that the general to

[1] *Blackwood's*, LXXXVII (March, 1860), pp. 335–6.
[2] See above, p. 98.

122

shall be such as never to make the reader forget the main purpose of the book.[1]

This very leisurely approach to the question of form in prose fiction, however, was rapidly becoming a thing of the past, and it was Lewes' much more stringent ideals that became dominant after 1870.

So insistent had the novel-drama analogy become in 1862 that Bulwer-Lytton felt called upon to amplify the distinctions he had made earlier between novels and plays in 'The Art of Fiction' of 1838. He complained in *Caxtoniana*, a series of essays written for *Blackwood's*, that formal criticism had grown too rigid in its demand for unity and showed no real conception of the novel as a distinct form. Too often, he claimed, reviewers apply to the novel 'rules drawn from the drama, and they are not only inapplicable, but adverse, to the principles which regulate the freedom of the novel'.[2] In this essay freedom is the key word. (Justin MacCarthy posited a direct relation between the vigour of the novel in 1864 and the novelist's freedom from any code of critical laws.[3]) Prose fiction needs 'an immense variety in modes of treatment—a bold license of loose capricious adaptation of infinite material to some harmonious unity of interest, which even the most liberal construction of dramatic license cannot afford to the drama'. The only kind of unity one could demand is that all the action bear 'upon some ulterior idea for which the action is invented'.[4] In other words it was thematic unity that the critic should look for, not the kind of tidy structures found in a play.

Don Quixote and *Wilhelm Meister* gave the standards that critics should use. In each, though there were seemingly many unrelated episodes, characters who appeared and disappeared without any effect on any single issue, loose ends which the author did not bother to tie up in one dénouement,[5] there was a single underlying meaning in all the action, one main theme. The great novelists unite 'an interior symbolic signification with an obvious popular interest in character and incident. . . .' But

[1] *Op. cit.*, III, 40–1. [2] *Blackwood's*, XCIII (May, 1863), 558.
[3] *Westminster Review*, LXXXII (July, 1864), 24–6.
[4] *Blackwood's*, XCIII (May, 1863), 558.
[5] The term *dénouement*, according to Bulwer, could apply only to plays, not novels.

this meaning must not be rendered 'so distinct and detailed as to become obviously allegorical' unless, as in *The Pilgrim's Progress*, the work is avowedly an allegory. The novelist will also err if he admits any dialogue not closely bearing on his purpose and 'whenever he fails in merging the two [symbolical meaning and incident] into an absolute unity at the end'.[1] Thus for Bulwer, unity of action in the Aristotelian sense is unnecessary in a novel; all that is necessary is unity of theme.

The author of the essay 'Mr. Trollope's Novels' in the *North British Review* of May, 1864, maintained that the drama, because of its closely-knit structure, is a less realistic medium than prose fiction. The plot of a play

generally implies at once an isolation and interdependence of characters and interests which never found its counterpart in real life since this world began. Ten or twelve people are so absolutely cut off from the rest of mankind, and linked so closely to one another, that the most insignificant cannot move an arm without hastening or retarding a catastrophe. . . .

In novels, this critic asserts,

there is no reason that we can see, why the people should not hang together as loosely as in real life. . . . A novel is not a drama; and we have time, in our way to the conclusion, to pause upon details and to wander into byways. If the novelist can trust himself to let his story stand still, while he elucidates a nicety of character, or describes a picturesque or humorous situation . . . ,

why shouldn't he? But a novel must have 'unity of feeling and interest', so that 'if the scenes for the sake of which the story stands still, in no way concern the principal characters, and are remote from the leading interest of the piece, their introduction at all is a blot. . . .' Thus the scenes concerning Mr. Moulder in *Orley Farm* are faulty because they have so little connection with Lady Mason. Concerning the criticism often made against Trollope that he is undramatic, that he describes when he should represent, the author of this essay asks why it is necessary for the novel 'to conform to the conditions of the drama'. 'The dramatist who describes his characters instead of making them reveal themselves, fails in the principal object of his art. But the novelist is tied down by no such rigorous rules. It is his privilege

[1] *Blackwood's*, XCIII (May, 1863), 554.

to describe. . . . As long as he can do so without becoming tedious. . . .'[1]

The same subject had been raised earlier in the *North British Review*, 1856, where the chief difference between the novel and the drama was seen to stem from the length of time represented in each genre. 'The drama presupposes the characters already formed, and depends for its interest on one great action, to which all its personages contribute. The novel represents a course of life, or one phase of life spread over a considerable time. . . .' Consequently novels might contain many individuals who did not influence 'the main event'; they might be important, rather, for the development of the character of the protagonist.[2]

Some critics, however, recognized the validity of the analogy between the drama and certain novels, yet would not try to fit all novels to one kind of structure. For example, the author of 'Recent Works of Fiction' in the *Prospective Review* of 1853, divides his subject into two classes, the epic and the dramatic, and the rules of construction for each more or less conform to its prototype. Since the aim of the epic is a comprehensive survey of life, the epic novel is 'necessarily slow in . . . [its] development', allowing much 'digression and disquisition' and 'the readers, like travellers through a pleasant country, instead of hurrying to the goal, are contented to linger by the way, and to enjoy the rich prospects which open round them as they advance'. But the dramatic novel unfolds very differently since it 'exhibits the concentrated essence of life, rather than life itself'. As a result, it will be characterized by rapid action, a small number of characters and a very limited 'field of view'.[3] This distinction is very similar to the one we have previously noticed between the dramatic and the panoramic novel.[4]

In a similar way, Walter Bagehot would divide all novels into the ubiquitous or miscellaneous, which attempts to treat all of life and in which nothing would really be irrelevant, and the sentimental, using the term in Schiller's sense of pertaining to the sentiments or emotions. Since the latter kind is a love story, it must be restricted to the actual love affair that is its ostensible object. The trouble with Dickens was that he was

[1] XL, 372–4. [2] XXVI, 209. [3] IX, 224.
[4] See above, p. 111.

actually writing ubiquitous novels while very often pretending to be writing sentimental ones about one or more pairs of lovers. Consequently in a typical Dickens novel, the love story was not consonant with the rest.[1]

Bagehot's most interesting treatment of the question of unity in prose fiction, however, appears in an essay not included in Hutton's edition of *Literary Studies*, probably because it dealt with a group of rather ephemeral novels. In 'A Novel or Two', printed only in the *National Review* of October, 1855, he tries to indicate the relationship that characters should bear towards each other and towards the book as a whole. The novelist 'must enter into each [character] individually, and he must bind them all together. He must be in each and over all . . . [and] imbue his tale with the feelings of the secret relation between the characters which suggests the reason why their destinies are interwoven, and which determines the limits of their mutual influence on each other's career.' In other words, a novel is well constructed if the author can 'give a unity of meaning to the whole, as well as individual life to the parts'. Bagehot's chief objection to most contemporary writers is that they neglect the tale 'in delineating the character', so that a part becomes more important than the whole. Bagehot insists as strongly as Aristotle that the plot, conceived of as the action, is the soul of any work, and the characters must be considered as component parts. 'In the tale—the action—lies the proper fusing power for the individual elements', and a novel should never be considered as 'a bundle of fictitious biographies . . . [tied] mechanically together'. Moreover, without a true plot, that is, without an action conceived of as an 'organic whole', the delineation of character will be ineffective. 'The characters cannot be fairly elaborated in their mutual relations, unless the conception of the principal relations germinate in the author's mind simultaneously with the conception of the characters themselves.' [2]

Bagehot, however, makes clear that by action he does not have in mind Charles Reade's kind of startling incident, which is designed to reduce the reader to wondering what will happen next. All incident is to show the development of character and to make manifest 'the genial beauty and stormy greatness of

[1] 'Charles Dickens', *The Works of Walter Bagehot* (London, 1915), III, 73–107. [2] I, 336–8.

human nature'. The subject matter of great literary art should be the great passions, but 'without running into the absurdities of the passionate, stage-effect sort of novelists. . . .' [1]

4. PLOT AND CHARACTER

Wilkie Collins, in the Preface to *The Woman in White*, apparently was in agreement with Bagehot.

> I have always held to the old-fashioned opinion that the primary object of a work of fiction should be to tell a story; and I have never believed that the novelist who properly performed this first condition of his art, was in danger, on that account, of neglecting the delineation of character—for this plain reason, that the effect produced by any narrative of events is essentially dependent, not on the events themselves, but on the human interest which is directly connected with them. . . . It is not possible to tell a story successfully without presenting characters. . . .[2]

Collins, however, seemed unaware of how uninteresting his characters were, and no matter how much he insisted that his stories were really about the struggle between good and evil, most of his critics have persisted in seeing nothing more in them than a fascinating and ingenious series of events. Even Dickens finally came to realize that Collins' elaborate construction was not enough, and he wrote to Wills in 1868: 'I quite agree with you about *The Moonstone*. The construction is wearisome beyond endurance. . . .' [3] Many of Dickens' own novels were equally complicated, but, as Edmund Wilson has brilliantly demonstrated, the plot complications never exist for their own sake.

George Eliot seemed to a critic writing in the *National Review* in July, 1860, best to exemplify the intimate connection that should exist between plot and character. She rigorously eschewed 'all those artificial enhancements of interest which do not arise fairly out of the moral constitutions of the characters . . .' and all the 'adventitious effects' of conventional romance, so that in her greatest works up to that date, 'Mr. Gilfil's Love Story' and *Adam Bede*, there was 'the simplest possible unfolding of the tragedy. . . .' The presence of 'any extraneous or chance elements' would necessarily produce 'a less profound and single

[1] *Ibid.*, pp. 340–1.   [2] (New York, n.d.), I, 4–5.
[3] *Dickens Letters*, III, 660.

effect on the imagination' and destroy the 'solemnity . . . [of] the movement of the principal action in the story'. This critic, who, if he is not Walter Bagehot, shares many of his ideas, complains, however, of 'an occasional looseness of texture' in her narratives, 'the characteristic tendency of the author to sketch in freely all her imagination has grasped, without reference to unity of design. . . .' This tendency shows itself in the fact that 'some of the principal figures, quite essential to the whole effect of the tale, stand too much outside the thread of the story, and take no part in its evolution'. Unity of design, the author of 'The Novels of George Eliot' goes on to explain, is not one of the 'mere technical or formal rules of art'. 'There is a greater vividness of impression, a more concentrated effect produced on the mind, when the course of the narrative works *in conjunction* with the power of the artist to engrave the picture upon the memory, than when they work apart.' Because of the position of figures like Seth Bede, Bartle Massey, and Mr. Craig, 'the group of characters painted [in *Adam Bede*] is a far more perfect work of art than the story . . . which includes them'.[1] But it is the structure of *The Mill on the Floss* that is found to be radically defective. The brother-sister relationship, which occupies two-thirds of the book and is 'a masterly fragment', is in no way connected with Maggie's love story in the last third. The 'tangent into a new field', Maggie's incomplete elopement with Stephen Guest, 'turns on a moral problem foreign to the main subject'. Hence the book lacks unity of theme and fails as a work of art.[2]

The traditional distinction between character and plot, of course, stems from Aristotle's *Poetics*. Aristotle knew very well he was dealing with an entity no one of whose parts had any real separate existence. Breaking a play down into its elements —plot, character, thought, melody, diction, and spectacle— was merely a dialectical strategy, so that he could examine each element in turn. Later critics, however, thought of the two most important elements in a literary work, plot and character, as in some way independent of each other, especially in the Shakespeare criticism of the late eighteenth and nineteenth centuries, when the delineation of character seemed to be an end in itself, rather than one subordinate element in the creation of a total

[1] XI, 206–8. [2] *Ibid.*, pp. 214–16.

pattern. The strange use of the term plot in much mid-Victorian criticism is a reflection of this point of view. George Brimley, for example, came to the conclusion that *Henry Esmond*, certainly Thackeray's most carefully constructed novel, had no plot.[1] According to one *Westminster* reviewer, 'plot-interest, after all, is but of comparatively little value when compared with the power of drawing character. The greatest novels, "Gil Blas", "Don Quixote",—the plays of Shakespeare, which are but intensely dramatic novels in verse—have no plot',[2] and a critic of *Fraser's* thought the whole idea of plot childish: 'Few men feel interest in a plot after nineteen . . . from that time forward they look only to the development of character. . . .'[3] Plot, for a writer in the *British Quarterly Review*, is conceived of as a necessarily unimportant and artificial framework: 'The test of value in works of fiction being in our opinion the amount of truth they contain, we are but slightly interested in the question of Mr. Macdonald's success or failure in the construction of his plots. (We have seen that Meredith also, at times, thought of his plots as a kind of artificial box containing his characters.) In the same essay, 'Works by George Macdonald', the historical importance and value of Thackeray's work are 'closely connected with his habit of almost entirely dispensing both with plots and heroes'.[4]

For most of these critics, however, the word *plot* probably denoted the conventional plot devices of melodrama, what Bagehot called 'imported incident', rather than 'action', action being the logical working out of a certain initial situation and springing from the nature of the characters.[5] Using terminology from Carlyle's essay on Scott, G. H. Lewes had made the same distinction in the *Leader* of July 30, 1853, when he tried to explain how the ending of a certain novel about a miser was not inevitable. 'Instead of drawing his dénouement *ab intra*, from the elements of his drama, he draws it *ab extra*, invoking a *deus ex machina*, in the shape of a Plague.'[6] (Of course the same objection could easily be made and was made to the ending of *The Mill on the Floss*.) Character and action must be strictly related, and in 1866 Lewes complained of the increasing reliance on

[1] *Essays*, p. 254.   [2] LXXXVII (January, 1867), 575.
[3] XLIII (January, 1851), 88.   [4] XLVII (January, 1868), 21.
[5] *National Review*, I (October, 1855), 346.   [6] IV, 739.

what the 'sensation novelists' called 'striking incident', when such incidents do not arise out of 'the natural evolution of . . . [the] story'. They are only useful because 'they serve to bring into a focus the diffused rays of character and emotion'.[1]

The author of the very important essay 'Balzac and His Writings', in the *Westminster Review* of July, 1853, pointed out that one of Balzac's great contributions to the French novel was the eliminating of conventional and arbitrary plots. The *Comédie Humaine* differs from earlier novels 'not only in the truthfulness of the characters, but also in the simple and natural motives of the intrigue, which . . . has its origin in the hearts of the characters'.[2] George Eliot had made the same point about her own novels when she wrote to John Blackwood in February, 1857, that her stories grew from the 'psychological conception of the dramatis personae',[3] and two years earlier as reviewer for the *Westminster Review*, she criticized *Aspen Court* for lacking 'natural development of character and incident'.[4]

The *North British Review* predicated the same close relationship between plot and character in an essay on Jane Austen: 'In all the novels the plots are equally natural. . . . The events grow out of one another; and the characters of the actors are the sufficient reasons of the acts which are related. The action is such as is necessary to display the characters, not such as is invented for the purpose of mystifying and surprising the reader.'[5] The writer clearly realized that character can not be separated from plot in a novel, otherwise the work would tend to be a series of Theophrastian characters. 'A character . . . unfolded itself to her, not in statuesque repose, not as a model without motion, but as a dramatic sketch, a living history, a composite force, which could only exhibit what it was by exhibiting what it did.'[6] As another critic, writing in *Fraser's* December, 1852, said, 'Characterization that is not put into motion, tested and displayed in the actual operations of life, resolves itself into essay writing.'[7] A writer in *Blackwood's* in January, 1863, noted the increasing tendency to say 'the plot is nothing, the character is all'. But, he argued, how can people be delineated without circumstances, which are equiva-

---

[1] *Fortnightly Review*, VI (December 1, 1866), 893.   [2] LX, 209.
[3] *George Eliot Letters*, II, 299.   [4] LXIV (October, 1855), 611.
[5] LII (April, 1870), 141.   [6] *Ibid.*, p. 137.   [7] XLVI, 634.

lent to plot; 'if a person is depicted as yielding to a temptation, there must be an intelligible temptation offered. . . .' [1]

For Trollope, however, plot and character are completely separable and plot 'is the most insignificant part of a tale'. In his *Autobiography* he states, 'A novel should give a picture of common life enlivened by humour and sweetened by pathos. To make that picture worthy of attention, the canvas should be crowded with real portraits. . . . To my thinking, the plot is but the vehicle for all this. . . .' [2] Since he thought of plot as 'the contrived arrangement of incidents by which interest is excited',[3] that is, some arbitrary series of events not necessarily springing from the nature of his characters, it is no wonder that he thought time spent on working out a plot was time wasted. 'I have never troubled myself much about the construction of plots. . . .' Moreover, he candidly tells his readers that he usually started writing a novel without any clear idea of how it would end.[4]

But in spite of the way Trollope seemed to minimize the importance of structure, he did insist that the action of a novel be unified. 'There should be no episodes in a novel. Every sentence, every word . . . should tend to the telling of the story.' [5] One may ask, however, which story? In a novel like *The Last Chronicle of Barset* or *Orley Farm* there are many stories told, and the relation between them often seems quite tenuous indeed. In other novels, though, subplots do become part of one whole, as in *Can You Forgive Her?* with the contrast between the stories of Alice Vavasor and Lady Glencora and the parody provided by the comic underplot of Mrs. Greenough; or in *The Eustace Diamonds* and *The Way We Live Now*, where all the plots become part of a bitterly satiric picture of society. It is in these great novels that Trollope's theory and practice become one.

Though . . . [the] story should be all one, yet it may have many parts. Though the plot itself may require but few characters, it may be so enlarged as to find its full development in many. There may be subsidiary plots, which shall all tend to the elucidation of the main story, and which will take their places as part of one and the

---

[1] XCIII, 92.
[2] *An Autobiography* (Berkeley and Los Angeles, 1947), pp. 106–7.
[3] *Trollope Letters* (London, 1951), p. 217.
[4] *Autobiography*, p. 194.   [5] *Ibid.*, p. 198.

same work,—as there may be many figures on a canvas which shall not to the spectator seem to form themselves into separate pictures.[1]

In his practical criticism, Trollope, strangely enough, seems to emphasize the importance of form. *Vanity Fair, Pendennis*, and *The Newcomes*, in spite of their style and their evidence of great imaginative power and perception of character, are for him 'comparatively idle books. His [Thackeray's] only work, as far as I can judge them, in which there is no touch of idleness, is *Esmond*. . . . All his full-fledged novels, except *Esmond*, contain rather strings of incidents and memoirs of individuals, than a completed story. But *Esmond* is a whole from beginning to end. . . .'[2] Trollope decided that *Esmond* was the best English novel because of its formal perfection, a judgment in which he was joined by a strange bedfellow, Walter Pater.

5. GEORGE ELIOT ON FORM

George Eliot's response to *Rachel Ray* must have been very gratifying to Trollope, for she wrote in October, 1863, that she was much struck with the way he organized his material into 'a strictly related, well-proportioned whole, natty and complete as a nut on a stem. Such construction is among the subtleties of art which can hardly be appreciated except by those who have striven after the same results with conscious failure.'[3] (One wonders here if she were referring to *The Mill on the Floss* or to *Romola*.) She herself was extremely sensitive to criticisms of the unity of her work, and one of the very few times she answered a critic was August, 1863, in a letter to R. H. Hutton. He had felt that there was too much undigested material in *Romola*, which had very little connection with her plot, and she felt bound to vindicate her very conscientious striving after unity. 'Perhaps even a judge so discerning as yourself could not infer how strict a self-control and selection were exercised in the presentation of details. I believe there is scarcely a phrase, an incident, an allusion that did not gather its value to me from its supposed subservience to my main artistic objects.' The

[1] *Autobiography*, p. 199.
[2] *Thackeray* (New York, n.d.), p. 121.
[3] *George Eliot Letters*, IV, 110.

method of *Romola*, she points out, even though it is a historical novel, is really no different from that of her English novels.

It is the habit of my imagination to strive after as full a vision of the medium in which a character moves as of the character itself. The psychological causes which prompted me to give such details of Florentine life and history as I have given, are precisely the same as those which determined me in giving the details of English village life in 'Silas Marner'. . . .[1]

After reading the manuscript of *Middlemarch*, John Blackwood, her publisher, noted that 'there will be complaints of the want of the continuous interest of a story. . . . Each group you introduce is a complete little book or study in itself.' In her answer we can again detect some irritation because she felt misunderstood. 'I don't see how I can leave anything out, because I hope there is nothing irrelevant to my design—to show the gradual action of ordinary causes. . . .'[2] She said the same thing in the novel itself by means of an extended metaphor: when a candle is held up to a metal surface, the apparently random scratches seem to take on form and shape. Her annoyance was even greater after the publication of *Daniel Deronda* because of 'the laudation of readers who cut the book into scraps and talk of nothing in it but Gwendolyn. I meant everything in the book to be related to everything else there.'[3] But even though it is easy to demonstrate that everything in the book is strictly relevant to some design she had in mind, readers from Henry James to F. R. Leavis have continued to isolate the Gwendolyn story from the rest of the book.

In spite of her preoccupation with structure, however, the *Edinburgh Review* of October, 1866, thought her 'power of constructing a fable . . . not equal to her skill in delineating character' and found fault with the structure of *Felix Holt* because George Eliot failed to fuse her two plots, that involving the fortunes of Felix and Esther and that involving the Transomes.

The story has the defect of running in two parallel lines with only an occasional and arbitrary connexion. . . . Either half of the story would have stood by itself, if Esther Lyons had not been employed as a link between the Minister's little house in Malthouse Yard and the stately park with the bad title.

[1] *Ibid.*, p. 97.   [2] *Ibid.*, V, 168.   [3] *Ibid.*, VI, 290.

George Eliot's attempt to make the story of the title to the Transome estate tie the whole novel together failed according to this critic because 'although it is the subject of significant allusion in the introductory chapter, and of incessant anxiety and uncertainty through the entire course of the narrative, [it] exercises no eventual influence on the fortunes of the principal personages'.[1]

6. ORGANIC UNITY

The use of subplots in themselves, however, so far as I have been able to determine, was never questioned in the eighteen-fifties and sixties by any English critic. According to Van Meter Ames, behind the use of multiple plots in English imaginative literature, from the Elizabethan drama to the Victorian novel, lies the feeling that 'life does not present itself as a simple unit (in accord with the British philosophy of pluralism and empiricism)'. The French, on the other hand, 'have been monistic, their novels being lengthened short stories, exhibiting little development of character and brooking no digression, gaining in incisiveness but losing in scope, giving a single portrait where the English novel would give a group portrait'.[2]

But, as we have seen in this chapter, there was a very strong demand that all the material included in a single novel be unified, though that unity often eluded strict definition. As a critic in the *North British Review* of November, 1859, put it, using a favourite romantic metaphor, 'A plot should grow as a plant grows; and unless the writer can divine the organic relation between events—can master, as if by instinct, that law of life which makes one course of action draw with it, as its inevitable corollary or supplement, a given series of effects,—his plot will always manifest a certain crudeness and inconsequence,' and this order underlying a novel must be a 'coherent and vital order'.[3] Here certainly, as was so often the case in all Victorian criticism, the influence of Coleridge and German romantic criticism is very apparent.

Leslie Stephen also uses the term *organic unity*, and in his essay on Fielding it means more than the construction of a

[1] CXXIV, 438-44.   [2] *Aesthetics of the Novel* (Chicago, 1928), p. 178.
[3] XXXI, 390.

coherent plot. 'Fielding's great novels have a true organic unity as well as a consecutive story. . . .' For Stephen, Fielding's novels are distinguished by their 'seriousness of purpose' from 'the old type novel [like *Gil Blas*], developed by Smollett, which is but a collection of amusing anecdotes. . . .' It is this underlying purpose and seriousness that fuses Fielding's heterogeneous material into living wholes, and the excellence of the plot of *Tom Jones* 'depends on the skill with which it is made subservient to the development of character and the thoroughness with which the working motives of the persons involved have been thought out'.[2] In the version of his essay on Hawthorne that appeared in the *Cornhill Magazine* of December, 1872, there is another interesting attempt to define what unity should be in a novel, although Stephen was obviously not satisfied with it, since he removed the entire passage from the same essay when it appeared in *Hours in a Library*. 'Some central truth should be embodied in every work of fiction, which cannot be compressed into a definite formula, but which acts as the animating and informing principle, determining the main lines of the structure and affecting even its most trivial details.' Afraid of being misunderstood Stephen qualifies this statement by saying that 'critics who try to extract it as a formal moral, present us with nothing but an outside husk of dogma', and it cannot be packed into 'a single portable formula'.[2] James' Hugh Vereker had almost the same difficulty in explaining to his listeners what he meant by the figure in the carpet which gave unity to the whole *œuvre* of an author.

Certainly during this period critics and novelists began in a significant way to work out some of the most important concepts for the criticism of novels as a distinct branch of imaginative literature. The idea of point of view, the distinction between rendering and describing a scene, and the whole complicated question of unity in a novel as distinct from a play or any other art form had been all discussed quite fully by English critics before the publication in 1878 of Henry James' first collected critical essays.

[1] *Hours in a Library*, III, 4.   [2] XXVI, 717.

PART THREE

PART THREE

IV

MID-VICTORIAN
REALISM
Real Toads in Real Gardens

I. BACKGROUND

THE theoretical basis of realism, the most fruitful artistic movement of the mid-nineteenth century, is the idea that a work of art is an imitation or a mirror of the world outside of itself. *Mimesis*, as Dr. Abrams noted, is 'probably the most primitive aesthetic theory', and has had a very long and complicated history from its first appearance in the dialogues of Plato to its elaboration by such eighteenth-century writers on the theory of art as Sir Joshua Reynolds, Lessing, and Batteux.[1] It was only natural that these ideas should concern early theorists of the novel, since the form originated with Cervantes, Lesage and Fielding as a distinctly anti-romantic genre. Its basic premise was that romance writers distorted life and gave a false picture of reality; it was the job of the novelist to correct this picture, to show how things really happened.

The Progress of Romance by Clara Reeve, published in 1785, dealt with the whole field of prose fiction, but Miss Reeve,

[1] *The Mirror and the Lamp* (New York, 1953), pp. 8–14.

writing after the major work of the eighteenth-century novelists had been completed, felt forced to distinguish between two different genres, each with its own requirements. The prose romance, 'an heroic fable which treats of fabulous persons and things' [1] (earlier in the same work she characterized it as a 'fabulous story of such actions as are commonly ascribed to heroes, or men of extraordinary courage and abilities' [2]) should not be confused with the novel, 'a picture of real life and manners, and of the times in which it is written'. Continuing this distinction, she observed,

> The Romance in lofty language, describes what never happened nor is likely to happen.—The Novel gives a familiar relation of such things, as pass every day before our eyes . . . and the perfection of it is to represent every scene, in so easy and natural a manner, as to make them appear so probable . . . (at least while we are reading) that all is real, until we are affected by the joys or distresses, of the persons of the story, as if they were our own. [3]

Fielding, who was the first major English writer of novels in Miss Reeve's sense of the world *novel* had earlier come to a similar conclusion about the theory of the new literary form he was developing. The novelist, he asserted in the very important introductory chapter to Book VIII of *Tom Jones*, must keep within the bounds of probability, not alone of possibility, as the earlier French critic of the prose romance, Huet, had said. As a result Fielding committed himself to the portrayal of mixed characters, that is, neither wholly good nor wholly bad (though he himself came dangerously close to these extremes with Blifil and Squire Allworthy), and actions not only 'within the compass of human agency, and which human agents may probably be supposed to do' but also 'likely for the very actors and characters themselves to have performed'. Fielding, however, would have disagreed with Miss Reeve's restriction of the novel to the realm of the familiar, those things which 'pass every day before our eyes'. For Fielding, even though 'every good author will confine himself within the bounds of probability, it is by no means necessary that his characters, or his incidents, should be trite, common, or vulgar; such as happen in every street,

---

[1] The Fascimile Text Society (New York, 1930), p. 111.
[2] *Ibid.*, p. 13.   [3] *Ibid.*, p. 111.

or in every house, or which may be met with in the home articles of a newspaper'.[1]

Because Fielding's conception of character and situation was so bounded by the canon of probability, Scott thought of *Joseph Andrews* and *Tom Jones* as the first true English novels rather than *Pamela* and *Clarissa*. Richardson, he implied, merely domesticated the earlier prose romances, giving them a contemporary English middle-class setting, while retaining many of their conventions and character types. 'Richardson's novels are but a step from the old romance, approaching, indeed, more nearly to the ordinary course of events, but still dealing in improbable incidents, and in characters swelled beyond the ordinary limits of humanity.' It was only in *Tom Jones* that Scott first found 'truth and human nature itself'.[2]

But even in Fielding Scott could find traces of the romance from which the novel evolved:

The reader expected . . . a course of adventures . . . more interesting and extraordinary than those which occur in his own life, or that of his next-door neighbours. The hero no longer defeated armies by his single sword, clove giants to the chine, or gained kingdoms. But he was expected to go through perils by sea and land, to be steeped in poverty, to be tried by temptation, to be exposed to the alternate vicissitudes of adversity and prosperity, and his life was a troubled scene of suffering and achievement.

Although Fielding and his contemporaries professed to imitate nature, 'it was, as the French say, *la belle nature*'.[3] Even the character of Tom Jones, for Scott, was improved upon or idealized somewhat, for, no matter what follies he committed, he was 'studiously vindicated from the charge of infidelity or heart'. In order to find true realism—Scott of course did not use that term—one would have to go to the novels of Jane Austen: 'They belong to a class of fictions which has arisen almost in our times, and which draws the characters and incidents introduced more immediately from the current of ordinary

---

[1] *Tom Jones* (New York, 1943), pp. 337–8. For Huet on this subject see *History of Romances* (London, 1715), p. 99.

[2] *Miscellaneous Prose Works* (Boston, 1829), III, 75.

[3] According to Charles Batteux, the chief exponent of this theory, *la belle nature* is not 'le vrai qui est; mais qui peut être, le beau vrai, qui est représenté comme s'il existoit réelement, & avec toutes les perfections qu'il peut recevoir'. Abrams, *op. cit.*, p. 35.

life than was permitted by the former rules of the novel.' [1] The new novel, which Scott was describing in this essay on *Emma* in the *Quarterly Review* of October, 1815, was rigidly to eschew interest arising from the extraordinary and to avoid

alarming our credulity . . . [or] amusing our imagination by wild variety of incident, or by those pictures of romantic affection and sensibility, which were formerly as certain attributes of fictitious characters as they are of rare occurrence among those who actually live and die.

Instead, the newer novelist must become expert in 'the art of copying from nature as she really exists in the common walks of life, presenting to the reader, instead of splendid scenes of an imaginary world, a correct and striking representation of that which is daily taking place around him'. The characters, too, must 'conduct themselves upon the motives and principles which the readers may recognize as ruling their own [lives] and that of most of their acquaintances'. The comparison Scott draws towards the end of this review between *Emma* and the painting of the Low Countries was to be used for countless other novels in the course of the century.

The author's knowledge of the world, and the peculiar taste by which she presents characters that the reader cannot fail to recognize, reminds us something of the merits of the Flemish school of painting. The subjects are not often elegant, and certainly never grand; but they are finished up to nature, and with a precision which delights the reader.[2]

Scott, in this essay, included many of the points which were later to be almost endlessly discussed by critics for and against the realistic novel, but, though he obviously admired Jane Austen very much, he passed no judgment on the relative value of the new realistic novel and the older romance, both of which were flourishing in 1815. He did suggest, however, that the future belonged to the realists, in spite of the fact that he himself was to do so much with his 'big bow-wow' style of swashbuckling romance. It was, however, romance with a difference, and it should be remembered that the Waverley Novels were as

---

[1] *Quarterly Review*, XIV (October, 1815), 189–91.
[2] *Ibid.*, pp. 192–7.

important an influence on the *Comedie Humaine* as Jane Austen
was to be on *Middlemarch*. The materials of romance,

robbers, smugglers, bailiffs, caverns, dungeons, and mad-houses [we
have here some of Scott's most characteristic properties], have been
all introduced until they ceased to interest. And thus in the novel,
as in every style of composition which appeals to public taste, the
more rich and easily worked mines being exhausted, the adventurous author must, if he is desirous of success, have recourse to
those materials which were disdained by his predecessors as un-
productive, or avoided as only capable of being turned to profit
by great skill and labour.[1]

2. SIMPLE REALISM

But in spite of Scott's pronouncement that the traditional motifs
of romance were exhausted, the genre continued to be popular,
especially in the form of historical romance, during the thirties
and forties. The romance writer in this period opened new
territory with stories of the fabulous life led by aristocrats (the
'silver fork novel') and by criminals (the 'Newgate novel'), but
he still kept the old intention of 'alarming our credulity' and
'amusing our imagination by a wild variety of incident' or by
pictures of high-pitched 'romantic affections and sensibility'.
The type of novel that *Emma* represented, one which draws its
material from 'the current of ordinary life', seemed to be only
a minor current in the thirties and early forties, and if we can
trust Harriet Martineau, it was extremely difficult to find a
publisher for a book like *Deerbrook*, which dealt with middle-
class life in a realistic manner. John Murray rejected it in 1838,
she notes in her *Autobiography*, because the heroine came from
Birmingham and the hero was a surgeon. 'Youths and maidens
looked for lords and ladies on every page of a new novel.' [2]
Charlotte Brontë had much the same difficulty in 1846 with
The Professor, and for the same reason; yet, by the 1850's and
1860's critics were demanding that novels treat the same sort of
material that Harriet Martineau and Charlotte Brontë had
found so difficult to publish. For example, *Fraser's* in October,
1851, praised a novel called *The Story of a Family* because of its

[1] *Ibid.*, p. 192.
[2] Ed. Maria Weston Chapman (Boston, 1877), I, 415.

'naturalness': 'It is perfectly quiet, domestic, and truthful . . . and in the most pathetic incident there is nothing irreconcile-able with every-day experience.'[1] Another *Fraser's* essay in January, 1860, explained why everyday experience provided the best material for the novelist:

These are the very events and feelings upon which the happiness or misery of most of us depends; and the field which embraces them, to the exclusion of the wonderful, the sentimental, and the historical, is surely large enough, as it is certainly the one which admits of the most profitable cultivation. In the end, too, the novel of daily real life is that of which we are least apt to weary. . . .[2]

Macmillan's Magazine in August, 1861, carried an essay by J. M. Ludlow, '*Elsie Venner* and *Silas Marner*', which found fault with American novels for turning away from domestic realism. 'It seems as if the ablest American writers were now unable to look ordinary life steadily in the face, to see its beauty and its noble-ness, and to depict it with the loving care of the true artist.' American literature was being undermined by 'this search after and study of the singular and exceptional', and when American writers did handle ordinary domestic life, they treated it 'only as a framing or as a background for the abnormal, the improb-able, the fantastic'.[3] These observations of Ludlow on Haw-thorne, Poe, and Holmes were meant not as a purely descriptive statement but as a value judgment: novels that dealt with the improbable or fantastic were not as good as those dealing with the ordinary or the normal, and it was for this reason that *Silas Marner* was superior to *Elsie Venner* or *The Marble Faun*.

As a critic Trollope seemed to be in substantial agreement with the position represented by Ludlow and the writers for *Fraser's Magazine*, for in his *Autobiography* he specifically says, 'A novel should give a picture of common life enlivened by humour and sweetened by pathos.'[4] He describes *Framley Parsonage* in those terms: 'The story was thoroughly English. There was a little fox-hunting and a little tuft-hunting, some Christian vir-tue and some Christian cant. There was no heroism and no villainy.'[5] Heroism and villainy, as a matter of fact, were strictly proscribed in Chapter XXXV of *The Eustace Diamonds*,

[1] XLIV, 389.   [2] LXI, 31.   [3] IV, 308–9.
[4] (Berkeley and Los Angeles, 1947), p. 107.   [5] *Ibid.*, p. 121.

'Too Bad for Sympathy', because they were so rarely met with in ordinary experience.

Our own friends around us are not always merry and wise, nor, alas always honest and true. They are often cross and foolish, and sometimes treacherous and false. . . . We cannot have heroes to dine with us. There are none. And were these heroes to be had, we should not like them [this is precisely what Lytton Strachey showed in his 'Florence Nightingale' and 'General Gordon']. But neither are our friends villains. . . .

Therefore, Trollope concludes, characters in novels should be neither better nor worse than the people we usually have to dinner.[1]

But when he criticizes those of his novels which were closest to ordinary, everyday existence, namely *The Belton Estate*, *Rachel Ray*, and *Miss Mackenzie*, he finds them merely 'readable', and they contain scenes which are 'true to life' but otherwise have 'no peculiar merits, and will add nothing to my reputation as a novelist'.[2] The fact that a novel is a transcript of ordinary life is not enough: 'He who can deal adequately with tragic elements is a greater artist and reaches a higher aim than the writer whose efforts never carry him above the mild walks of everyday life.'[3]

Realism, however, as many critics discovered, was not basic-ally a question of subject matter; it was a matter of the writer's attitude towards and treatment of his subject matter. Thack-eray's handling of the Newgate theme in *Catherine* and *Barry Lyndon* was obviously not the same sort of thing that Bulwer or Ainsworth had done, nor was his treatment of the Crawleys, Southdowns, and Steynes like that of Lister or Mrs. Gore. For Thackeray himself, Dickens' art, even though it usually treated middle-class life, was somehow illegitimate; Dickens misused the novel form.

I quarrel with his Art in many respects: which I don't think represents Nature duly; for instance Micawber appears to me an exaggeration of a man, as his name is of a name. It is delightful and makes me laugh: but it is no more real than my friend Punch is: and in so far I protest against him . . . holding the Art of Novels *is* to represent nature: to convey as strongly as possible the sentiment

---

[1] Modern Library edition (New York, n.d.), pp. 317–18.
[2] *Autobiography*, p. 163.   [3] *Ibid.*, p. 190.

of reality—in a tragedy or a poem you aim at producing different emotions; the figures moving, and their words sounding, heroically: but in a drawing room drama a coat is a coat and a poker is a poker. . . .[1]

In 1841 an anonymous critic in the *Athenaeum* had defined the novel in a very similar way, but he left open another approach, equally legitimate, to prose fiction:

Is it not that a *novel* is, or aims at being, a picture of daily life,— a reflex of human nature under the modifications of an actual state of society? . . . A *romance*, on the contrary, pretends to no such fidelity of delineation. It strives to paint man as a being of passion alone; its view of life is taken by the flare of torches; artificial lights and abrupt shadows—dazzling brilliancy and fathomless gloom— such are the laws of its chiar-oscuro, such the effects it loves to produce. Everything it presents is rendered wildly picturesque, mysteriously undefined, by the flickering glare which is thrown over the picture. In short, the Novel, while it strives to arrest our attention by exciting sympathy and surprise, appeals to the observant and reasoning faculties also;—the Romance, on the contrary, addresses itself to the imagination alone. . . .

But the age of romance is almost over because it 'is at variance with the spirit of the present age. The nineteenth century is distinguished by a craving for the positive and the real—it is essentially an age of analysis and criticism . . . and these faculties are . . . the natural antagonists to the imagination. Hence the present dearth of Poetry and the death of Romance. . . .' [2]

In October, 1853, the *Westminster Review*, in a rather long article, attempted to give a connected history of the novel. The author, who Professor Haight, on internal evidence, believes may be George Eliot, again relates changing approaches to fiction to the changing spirit of the period: 'We feel the chasm which separates one age from another as completely in the style of fiction which has prevailed, as in the phase of religious belief, or of scientific knowledge, which has peculiarly distinguished each period. . . .' Since the present age, according to Comte's scheme, is no longer theological or metaphysical, but positive, modern novelists will restrict themselves

more and more to the actual and the possible; and our tastes would be offended were they greatly to overstep these limitations, for a

[1] *Thackeray Letters*, II, 772–3.   [2] September 25, 1841, p. 740.

scientific, and somewhat sceptical age, has no longer the power of believing in the marvels which delighted our ruder ancestors. The carefully wrought story, which details in orderly chronological sequence; which unfolds character according to those laws which experience teaches us to look for as well in the moral as the material world; and which describes outward circumstances in their inexorable certainty, yielding to no enchanter's wand ... is ... [not met with] until science and letters have reached a high place and are established firmly enough to influence the popular mind. ...

The author of this essay, however, very soon forgets his historical approach to his subject: 'The flimsiest modern novel ... is infinitely superior in artistic arrangement ... to even the most readable of ancient fictions' [1] because of the constitution of the human mind itself.

There is an instinct in every unwarped mind which prefers truth to extravagance, and a photographic picture, if it be only of a kitten or a hay-stack, is a pleasanter subject in the eyes of most people (were they brave enough to admit it), than many a glaring piece of mythology, which those who profess to worship High Art find themselves called upon to pronounce divine. [2]

In the same year the *Westminster* ran two other important essays devoted to the subject of realism in fiction. One, a survey of Thackeray's work up to *Henry Esmond*, found Thackeray to have been the most influential of all English novelists in directing fiction back to 'nature and truth', 'nature and truth' meaning 'the men and women who compose the sum of that life in the midst of which we are moving'. Thackeray's purpose, which is one that should motivate all novelists, is to show these men and women 'in situations such as we might see them in any day of our lives' in order 'to probe the principles upon which the framework of society in the nineteenth century is based ... to

[1] LX, 343-5.
[2] *Ibid.*, p. 358. This kind of aggressive philistinism certainly seems very far from the characteristic way George Eliot's mind functions, as do the judgments made on various novelists in the course of this essay: e.g. 'Without brilliance of any kind—Without imagination, depth of thought or wide experience, Miss Austen, by simply describing what she knew and had seen, and making accurate portraits of very tiresome and uninteresting people, is recognized as a true artist, and will continue to be admired, when authors more ambitious ... will be neglected and forgotten.' (*Ibid.*, p. 358.)

paint life as it is, coloured as little as may be by the hues of the imagination. . . .' [1] That there is a real continuity between English realistic theory in the fifties and the later naturalism is evident from the scientific, specifically sociological, intention posited here. For the next sixty years, critics of fiction in both England and France continued to ask the same questions: can —or should—the novelist give an exact transcript of 'life as it is?' and what is the purpose of this transcript?

The other essay, 'Balzac and His Writings', the first extended and serious piece of criticism Balzac received in an important English periodical, attempted to place its subject in the post-revolutionary literary and artistic movements in France. 'The reform in art, to which the name romanticism has been given . . . by abolishing the conventional models, led naturally enough to the adoption of real and natural models, and to the exact imitation of nature.' This new movement, 'only a continuation or branch of what had before been absurdly styled "romanticism",' has been given the name 'realism' in France, and its followers are called 'realists' because they 'copy from nature, and, above all, from modern nature, and the nature that surrounds them. . . . The head of this realist school was Honore de Balzac. . . .' [2] The author of this essay was careful to point out, however, that though Balzac's characters are always 'true in nature', they are not necessarily 'of a kind met with every day. "The characters of a novel," says Balzac, "must be more logical than those of history." ' [3] Here, as Robert Gorham Davis has shown, is probably the first use of the term *realism* in English criticism,[4] although the term *realist*, as Professor Davis did not realize, was used two years earlier in *Fraser's* of January, 1851, and applied to Thackeray—he was called 'chief of the Realist school' [5]—but there was no attempt made in that essay to define the term. Both of these uses antedate 1856, the year given by the *OED*, which ascribes to *Modern Painters*, Volume IV, the introduction of the terms *realism* and *realist* from France into England. Although David Masson, in the article '*Pendennis and Copperfield*: Thackeray *and* Dickens' in the May, 1851, issue of

---

[1] LIX (April, 1853), 272–4. [2] LX (July, 1853), 203. [3] *Ibid.*, p. 212.
[4] 'The Sense of the Real in English Fiction', *Comparative Literature*, III (1951), 214.
[5] XLIII, 86.

the *North British Review*, refers to the real and ideal styles of art, explaining that he derived these terms from the criticism of painting,[1] he did not add the suffixes *-ist* and *-ism* until he re-used this material in his *British Novelists and Their Styles* of 1859. By that time apparently *realist* and *realism* had been thoroughly naturalized in England.

In France, according to Bernard Weinberg in *French Realism, The Critical Reaction 1830–1870*, the term *realism* was first applied to art in the 1830's, although it was confined to painting. (Before then, it had been only a metaphysical term.) It was not given any real prominence, however, until 1846, when Houssaye published his *Histoire de la peinture flamande et hollandaise*. Only then was *réalisme* used for literature, specifically referring to Mérimée and Balzac. Only in 1851 did the words *réalisme* and *réaliste* gain currency as names of a kind of novel and novelist and all through the fifties they were often italicized as neologisms.[2] As we can see, these new critical terms established themselves in the vocabulary of France and England at about the same time, though they were used with much more frequency in France, where there was a more clearly marked school of writers who could be labelled *réalistes*.

3. THE REDUCTIO AD ABSURDUM

For many English critics of the early fifties it was chiefly Thackeray who seemed to be fixing new canons for the novel and establishing a new type of book. The *Quarterly Review* of September, 1855, described *The Newcomes* as 'the most minute and faithful transcript of actual life which is anywhere to be found'. The words *copy, transcript, photograph*, and *daguerreotype*, as we shall see, were used by both defenders and attackers of the new movement.

Mr. Thackeray looks at life under its ordinary aspects, and copies it with a fidelity and artistic skill which are surprising. Men, women, and children talk, act, and think in his pages exactly as they are talking, acting, and thinking at every hour of the day. . . . Just as the stream of life runs on through these volumes, so may it be seen to flow in the world itself by whoever takes up the same position on the bank.

[1] XV, 68–70.   [2] (Chicago, 1937), pp. 117–19.

The ordinary novelist, for this reviewer, tends to

describe characters under exceptional circumstances, to show them influenced by passions which seldom operate in their excess with each individual, and to make them actors in adventures which in their aggregate happen to few or none. It is the picked passages of existence which they represent, and these again are often magnified and coloured beyond the measure of nature.[1]

With this extreme kind of realism, which almost seems to preclude any sort of selection on the part of the artist or any artistic shaping, Thackeray might have agreed in theory, even though it is obviously impossible in practice. According to the *Saturday Review* of September 7, 1861, 'The highest art is the nearest approach to nature,' and the best novelists are those who 'drew from life, having studied human nature, in all its varieties, as it is, and not through the distorting medium of their own fanciful conceptions'.[2]

An equally thorough-going statement of the doctrinaire realist position was given in 1855 by Fitzjames Stephen in 'The Relation of Novels to Life'. Every novel, according to Stephen, should strive to give 'a perfect representation of life',[3] specifically the life of a single man, and, as a result, prose fiction hardly belongs to the realm of imaginative literature at all. 'The first requirement of a novel is, that it should be a biography—an account of the life or part of the life, of a person.' Since the novel is a 'fictitious biography', it should have no more plot than a *bona fide* biography; it merely relates anything of importance that happened to a given individual. In a drama Stephen sees the importance of form and unity since it is 'the representation of an incident',[4] but in a novel plot, or even any sort of story thread, distorts the representation of life. In a well-constructed plot 'the personages have apparently a much closer connexion, and more intimate sympathy with each other, than they would have under similar circumstances in real life'; in *Robinson Crusoe* and the other imaginary biographies of Defoe, on the other hand, characters 'appear and disappear as they do

[1] XCVII, 150–1.   [2] XII, 251.
[3] *Cambridge Essays* (London, 1855), p. 181.
[4] *Ibid.*, pp. 148–51. This idea of the novel as a fictitious biography can be found earlier in Carlyle's essay 'Biography', *Works* (London, 1887), pp. 250–1.

in life'.[1] When he applied this critical apparatus to *David Copperfield*, which he thought of as the autobiography of the hero, he found the book indecorous. We should consider 'what would be the feelings with which we should look upon a man who so described his life. . . . What would be thought of a real autobiography disclosing all a man's most secret thoughts and most sacred affections? It would be considered a great breach of decency: and why is this less an offence in a novel than it is in real life?' [2] Stephen's ideal in autobiography is obviously much closer to John Stuart Mill's than to Rousseau's.

The same kind of confusion between art and life can be found in a *Quarterly* essay of October, 1860, on George Eliot, the same one that complained that the number of deaths in her first three books was out of proportion to the number in real life.[3] The author of this review does not like her novels because in them he is forced to meet people he would ordinarily avoid. 'She knowingly forces *dis*agreeable people on us, and insists that we shall be interested in their story. . . .' [4] Life and art are further confounded by a critic writing in the *North British Review* of May, 1864. The realistic novelist must imitate life not only in the subject matter of his book but also in his form, or rather lack of form. He agrees with Stephen that 'the realist in fiction is careless about plot. His sole object is to describe men's lives as they really are; and real life is fragmentary and unmethodical.' [5] Since the idea of plot presupposes method and form, they must go in the interest of realism.[6]

4. ART IS NOT LIFE

Fitzjames Stephen's attempt to take the novel out of the realm of art completely—to make it, in Aristotelian terms, conform to the lower truth of history (for biography is but a branch of

---

[1] *Cambridge Essays*, p. 164.   [2] *Ibid.*, pp. 189–90.
[3] See above, p. 65.   [4] CVIII, 476.   [5] XL, 372.
[6] See also the *Edinburgh Review*, CX (July, 1859), 223–4: 'A novel is good in proportion to its truth to nature; no matter where the scene is laid, or what the characters may be. . . . Given a thread of some story [and the story obviously is unimportant], we only require personages engaged to act as they would in real life.' George Eliot's characters for this reviewer are 'persons with whom we might become acquainted, rather than . . . imaginary human beings'.

history in its subservience to what actually happened rather than what could or should happen) instead of the higher truth of poetry—met with many critical rejoinders.

The author of 'Religious Novels' in the *North British Review* of November, 1856, grants that the novel is closer to the character of a fictitious biography than the drama, for 'the drama presupposes the characters already formed, and depends for its interest on one great action, to which all the personages contribute'. The novel is much more concerned with the development of a character, and often 'represents a course of life, or one phase of life spread over a considerable time. . . .' But there the analogy between novel and biography ends, for the novel aims 'at representing certain critical phases of life . . . which generally call out . . . whatever is most passionate and enthusiastic in character'. If one actually examines the best novels instead of forming '*a priori* ideas of what . . . [they] ought to be', he will find 'that the novelist, like the dramatist or any other artist, limits his materials, selects those which are most suited to his purpose, and intensifies their action somewhat beyond the actual results of experience. This seems to us to be required by the necessary distinction between art on the one hand, and life on the other.' The novel, in short, does not 'imitate life exactly' but presents 'in an artistic shape, and yet in one which is felt in the main to be true to nature and experience . . . aspects of life and phases of character. . . .'[1]

An essay which appeared in the same review two years later condemned *John Halifax, Gentleman* for having a 'number of successive plots . . . threaded together in place of a single comprehensive plot' and concluded that it was 'a fictitious biography, rather than a novel', and as such, defective. A work of art should not have

different centres of interest and different groups of events . . . artificially amalgamated into one work. In a real biography the interest lies in seeing the whole issues of a single life; and the reason for threading together periods which, as artistic effects, are complete in themselves, is obvious, namely,—that in real life, and by one greater than any artist, they were so threaded together. But there is no such excuse for a fictitious biography that does not form an artistic whole.[2]

[1] XXXVI, 209-10.   [2] XXIX (November, 1856), 472.

Trollope, in many of his novels, certainly did not seem very much concerned with artistic wholes; yet he too ranged himself against the idea that a novel is an imaginary biography, which, unawares, he combined with the later theory of the novel as a slice of life in his criticism of all of Thackeray's novels except *Henry Esmond* and *Barry Lyndon*. '*The Newcomes*, therefore, like Thackeray's other tales, is rather a slice from the biographical memoirs of a family, than a romance or novel in itself.' Trollope would not consider a work a novel unless it had a definite structure.[1] Indeed, critics throughout the fifties and sixties grew more and more insistent upon a strict view of unity in the novel ('close texture and welded interest of the whole'[2]) that would preclude any harking back to the older picaresque tradition of Smollett and early Dickens. The discussion of form and structure during this period clearly pointed towards the 'well-made' novel on the French model that was to be so important during the next four decades.

5. BULWER AND DICKENS—THE ATTACK ON REALISM

The critical term most often opposed to *realism* was *idealism*, and the most articulate advocate of the latter was Bulwer-Lytton. In an essay of 1838 he defined art as 'the process by which we give to natural materials the highest excellence they are capable of receiving', so that mere technical correctness in copying could not be called art at all. In order to evaluate any work we should ask ourselves not 'how far it resembles what we have seen so much as how far it embodies what we can imagine'. Art concerns itself only with the realm of ideals; it is not the imitation but the 'exaltation of nature'.[3] This anti-mimetic theory was very closely related to the aesthetic speculation of the German post-Kantian philosophers, whom Bulwer, in his enthusiasm for the German Romantic movement, read widely.

The transcendental formulation of his ideas was made much more explicit when Bulwer expanded his critical theories in the series of essays he wrote for *Blackwood's* in 1862 and 1863.

---

[1] *Thackeray*, p. 113. See above, p. 132.
[2] *North British Review*, XXIX (November, 1856), 471.
[3] *The Critical and Miscellaneous Writings of Sir Edward Lytton Bulwer* (Philadelphia, 1841), I, 52–3.

Art . . . is the effort of men to express the ideas which Nature suggests to him of a power above Nature, whether that power be within the recesses of his own being [the imagination, in the romantic sense of the word], or in the Great First Cause of which Nature, like himself, is but the effect. Art employs itself in the study of Nature, for the purpose of implying, though but by a hint or a symbol, the supernatural.

The term *supernatural* does not necessarily have a religious meaning but is almost equivalent to the human imagination. This faculty, according to Bulwer, is 'the supernatural in man', because it is the only means man has of transcending nature. Art, the product of the imagination, must also, by this strange logic, transcend nature and never copy it.

We not only degrade but altogether mistake and falsify [art], if we call it the imitation of Nature. . . . [Art] is a selection from Nature of certain details arranged into a whole, to which no whole in Nature has resemblance, and intended to convey ideas of something which man conjectures or divines to be supernatural by reason of the supernatural within himself.[1]

Bulwer, as we have seen, does not deny that the primary material of the novel comes from the world external to the novelist—matter of fact or positive truth as nineteenth-century philosophy called it: '*The artist never seeks to represent the positive truth, but the idealised image of a truth* [italics Bulwer's]. As Hegel well observes, "That which exists in nature is a something purely individual and particular. Art, on the contrary, is essentially destined to manifest the general." ' Hence for Bulwer all things and all phenomena are generalized when they are transformed into ideas or ideals of the mind.[2] Characters in a novel, as embodiments of ideals created by the human imagination from the raw facts of experience, are not individuals but types or symbols. It is a serious critical mistake according to Bulwer to think of them and judge them by their correspondence to people we know. The great characters of literature were never meant to be real people, but that is not to say that they are mere abstract figures either. The artist seeks 'to show the effects of [a] passion upon certain given forms of character under certain situations: And he secures the individuality required, and

---

[1] XCII (August, 1862), 163-4.   [2] XCIII (May, 1863), 549.

avoids the lifeless pedantry of an allegorized abstraction, by reconciling passion, character, and situation with each other; so that it is always a living being in [*sic*] whom we sympathize.' But though individual, he insists, every great character will be typical, as Don Quixote is a representation of 'that extravagant generosity of enthusiasm for the redress of human wrongs, which, even in exciting ridicule, compels admiration and conciliates love'. We are not, however, while reading Cervantes, to ask ourselves if Don Quixote is like anyone we know or are ever likely to know. The greatness of the character, far from being in its likeness to an individual Cervantes found in life, is in its 'fidelity to a certain nobleness of sentiment, which, however modified, exists in every genuinely noble nature'.[1]

But Bulwer's 'general truths' seem dangerously near a kind of never-never land to which he periodically escaped to forget all about unpleasant reality, and one wonders what kind of truth fiction can embody when it builds up a world in which there is no 'servile copy of particulars'. We come to fiction, he writes in this same essay,

with a desire to escape, for the moment, out of this hard and narrow positive world in which we live; to forget, for a brief holiday, disputes between High and Low Church, Tories and Radicals—in fine, to lose sight of *particulars* in the contemplation of *general* truth. We can have our real life, in all its harsh outlines, whenever we please it; we do not want to see that real life, but its ideal image, in the fable land of art.[2]

This description would more likely fit William Morris' prose romances or Rossetti's ballads than any of the great nineteenth-century novels. How much of 'real life' can be left in such a conception? for Bulwer seems to prefer his general truths to be completely emptied of all particulars, all content, and we are left with a very shadowy world indeed, something like a painting of Burne-Jones, or of Dufy.

Dickens never would have subscribed to any theory that considered art as escape,[3] and in his world the 'harsh outlines' of 'real life' were very much in evidence, even, most critics complained, too much intensified. He did agree, however, with

---

[1] *Ibid.*, pp. 552–3. [2] *Ibid.*, p. 550.
[3] See above, pp. 23–5.

Bulwer's defence of what hostile critics like Thackeray called exaggeration. According to Bulwer, here was the very essence of art, and appropriately, Forster in his *Life of Dickens* quotes a manuscript note by Bulwer:

> The greatest masters of the novel of modern manners have generally availed themselves of capital Humour for the illustration of manners; and have with a deep and true, but perhaps unconscious, knowledge of art, pushed the humour almost to the verge of caricature. For, as the serious ideal requires a certain exaggeration in the proportions of the natural, so also does the ludicrous.

Aristophanes, Cervantes, and Fielding—all of them employed 'the admirable exaltation of the humorous by means of the exaggerated', or what the Victorian critics called caricature. Bulwer concludes that modern ideas of probability and verisimilitude had really very little to do with art. 'It follows, therefore, that art and correctness are far from identical, and that the one is sometimes proved by the disdain of the other.' [1] Dickens himself tried to indicate the relationship between objects and characters in his books and those in the world by the phrase 'fantastic fidelity'.[2]

Dickens saw a very distinct connection between his own art and that of the folk and fairy tale and realized his methods were very far from those of the realistic novelists of the mid-century. As far as he was concerned, the prevailing emphasis on verisimilitude was beside the point, since he was consciously using distortion and fantasy:

> It does not seem to me to be enough to say of any description that it is the exact truth. . . . The exact truth should be there; but the merit or art in the narrator is the manner of stating the truth. . . . In these times, when the tendency is to be frightfully literal and catalogue-like—to make the thing, in short, a sum in reduction that any miserable creature can do in that way—I have an idea (really founded on the love of what I profess), that the very holding of popular literature through a kind of popular dark age, may depend on such fanciful treatment.[3]

The paintings of the Pre-Raphaelites he saw as an example of the modern tendency to be 'frightfully literal and catalogue-

---

[1] Ed. J. W. T. Ley (New York, n.d.), p. 726.   [2] *Ibid.*
[3] *Ibid.*, pp. 727–8.

like', and he attacked them, chiefly Millais' 'Christ in the House of his Father', which depicted Jesus as a common carpenter and included all the familiar details of a contemporary carpenter's shop. Art should not merely be 'the faithful portraiture of shavings, or the skilful colouring of drapery'; rather it should 'inform' objects 'with mind and sentiment'.[1]

Dickens had no objection to the use of modern life in art, but he believed very strongly that the artist must transform his raw material, and in the preface to *Bleak House* he wrote: 'I have purposely dwelt upon the romantic side of familiar things.'[2] The first number of *Household Words* began with a similar statement of purpose: 'To show to all, that in familiar things, even in those which are repellent on the surface, there is Romance enough, if we will find it out. . . . The mightier inventions of this age are not, to our thinking, all material, but have a kind of souls in their stupendous bodies. . . .'[3] All through *Household Words* and *All the Year Round*, in articles like 'Poetry on the Railway', 'Twenty Miles', and 'The Poetry of Fact',[4] Dickens insisted that the conventional subject matter of poetry was worn out and that the poet should turn to the products of the industrial revolution taking place around him, which he was studiously trying to ignore. The Pre-Raphaelite painters, however, instead of revealing beauty in surface ugliness and transforming everyday objects into things of beauty, merely rendered extremely awkward and ugly the things they so painstakingly and literally copied.

He felt the same way about the stories he read as an editor. In rejecting one story as too commonplace, he explained: 'something more is wanted in such a narrative, than its literal truth. . . .' The story was not 'told artistically',[5] and very often to Dickens art and literal truth seemed incompatible.

But in spite of his dislike for treatment that was literally realistic and nothing more, he was opposed to any art which seemed to separate itself too much from life. Coming out of an exhibition of orthodox academic painting, he noted in

[1] *Household Words*, I (June 15, 1850), 265–6.
[2] Preface, *Bleak House* (London, 1948), p. xiv.   [3] (March 30, 1850), 1.
[4] See *Household Words*, XI (June 2, 1855), 414–18; X (September 2, 1854), 68–72; *All the Year Round*, XVIII (September 14, 1867), 277–9.
[5] *Dickens Letters*, II, 236.

Household Words, 'was like the transition from Madame Tussaud's waxworks, or a tawdry fancy ball in the Sleeping Beauty's palace during the hundred years of enchantment, to a windy mountain or the rolling sea', and the two sentries at the door seemed to him allegorical personages keeping life out. What he objected to specifically was what any good academician would have called the idealizing tendency of the pictures: all the models were perfectly proportioned, the men with large chests and the women with long lashes; all the metal objects seemed to be polished up specially for the exhibition, and there were no signs of passion in any of the paintings—all was perfectly decorous and lifeless.[1] For a similar reason he had a strong antipathy to the novels of Charlotte Yonge, especially to *The Heir of Redclyffe.* The dilemmas of her people were completely unreal to him and the 'characters . . . simply impossible. They have no types in nature. . . .'[2]

There were at least three distinct attitudes Dickens took towards the criticism of his novels that, based wholly on the ground of probability or verisimilitude, accused him of caricaturing and exaggerating. He could on occasion insist that everything in his novels was literal truth, sometimes very much toned down rather than exaggerated. 'Mr. Squeers and his school are faint and feeble pictures of an existing reality, purposely subdued and kept down lest they be deemed impossible.'[3] This kind of self-defence was in danger of becoming absurd when in the preface to *Bleak House* he listed his authorities for Krook's spontaneous combustion. Lewes' attacks on this episode in the *Leader,* however, with his much more impressive counter-authorities, were even more ridiculous, and neither Lewes nor Dickens seemed to realize that the whole controversy was beside the point.[4]

Yet Dickens did, on other occasions, call his method of delineation deliberately fanciful, an attempt to get away from the modern tendency of 'catalogue-like' literalism.[5] All stories,

[1] XVII (March 13, 1858), 289.

[2] XIX (December 18, 1858), 51. See above, p. 100, where he objects to Pearl in *The Scarlet Letter* for the same reasons.

[3] Preface, *Nicholas Nickleby,* Everyman's Library (London, 1907), p. xvii.

[4] See Gordon S. Haight, 'Dickens and Lewes', *PMLA,* LXXI (1956), 166–79.

[5] See above, p. 156.

by their very nature, he said, are bound to seem improbable, and improbability is 'allowable in them', but it is the author's part to force his readers to suspend their disbelief. Dickens once rejected a novel because, as he explained to his sub-editor, 'it is all working machinery, and the people are not alive. I see the wheels going and hear them going, and the people are as like life as machinery can make them—but they don't get beyond the point of moving waxwork. It is very difficult to explain how this is, because it is a matter of intuitive perception and feeling. . . .' One of the most important scenes seemed completely improbable to him because of the author's failure to make the most of his material, 'whereas if the scene were truly and powerfully rendered', then 'the reader must accept it whether he likes it or not'.[1] Truth is here certainly a function of the novelist's imagination and skill in rendering his scene and not the pedantic literalism of the critics who demanded that the novel become a superficially accurate copy of a certain specific *milieu*.

The third defence of his art against charges of distortion and caricature was 'The Spirit of Fiction', which we have already discussed in the first chapter. There, each great novelist is said to have his own way of seeing the world, and charges of exaggeration stem from the difference between the way ordinary men and men of genius see events.[2]

6. REALISM WITH A DIFFERENCE: GEORGE ELIOT, MEREDITH, LEWES

When Frank O'Connor in *The Mirror in the Roadway* finds that there is only one set of conventions for the nineteenth-century novel, that of the kind of realism practised by Trollope, Flaubert, and Tolstoi, for which he uses the analogy of the flat and undistorting mirror, he is certainly oversimplifying the views of the novelists and critics of the period. 'When Trollope criticizes Dickens, it is for his lack of verisimilitude, but when Dickens defends himself, it is not on the ground that verisimilitude is of no importance; on the contrary.' In support of this statement he gives Dickens' assertion that all he says about Chancery and Mr. Squeers' school is the literal truth. O'Connor

---

[1] *Dickens Letters*, II, 653.   [2] See above, pp. 27–8.

contends that this kind of 'truthfulness', which refers to objects in the exterior world mirrored exactly in the work of art, is an inherent element in the nineteenth-century novel, 'and any criticism which disregards . . . [verisimilitude], disregards the conventions on which it is based, and, as close as makes no difference condemns itself to irrelevance'.[1] O'Connor meant, of course, criticism which discusses Dickens' novels as fantasy and is concerned with symbolic meanings and overtones in the works of the mid-Victorian novelists. But O'Connor does not really seem aware of how widespread explicit opposition to realistic theory was or how tinged with idealism many realistic theories became.

George Eliot is a good example of how a relatively simple view of realism became gradually modified. At the beginning of her career as a novelist, she thought one of the most important requirements of a novel was that it image the world outside the artist's mind, the world of external reality, as faithfully as possible, and she used the traditional figure of the mirror for her art. 'My strongest effort is . . . to give a faithful account of men and things as they have mirrored themselves in my mind.' But she was aware, as so many proponents of realism in fiction were not, that art could never be a mere slice of life: 'The mirror is doubtless defective; the outlines will sometimes be disturbed, the reflection faint or confused; but I feel as much bound to tell you as precisely as I can what that reflection is, as if I were in the witness-box narrating my experience on oath.' [2] In this context, significantly, she seemed to deprecate the fact that some distortion of external reality is inevitable when it is transformed—one should almost say translated, rather—into art and she felt it to be the duty of the artist to keep this distortion down to a necessary minimum.

Idealism, the competing aesthetic doctrine of the fifties, seemed untenable to her at this period, the time of *Adam Bede*. According to some idealists, art should not be primarily the representation of external reality but the embodiment of ideas in the mind, only derived remotely from experience, or, among the more thorough-going Berkeleyans, not derived from experience at all. Other idealists, although they believed that art

[1] (New York, 1956), pp. 8–10.
[2] *Adam Bede*, Cabinet Edition, Vol. I, chap. XVII, 265–6.

gets its material from the world of external reality, believed this material must be presented in a form more beautiful, more perfect, or more typical than it could ever be found in the world of everyday experience. These theories of *la belle nature* or typical form,[1] however, were for George Eliot violations of the oath of the artist as witness to the truth; they would cause her to be radically insincere. That is the reason she gives for not portraying Mr. Irwine in *Adam Bede* as an ideal clergyman:

> Certainly I could, if I held it to be the highest vocation of the novelist to represent things as they never have been and never will be. Then, of course, I might refashion life and character entirely after my own liking; I might select the most unexceptional type of clergyman, and put my own admirable opinions into his mouth on all occasions. But my strongest effort is to avoid any such arbitrary picture. . . .[2]

Three years earlier in the controversy over aesthetics provoked by the successive volumes of *Modern Painters*, she championed Ruskin against the academicians. About Volume III she wrote: 'The truth of infinite value that he teaches is *realism* —the doctrine that all truth and beauty are to be attained by a humble and faithful study of nature, and not by substituting vague forms, bred by imagination on the mists of feeling, in place of definite, substantial reality.' [3] (Of course, this statement does not bear much relation to the very able and subtle handling of the Renaissance doctrine of idealism that Sir Joshua Reynolds set forth in his *Discourses*.) In her journal we can see how important realism was to her at that time. During a visit to Ilfracombe she speaks of her desire to know the names of things—rocks, plants, streams.

> The desire is part of a tendency that is now constantly growing in me to escape from all vagueness and inaccuracy into the daylight of distinct, vivid ideas. The mere fact of naming an object tends to give definiteness to our conception of it—we have then a sign that at once calls up in our minds the distinctive qualities which mark out for us that particular object from all others.[4]

---

[1] See above, pp. 139, 153–5.
[2] *Adam Bede*, p. 265.
[3] *Westminster Review*, LXV (April, 1856), 626.
[4] *George Eliot Letters*, II, 251.

The same attitude became the basis of one of the best of her critical essays in the *Westminster Review*, 'Worldliness and Other-Worldliness', a revaluation of the then popular eighteenth-century poet Edward Young, whom she had once admired very much. Now she finds *Night Thoughts* full of vagueness and generality, which for her at this period is a sign of 'deficient intellectual activity and deficient feeling'. The repeated use of abstraction and generality she sees as symptomatic of his worst faults, a radical insincerity and a want of genuine emotion.

> Emotion links itself with particulars, and only in a faint and secondary manner with abstractions. An orator may discourse very eloquently on injustice in general, and leave his audience cold; but let him state a special case of oppression, and every heart will throb. . . . Strong emotion can no more be directed to generalities apart from particulars, than skill in figures can be directed to arithmetic apart from numbers.[1]

Young's grandiloquence about life, death, immortality, eternity, lead him continually to such false and 'vicious' imagery as:

> His hand the good man fixes on the skies,
> And bids earth roll, nor feels her idle whirl.

By realizing the image literally, George Eliot (and this is characteristic of much of her criticism of bad poetry) points out how 'the monstrous absurdity of a man's grasping the skies, and hanging habitually suspended there, while he contemptuously bids the earth roll, warns you that no genuine feeling could have suggested so unnatural a conception'.[2]

In contemporary English fiction also she found insincerity and false conceptions—especially false conceptions of the different social classes. Here dead literary traditions and clichés which no longer had any reference to reality were the distorting factors. In drawing the characteristics of the peasantry, most contemporary social novelists, while professing to represent the people as they were, only drew upon the conventions of idyllic literature; e.g. all peasants are jocund, bashful, moral, and likely to 'refresh themselves, not immoderately, with spicy nut-brown ale'. Such a perversion George Eliot thought fatal, because it turned men's sympathies towards a 'false object instead of the true one'. The social classes could not be linked

---

[1] *Westminster Review*, LXVII (January, 1857), 30–1. [2] *Ibid.*, p. 27.

so long as we are taught to feel for the 'heroic artisan' or 'sentimental peasant' and not 'for the peasant in all his coarse apathy, and the artisan in all his suspicious selfishness'. It was this idealizing disposition in the English mind which she held accountable for the false psychology of Dickens, productive of such stereotypes as preternaturally virtuous children and fallen sisters. Dickens' art, in its simplification of social types, epitomized the false assumption of so many mid-Victorian minds, that there was only one thing needful. This, she felt, could not coexist with a real knowledge of the people—'a thorough study of their habits, their ideas, their motives'. She saw the futility of those who believed 'that all social questions are merged in economical science, and that the relations of men to their neighbours may be settled by algebraic equations'; and of those who dreamed 'that the uncultured classes are prepared for a condition which appeals principally to their moral sensibilities' —a probable reference to the Christian Socialists; and finally, in an obvious allusion to the aristocratic dilettantism of the Young England movement, of those who attempted 'to restore the "good old times" by a sort of idyllic masquerading, and to grow feudal fidelity and veneration as we grow prize turnips, by an artificial system of culture'.[1]

Rachel Gray, by Julia Kavanagh, a novel published early in 1856, was an attempt to treat lower middle-class life honestly, and George Eliot, reviewing it in the *Leader*, praised the author's effort 'to impress us with the everyday sorrows of our commonplace fellowmen, and so to widen our sympathies'. But for George Eliot, *Rachel Gray* was unsuccessful in its picture of the religious life of 'that most prosaic stratum of society, the small shop-keeping class' because its religion was merely 'an abstract piety . . . which smacks neither of the Church nor of the meeting house'. Apparently Miss Kavanagh was afraid to show the provinciality and crudity of the religion of her characters, and in her attempt to 'idealize' it—to make it 'an Evangelicism which has no *brogue*'—made it completely unreal. Here George Eliot discerned a magnificent field for the writer of fiction, 'a really new sphere for a great artist who can paint from close observation, and who is neither a caricaturist nor a rose-colour sentimentalist',[2] and it was she herself who took up this

[1] *Ibid.*, LXVI (July, 1856), 53–5.   [2] VII (January 5, 1856), 19.

challenge the same year with *Scenes from Clerical Life*, which began her career as a novelist and ended her career as a critic.

One of the last essays she wrote for the *Westminster Review* dealt with the ways women specifically could sin against her literary ideals: the natural development of character, close and genuine presentation of the complexity of life, and plot developing out of the mutual relations of the characters. 'Silly Novels by Women Novelists', a merciless attack on almost all English novels written by women except those of Jane Austen, Charlotte Brontë, and Mrs. Gaskell, divides its subject into the 'mind-and-millinery', the 'oracular', the 'modern-antique', and the 'white neck-cloth' species.[1] The reason for the fatuity of the entire genus is the 'amazing ignorance' of most women, 'both of science and life',[2] due partly to the inadequate education offered to women in England at that time, but mostly to the Victorian domestic ideal, which she disliked intensely (at least in the 1850's when she felt her own anomalous position in Victorian society most keenly). She points out in her article on Madame de Sablé that only in France did women have a decisive effect on the literature and thought of the country. French 'laxity of opinion and practice with regard to the marriage tie' resulted in extra-marital unions formed only on inherent fitness and mutual attraction, and hence tended to bring women more into the main stream of culture. The French mistress, forced to develop her intelligence to a greater extent than the English wife, as the 'sharer not of [her lover's] joys and sorrows only, but of [his] ideas and aims' was, unlike the English wife, generally admitted 'to a common fund of ideas, to common objects of interest with men'.[3] Gallantry and intrigue then, although not attractive ideals in themselves, 'certainly serve better to arouse the dormant faculties of woman than embroidery and domestic drudgery'.[4] (We think of Agnes Wickfield as the type of the English wife and compare her with Becky Sharp, whose intelligence disqualified her for the English social structure, and who was, besides, of French extraction.) Furthermore, George Eliot implies in *Middlemarch*, even the time of St. Theresa was better than the mid-nineteenth century

[1] *Westminster Review*, LXVI (October, 1856), 442–61.
[2] *Ibid.*, p. 449.   [3] *Ibid.*, LXII (October, 1854), 472.
[4] *Ibid.*, pp. 451–2.

or women of creative impulse: Dorothea would have had a
convent to reform and her large soul a more effective outlet
han she had as Mrs. Ladislaw. The lack of a recognized social
outlet for their powers led women to cultivate their emotions
or their own sake, and as a result their novels were sentimental.
All is seen through 'the pink haze of visions and romance. . . .
Women have not to prove that they can be emotional, and
rhapsodic, and spiritualistic. . . . They have to prove that they
are capable of accurate thought, severe study, and continuous
elf-command.' [1]

George Eliot's theory of realism, of course, was not merely
limited to 'a humble and faithful study of nature', the phrase
she applied to Ruskin. There was as much room in her aesthetic
for a poet like Dante as there was in Ruskin's for a painter like
Tintoretto. She did assert, however, that even in a poem like
The Divine Comedy, where certainly literal and everyday reality
is transcended, there must be a basis of hard realism. A great
imagination, such as Dante's, never attenuates or falsifies
reality but is 'at once the most precise and homely in [its] reproduction of actual objects, and the most soaringly at large in
[its] imaginative combinations'. [2]

About her own work, she writes of the deliberate use of non-
realistic devices:

The various *strands* of thought I had to work out forced me into
a more ideal treatment of Romola than I had foreseen at the outset
—though the 'Drifting Away' [Chapter 61] and The Village with
the Plague [Chapter 68] belonged to my earliest vision of the story
and were by deliberate forecast adapted as romantic and symbolical
elements. [3]

The genesis of *Silas Marner* is described as anything but that of a
realistic novel relying for its effect on an exact copying of a
certain *milieu*. 'It came to me first of all, quite suddenly, as a
sort of legendary tale, suggested by my recollection of having
once, in early childhood, seen a linen-weaver with a bag on his
back. . . .' [4] It seems inevitable that she connected the story
with Wordsworth—a quotation from *Michael* stands as the
epigraph—as her method here is almost identical with that of

[1] *Ibid.*, LXVI (October, 1856), 576–8.
[2] *Theophrastus Such*, Cabinet Edition, p. 195.
[3] *George Eliot Letters*, IV, 104.   [4] *Ibid.*, III, 382.

the *Lyrical Ballads*: familiar material is transformed by the imagination so that in some way it has the effect of fantasy, or what Coleridge called 'the original gift of spreading the tone, the atmosphere, and with it the depth and height of the ideal world around forms, incidents, and situations, of which, for the common view, custom had bedimmed all the lustre, had dried up the sparkle and the dew drops.' [1]

But the greatest change from her earlier critical theory as a periodical reviewer in the mid-fifties, when her emphasis was on fiction as a picture of real life, was in the importance of the place of ideas in the design of the novel. She came more and more to believe that the only true line of development for the English novel must be in what Arnold called 'the application of ideas to life'. But these ideas must become 'thoroughly incarnate', must be represented by 'breathing individual forms' grouped 'in the needful relations, so that the presentation will lay hold on the emotions as human experience—will . . . "flash" conviction on the world by means of aroused sympathy'. The picture must never lapse into the diagram, else it is no longer 'aesthetic teaching', but the 'most offensive of all teaching'.[2] It can easily be seen that wherever George Eliot violated her own critical canons, she failed most miserably—as in the dreary expanse of her blank verse tragedy, *The Spanish Gypsy*, the lifeless half of *Daniel Deronda*, and her conception of the character of Felix Holt.

When Meredith was a reviewer for the *Westminster*, his ideas on the question of realism were so close to those of George Eliot that one might easily attribute his essays to her. Answering one of Ruskin's forgotten critics, Edward Young, who in 1857 wrote a book called *Pre-Rafaellitism; or a Popular Enquiry into some newly-asserted Principles connected with the Philosophy, Poetry, Religion, and Revolution of Art,* Meredith stated that realism 'is the only basis of art'. Idealism was dangerous because 'it weans the mind from the significant humanity of things. And therefore is idealism, as a school, false—a mere copying of phantoms.' Young apparently had especially disliked Holman Hunt's 'Scapegoat', a once-famous Pre-Raphael-

---

[1] *Biographia Literaria* (London, 1906), p. 45.

[2] *George Eliot Letters*, IV, 300–1. Concerning her dislike for didacticism see above, pp. 43–5.

te painting. Young wanted an 'ideal', that is, a generalized landscape, rather than the very detailed one that Hunt had gone to Palestine to copy. Meredith rejoined, 'But surely that grandeur of desolation—the sense of having before you the actual scene—is infinitely more impressive than anything idealism could convey? It seems to us all the difference between history and fiction.' [1] Oddly enough, Meredith here seems to say that Hunt's precise documentation is more valuable as art than an imagined background would be, and he shifts the grounds of the discussion from that of the general versus the particular to that of the true versus the false, the true being the exact copy, and the false, the invented scene. Here Meredith reverses the traditional distinction, stemming from Aristotle, between history and fiction. But the realistic artist, he maintains, does not *merely* copy nature; he takes nature only as his *point d'appui*: 'The tendency of art is to excellence. . . . It will not for ever walk earth and pore on nature. It has the quality of flame once kindled.' Hence all great art seems to become idealistic, but if one examines it closely, it is basically realistic; that is, its material comes only from the external world, not the private fancy of the artist: 'The substantial has a shadow, the insubstantial none. The greatest idealists sprang from a school of hard realism.' (That is almost precisely what George Eliot was later to write about Dante in *Theophrastus Such*.) Hunt's 'Scapegoat', then, as great art, transcends the raw material from which it is derived, even though, inconsistently, Meredith classified it as 'history' rather than 'fiction'. 'We trust Mr. Young will live to see that the artist's pilgrimage to the Holy Land has been productive of results even nobler than the rose-flushed mountains of Moab and the rotting salt levels of the Dead Sea in that marvellous landscape.' [2]

A similar distinction between realism and idealism appears in a letter Meredith wrote in 1864:

One may find as much amusement in a Kaleidoscope as in a merely idealistic writer: and, just as sound prose is of more worth than pretentious poetry, I hold the man who gives a plain wall of facts higher in esteem than one who is constantly shuffling the clouds and dealing with airy, delicate sentimentalities, headless and tailless imaginings. . . .

[1] LXVII (April, 1857), 608.   [2] *Ibid.*

Art, Meredith held, must come to terms with reality, must be rooted firmly in reality and must never be a means of escape. 'Realism', he writes in the same letter, 'is the basis of good composition: it implies study, observation, artistic power, and ... humility.' Using his favourite term for reality, earth (almost an equivalent for all the meanings the word *nature* accrued in the nineteenth century), he tells why he dislikes Bulwer-Lytton's kind of idealism: 'Does not all science (the mammoth balloon, to wit) tell us that when we forsake earth, we reach up to a frosty, inimical Inane? For my part I love and cling to earth, as the one piece of God's handiwork which we possess. I admit that we can refashion; but of earth must be the material.' [1] Here we can see how closely connected his literary theory is with the body of ideas underlying all his novels and poetry. The novelist is free to shape his material as he wishes as long as he does not falsify human nature. In this way art becomes more than documentation, than a mere transcript of reality. As soon as the artist ceases to copy and begins to stylize his raw material, Meredith says he 'idealizes', but in this sense the words *idealize* and *idealism* are used in an honorific rather than a pejorative sense.

Between realism and idealism there is no natural conflict: This completes that. . . . A great genius must necessarily employ ideal means, for a vast conception cannot be placed bodily before the eye, and remains to be suggested. Idealism is an atmosphere whose effects of grandeur are wrought out through a series of illusions, that are illusions to the sense within us only when divorced from the groundwork of the real.

The great writers—Shakespeare, Goethe, Molière, and Cervantes—'are Realists au fond. But they have the broad arms of Idealism at command. They give us Earth; but it is earth with an atmosphere.' [2]

Gradually, however, this balance between what Meredith called 'realism' and 'idealism' became upset in his literary theory as well as in his novels, and the latter gained importance at the expense of the former. 'Molière did not paint in raw realism,' he wrote in the *Essay on Comedy* of 1877. 'He seized his characters firmly for the central purpose of the play,

---

[1] *Meredith Letters*, I, 156–7.   [2] *Ibid.*

stamped them in the idea, and by slightly raising and softening the object of study, generalized upon it so as to make it permanently human.' [1] What he calls 'high notes and condensing' became much more prominent in the later books, 'a "pitch" considerably above our common human'. [2] Characters and situations in those novels seem more and more to be projections of ideas in Meredith's mind and consequently lose much of the magnificent actuality of the earlier novels. His novels, in Elder Olsen's fruitful antithesis, tend to become 'didactic' rather than 'mimetic' in intention. [3]

As certain as Meredith was that 'earth' was to be the stuff of any genuine novel, he believed, in common with most of his contemporaries, that 'unpleasant' facts should not be made too insistent in fiction. In a review of 'The Wedding Guests', a novel of 1857 dealing with the transmission of hereditary insanity, he doubted whether such a subject could ever be 'satisfactorily handled in a novel'. Yet that did not mean the novelist should avoid questions of social evil—and he himself was often attacked for dealing with transgressions of the Victorian sexual code, especially in *Richard Feverel* and *Rhoda Fleming*:

If life in the present is to be portrayed, some hard things must needs obtrude. The province of Art is to subordinate and soften them down. There are few subjects not legitimate to the novelist, but as we are happily constituted to shun and detest the sight of evil, it should be the novelist's care not to give what is painful undue prominence, and especially not to strike a doubtful chord in the mind. We look on life apprehending the bad and searching for the good. In the picture of life, this search should be assisted without compromising truth, and to do this, and not throw dust in our eyes, is to be a great and worthy artist. [4]

A very similar passage appears in the *Prospective Review* of 1853.

Literature . . . must be based upon reality; there is, however, a high and generous, as well as a low and grovelling, reality; and the true artist, in embodying the spirit of the age instead of introducing

---

[1] 'Essay on Comedy', *Comedy*, ed. Wylie Sypher (New York, 1956), p. 10.
[2] *Meredith Letters*, II, 399.
[3] *Critics and Criticism, Ancient and Modern*, ed. R. S. Crane (Chicago, 1952), p. 68.
[4] *Westminster Review*, LXVII (April, 1857), 615.

us to a region of sordid and vulgar fact, depicted with revolting minuteness, gives greater prominence to its ennobling elements, and though not ignoring the existence of evil, yet veils it in a poetic form. It is not the function of art simply to reproduce the noisy and turbulent present, but to impart rhythmical beauty to its manifold aspects, and by introducing us to a region of calmer and loftier thought to win us to a nobler life.[1]

Meredith, in spite of his belief that art should 'soften' reality, was nevertheless able to accept *Madame Bovary* as a great novel,[2] but he could not accept the *naturalistes*, and his attitude towards them was very similar to that of Arnold and Tennyson:

I have gone through the horrible book of Mendès, with the sensation of passing down the ventre de Paris and out at anus into the rat-rioting sewers, twisted world, tumbled amid the frothing filth, the deadly stench, the reek and roar of the damned. Cloacina sits on such productions; Dementia, born of the nameless, dissects them. Nigh the end of it, Zola seemed to me a very haven, Maupassant a garden. Who reads must smell putrid for a month. . . . It is the monsterization of Zolaism. O what a nocturient, cacaturient crew has issued of the lens of the Sun of the mind on the lower facts of life!—on sheer Realism, breeder at best of the dung-fly![3]

In *Diana of the Crossways*, Meredith defines his own literary creed as an attempt to steer a middle course between the extremes of sentimentalism, on the one hand, masked by the term idealism, which would completely deny man's relation to the lower animals; and naturalism, on the other hand, which would reduce man to the lower animals and deny him free will. 'Philosophy is the foe of both, and their silly cancelling contest. . . . Philosophy bids us to see that we are not so pretty as rose-pink, not so repulsive as dirty drab; and that instead of everlastingly shifting those barren aspects, the sight of ourselves is wholesome, bearable, fructifying, finally a delight.'[4] In other words the purpose of art is to reconcile man to reality, or in Wordsworth's terms, to wed man to nature in 'a great spousal song'. Naturalism, for Meredith, merely disgusts, and false idealism must lead to disillusion. But Meredith's gospel of ever-continuing progress through evolution may, ironically, be

---

[1] IX, 226.   [2] See above, p. 39.
[3] *Meredith Letters*, II, 401.
[4] Memorial Edition (New York, 1910), p. 15.

one more form of 'rose-pink' that he could not recognize as such.

Do but perceive that we are coming to philosophy, the stride toward it will be a giant's—a century to a day. And imagine the celestial refreshment of having a pure decency in the place of the sham; real flesh; a soul born active, wind-beaten, but ascending. Honourable will fiction then appear; a fount of life, an aid to life, quick with our blood.

Of the two extremes, Meredith preferred the naturalists to the idealists:

Worse than that alternative dirty drab, your recurring rose-pink is rebuked by hideous revelations of the filthy foul; for nature will force her way, and if you try to stifle her by drowning, she comes up, not the fairest part of her uppermost! Peruse your Realists— really your castigators for not having yet embraced Philosophy.[1]

In the 1850's G. H. Lewes, like George Eliot and Meredith, adopted a predominantly realistic position. He was, however, forced to modify it to such a degree that it bore very little relation to the ideas of those who demanded literal verisimilitude. One of Lewes' most reiterated points is that all successful novels must be based on the writer's actual experience. 'Unless a novel be built out of real experience, it can have no real success,' [2] he wrote in 1847, and in 1853 he still insisted: 'A novel must fuse one's own personal experience and observation' and not use material from other novels.[3] The worst thing he could say of a book is that it 'is not like life, but like novels',[4] and as a critic he waged a perpetual campaign against the stereotypes of character and incident in the fiction of the period.

When, however, Lewes reviewed *Modern Painters, Volume IV* in the *Leader*, June, 1856,[5] he felt called upon to qualify what he meant by experience. Lewes' essay is significantly entitled 'Imaginative Artists' because many writers had mistakenly assumed that there was a conflict between imagination and real experience (a dichotomy which appears again towards the end of the century in Zola's 'Le roman experimental'). Charlotte Brontë, for instance, made Jane Eyre write, 'My imagination

---

[1] *Ibid.*, pp. 15–16. [2] *Fraser's*, XXXVI (December, 1847), 691.
[3] *Leader*, IV (January 8, 1853), 44. [4] *Ibid.*, V (January 21, 1854), 66.
[5] *Ibid.*, VII (June 7, 1856), 545.

created, and narrated continuously; quickened with all o incident, life, fire, feeling, that I desired and had not in my actual existence.' [1] To this view of the imagination as a mean of escape from a drab life into an exciting world of wish fulfil ment, Lewes had opposed his own definition in his review o *Jane Eyre*: Imagination is 'that singular faculty of penetrating into most the secret recesses of the heart, and of showing a character in its inward and outward workings. . . .' [2] Far from helping us to escape from our experience, only through the imagination can we fully explore and understand reality. In his essay on *Modern Painters* Lewes observes that Ruskin's re marks apply to all the arts, not only to painting. 'When, for example, he lays down the canon, "It is always wrong to paint what you don't see," it is a canon as applicable to the poet (and novelist) as to the painter; and one, indeed, which has been iterated in these columns with almost wearisome pertinacity.' But to guard against a too simplistic idea of realism Lewes goes on to say, 'We have sometimes been misunderstood . . . to mean that only actual visible objects, or events actually experienced, should be chosen; whereas the vision and the faculty divine, although essentially consisting in *seeing* and in representing only what is seen, may be exercised upon things non-existent as well as existent.' Not all can see with the mind's eye. 'But no one should attempt to paint what he does *not* see; no one should feign to see or feel what he does not see or feel'—an injunction that can still sound revolutionary in Eastern Europe. '. . . If because *Jane Eyre* agitated novel readers, you, who never saw Mr. Rochester, and never were in love with your master, write Jane Eyrish novels, you are wasting your time and the reader's temper. Paint what you see, write what you have experienced, and the utmost success *possible for you* will be achieved,' he counsels the aspiring novelist. [3] Realism here is equivalent to sincerity, and this passage is almost a restatement of the Horatian maxim, 'Si vis me flere, dolendum est / Primum ipsi tibi.'

Lewes hated the prevailing form of idealism, especially

---

[1] *Jane Eyre* (London, 1908), chap. XII, p. 104.

[2] *Fraser's*, XXXVI (December, 1847), 687. See Franklin Gary, 'Charlotte Brontë and George Henry Lewes', *PMLA*, XI (1936), 518–54.

[3] *Leader*, VII (June 7, 1856), 545.

popular in Germany, which stated that 'art must elevate the public by "beautifying" life'; this doctrine seemed to him 'the natural refuge of incompetence, to which men fly, impelled by a secret sense of their inability to portray Reality so as to make it interesting'. In his essay 'Realism in Art: Recent German Fiction', which appeared in the *Westminster* for October, 1858, he dismissed any distinction between art and reality as false, for 'Art is a Representation of Reality'. (Lewes in his critical writings seemed as unaware as most of his contemporaries of the pitfalls lying in the word reality, with or without a capital *r*.) The only legitimate distortion allowable is due to the nature of the medium—'The canvas of the painter, the marble of the sculptor, the chords of the musician, and the language of the writer, each brings its own peculiar laws. . . .' Lewes also apparently rejected the classical distinction between the real and the true—*le réel* and *le vrai*. 'Realism is thus the basis of all Art, and its antithesis is not Idealism, but *Falsism*.' The painter who gives 'regular features' and 'irreproachable linen' to his peasants and makes his milkmaids into 'Keepsake beauties', and the writer who makes 'Hodge . . . speak refined sentiments in unexceptional English' are alike guilty of falsification. 'Either give us true peasants, or leave them untouched; either paint no drapery at all, or paint it with the utmost fidelity, either keep your people silent, or make them speak the idiom of their class' —this is the ultimatum he gives the artist.[1]

True idealism, then, for Lewes, has nothing to do with *la belle nature* or generalized forms but is derived from a way of seeing reality. If a painter or writer discerns and can express the deepest emotional life of the people he is representing, can discern, in other words, the 'poetry' of his subject, then his treatment can be called 'ideal'. But 'the sentiment must be real, truly expressed as a sentiment, and as the sentiment of the very people represented; the tenderness of *Hodge* must not be that of *Romeo*. . . .' It is here that imagination and sympathy come into play; it is through them that the artist is enabled distinctly to 'see' his subject, and through them the antithesis between realism and idealism is broken down. The highest example, for Lewes, of an idealistic work of art, 'The Sistine Madonna', is also a work of the highest realism.

[1] LXX, 493.

In the never-to-be-forgotten divine babe, we have at once the intensest realism of presentation, with the highest idealism of conception: the attitude is at once grand, easy, and natural; . . . in those eyes, and on that brow, there is an indefinable something which, greater than the expression of the angels, grander than that of pope or saint, is, to all who see it, a perfect *truth*; we feel that humanity in its highest conceivable form is before us, and that to transcend such a form would be to lose sight of the *human* nature there represented.[1]

With most products of Victorian realism, Lewes apparently had little sympathy. Instead of great subjects, grandly conceived, too many artists were spending their lives on trivia.

The rage for 'realism' [Lewes wrote in 1865] which is healthy in as far as it insists on truth, has become unhealthy, in as far as it confounds truth with familiarity, and predominance of unessential details. There are other truths besides coats and waistcoats, pots and pans, drawing-room and suburban villas. Life has other aims besides those which occupy the conversation of 'Society'.[2]

The same complaint had earlier been made by the *Prospective Review* in 1854: Too many novelists 'stifle . . . [themselves] with the minutiae of . . . [their] own experience' and show no imagination in their works.[3] Walter Bagehot in the *National Review*, October, 1855, had also complained of the 'strict experience school of writing' and the 'chatty school', both of which merely represented the 'surface of life'.[4] This kind of fiction, which depended on the accumulation of accurate details and in which verisimilitude was an end in itself, Lewes called 'detailism' to distinguish it from true realism.[5]

Through his distaste for novels which heaped up masses of detail, Lewes was often led to statements very close to a kind of neo-classicism. For example, of a novelist who tried to disarm his critics by claiming that all his events actually happened, he asserted, '. . . Incidents . . . must be true in *principle* rather than in fact.' The novelist must be able to present what is 'essential and typical in a subject [the last part of this quotation is very close to Sir Joshua Reynolds]'.[6] Earlier in the *Leader*

---

[1] LXX, pp. 493–6.

[2] *Principles of Success in Literature* (London, n.d.), p. 81.

[3] X, 473.   [4] I, 337–40.   [5] *Principles of Success in Literature*, p. 80.

[6] *Leader*, V (December 2, 1854), 1144.

Lewes had called art 'a selection of typical elements' from life, rather than a transcript of life or a mirror reflecting reality.[1] If the implications of such statements are developed fully, one would end up in the camp of the idealists.

Lewes found fault with many of the characters in *Shirley* because they were too strange, too unusual. And when Charlotte Brontë claimed that she had directly copied from nature precisely those characters who had been most objected to as unnatural, he replied, 'Art . . . deals with the broad principles of human nature, not with idiosyncracies. . . . The curious anomalies of life . . . are not suitable to a novel.' The characters of *Shirley*, moreover, were too harsh and too rude: 'They are, one and all, given to break out and misbehave themselves upon very small provocation. The manner and language of Shirley towards her guardian passes all permission.' Even if Yorkshiremen—and women—actually do talk in this way, decorum and propriety are here apparently more important for Lewes than realism: Currer Bell 'must learn . . . to sacrifice a little of her Yorkshire roughness to the demands of good taste, neither saturating her writings with such rudeness and offensive harshness, nor suffering her style to wander into such vulgarities as would be inexcusable—even in a man'.[2]

Lewes was most offended by the hero of the novel, Robert Moore, who 'is disgraced by a sordid love of money, and a shameless setting aside of an affection for Caroline in favour of the rich heiress'. Such behaviour may be true to nature, but it is not permitted in a hero, a figure whose position demands he have a 'noble' nature, be an 'ideal of manhood'.

In a subordinate character such a lapse from the elevation of moral rectitude, might have been pardoned; but in a hero—in the man for whom our sympathies and admiration are almost exclusively claimed—to imagine it possible, is a decided blunder in art—as well as an inconsistency in nature. A hero may be faulty, erring, imperfect; but he must not be sordid, mean, wanting in the statelier virtues of our kind.[3]

The heroes of George Eliot's later novels, Felix Holt and Daniel Deronda, perfectly illustrate Lewes' idea of what a hero

[1] IV (July 30, 1853), 740.
[2] *Edinburgh Review*, XCI (January, 1850), 160–1.
[3] *Ibid.*, pp. 163–4.

should be—figures deliberately drawn as ideals of manhood, and consequently never allowed lapses from 'the elevation of moral rectitude'.

7. SIMPLE IDEALISM

In October, 1852, the *Westminster*, which, probably because its sub-editor, Marian Evans, was usually committed to the realistic point of view, carried one of the most explicit statements of the idealist as opposed to the realist position in a review of *The Blithedale Romance*. Hawthorne's characters, according to the reviewer, are made to seem too much like real people; that is, they 'are too thoroughly individualized for dramatic cooperation, or for that graduated subordination to each other which tends to give a harmonious swell to the narrative, unity to the plot, and concentrated force to the issue'. Moreover, Zenobia's end is 'an outrage upon the decorum of art, as well as a violation of its purpose. That such things do happen, is no reason why they should be idealized; for the Ideal seeks not to imitate Reality, but to perfect it, . . . [show us what] *ought* to be true.' The function of the novelist is then 'to describe things that are not as though they were'.[1] It would be interesting to hear the comments of one of Swift's Houyhnhnms on this statement.

An essay in *Fraser's* of January, 1851, makes Thackeray's theory of realism directly responsible for the failure of *Pendennis*: Thackeray does not seem to be aware that there are necessary differences between people in real life and characters in literature. As a result there are too many contradictions left unresolved in the portrayal of Arthur Pendennis, and even Thackeray himself does not really seem to understand him

---

[1] *Westminster Review*, LVIII, 593–6. This essay is sometimes attributed to George Eliot. See James D. Rust, 'The Art of Fiction in George Eliot's Reviews', *RES*, n.s., VII (1956), 164–72. The author relies very heavily on this review of *The Blithedale Romance* for his exposition of George Eliot's theory of the novel. However, Professor Haight points out in *The George Eliot Letters*, II, 55, that the only evidence for this attribution is the fact that George Eliot had read the novel just before the review appeared, and that the rhetorical style would make her authorship of the essay doubtful; moreover, the content is not reconcilable with her critical position at this time. For example, we find in this review, 'Reality should only be introduced as to give effect to the bright ideal which Hope pictures in the future.'

since he has given no clue as to 'how a man can be an affection-
ate creature and a supercilious dandy, honest and generous,
selfish and sincere, spoilt by prosperity, and improved by it.
. . .' Besides, for this critic, Pendennis is too uninteresting a
person to sustain the weight of a whole novel.

Our author, in his capacity of chief of the Realist school,[1] might
ask us whether we can reconcile the contradictions apparent in the
character and conduct of our most intimate friends, even Jones or
Jenkins. We reply we did not *make* Jones or Jenkins; if we had we
should have made him several inches taller, many degrees hand-
somer. . . . Seriously, Pendennis is an unlucky creation. His virtues
and vices are all dubious, and on a small scale; we meet with so
many like him in real life, why should we have him forced upon us
in *ideal* life?[2]

The reviewer of *He Knew He Was Right* in the *British Quarterly
Review* was just as strongly opposed to any aesthetic based on
realism. 'A work of art should not be true to life, but should
idealize—that it may elevate it.' [3] The *Spectator* agreed that
realism was somehow incompatible with the idea that art
should be morally improving. Reade's *Peg Woffington* is too
much like reality. 'There is such a thing as being *too* natural
for purposes of art', because novels 'improve and elevate the
mind, by removing from nature that which is low, and raising
that which is selected for treatment'.[4]

Sam Weller, according to the author of 'Charles Dickens' in
Blackwood's of April, 1855, was one of the best examples of an
idealized character who became typical of his class. Dickens,
'while preserving a most perfect likeness, separates from all the
lower and coarser features of the class this thoroughly genuine
man'. Mrs. Bardell and her circle, on the other hand, are as
offensive to good taste as Sam Weller is inoffensive. 'Mr.
Dickens chooses to show us in such pictures the difference between a thorough Dutch portrait of a scene, and the refined
representation which seizes the necessary *truth*, but rejects the
prosaic *fact*, which is neither agreeable nor edifying.' [5]

[1] See above, pp. 148–9.
[2] XLIII, 86. For a similar demand for ideal characters see above, p. 68.
[3] L (July, 1869), 264.
[4] XXVI (January 1, 1853), supplement p. 4.
[5] LXXVII, 455.

The same distinction between truth and fact, which derives from the classical French distinction between *le vrai* and *le réel* (a variation of Aristotle's distinction between the truths of poetry and history), is made in another *Blackwood's* essay of the same year on Bulwer-Lytton.

> It is not the vocation of a novel-writer to startle us with exaggerated events, which are true only because they have happened, but to order his world on the general principles of nature as the outer world is regulated—to keep his eye on the broad truths of existence, instead of the special and distorted realities of some individual life; in a word, indeed, to be true to nature, and leave fact to the exposition of a less ambitious art.[1]

The reviewer of *Tara: A Mahratta Tale* for the *Saturday Review* was equally emphatic on the same point: 'The first and cardinal article of the novelist's profession should be general, not particular, truth.'[2] When Charlotte Brontë called Jane Austen more 'real than true',[3] she meant the same thing: Jane Austen's novels merely dealt with particular facts, not the only truths of human nature that mattered to her—the passions.

If, as the critic in *Blackwood's* April, 1855, wrote, the 'very highest aim of the writer of fiction' is the 'power of creating a real man, a real woman, and throwing upon these creations of his genius . . . ideal purity and generous grace',[4] then evidently any sort of exact correspondence between the characters of a novel and actual people the reader knows is not to be expected, and several months earlier in the same magazine Thackeray had been relegated to the position of 'historian of human nature' rather than poet, which every great novelist should be, because he never attempted 'to embody the purest ideal soul' in any of his characters.[5]

Seven years later, again in *Blackwood's Magazine*, an article on Charles Lever stated: 'To represent human beings precisely as they are, is not a necessary condition of art of any kind.' This critic, probably Robert Lytton,[6] illustrated his meaning with an example from painting: 'A deformed saint by Massaccio may

---

[1] LXXVII (February, 1855), 230.   [2] XVI (October 31, 1863), 587.
[3] Clement Shorter, *The Brontës* (New York, 1908), I, 388.
[4] LXVII, 453.   [5] *Ibid.* (January, 1855), p. 96.
[6] See above, p. 62.

be truer in art than a correct anatomical study by Mr. Etty,'
and the same conditions apply to literature.

Nor is there any reason why that extravagance of design which
dilates either human actions or human emotions, or even the situations of human life, to perfectly impossible proportions, should be in
itself a defect. For what is impossible in fact may be proper in art.
Ariosto is undoubtedly one of the greatest of narrative poets, and
it is probably in his extravagance that we shall find the secret of his
indefinable power.

Lever, in his very deliberate use of distortion, exaggeration and
caricature was, this critic showed, in the great tradition of
European narrative fiction: Cervantes, Lesage, Swift, Fielding,
Smollett, and Scott.[1] (If the author of this important essay
actually was Robert Lytton, then his theory of the novel was
very similar to his father's and Dickens'.)

W. C. Roscoe, as we have seen elsewhere,[2] thought realism
of the sort he analysed in his essays on Defoe and Thackeray
could actually interfere with the chief function of the novelist.
Defoe's works have an amazing 'life-likeness' because he is
'always occupied with the absolute existent realities of the
world; with men as he saw them move in actual life; with facts
as they actually happened'. As a result, 'he has no analytic
perception whatever'. 'The strange underlying forces and
essences which . . . the minds [of idealists as opposed to realists]
love to contemplate . . . have no interest for him. . . .' He is
'totally destitute of the power to fathom any intricacies of
human nature', and in spite of his 'enormous reconstructive
imagination', his 'creative imagination' is very narrow. 'He takes
up things just as he finds them; and when he wants to create,
he re-sorts them, or at most makes others exactly like them.'[3]
It is interesting that almost exactly the same criticisms were
later levelled at Zola by anti-naturalists like Brunetière.

As a matter of fact, the English reviews of the late fifties and
early sixties carried several trenchant statements which significantly prefigured the major attacks on the theory behind *Le
roman expérimental*. In 'Distortions of the English Stage: Macbeth' (*National Review*, October, 1863), all works of art, the
argument goes, must have a unifying idea, and only material

[1] XCI (April, 1862), 454.   [2] See above, pp. 51-2.
[3] *National Review*, III (October, 1856), 389-90.

related to that idea can be included in any work. Art cannot be 'simply the reproduction of nature', or in Zola's later metaphor, a slice of life as little distorted by the writer's personality or imagination as possible. Rather, for this critic, art 'is a crystallization out of nature of all elements and facts related by affinity to the idea intended to be embodied. These solely it should eliminate and draw to itself, leaving the rest as unessential. A literal adherence to all the accidents of nature is not only not necessary in art, but may even be fatal.' [1] The metaphor of the crystal is much more effective than a slice because a crystal has an organizing centre and so, a very determinate form.

An even earlier anticipation of the attacks against Zola's quasi-scientific theories occurs in an essay on George Eliot in *Bentley's Quarterly Review* of 1859. As soon as the individual soul or conscience ceases to be the centre of the novelist's world, his books become uninteresting. '. . . Persons who regard men as mere units of a demoralized society, must make them all on the same type. . . . Brute force, brute courage, and brute instincts . . . admit of little actual change of representation. . . . No man can maintain an interest in a world without souls, in a society which discards all high or useful aims and all notion of duty.' [2] George Eliot, for this critic, as for James and Brunetière also, was the opposite kind of novelist from the new scientific realist because she makes the focus of her novels the human conscience, and she always sees society as a collection of individuals who are in control of their destiny, even though they are very much influenced by the world that surrounds them.

8. THE ROLE OF THE IMAGINATION IN THE STYLIZATION OF REALITY

In spite of the novels of George Eliot, English realism in the late fifties and sixties seemed to many critics to limit itself more and more to the middle-class domestic novel. In the *National Review* for April, 1863, an article on *The Chronicles of Carlingford* by Mrs. Oliphant, an example of this genre, complained that the age could not 'create a literature of lofty idealism'; instead, 'the

[1] XVII, 292.   [2] I (July, 1859), 472.

novel of home life' has become the 'accredited' literary form. In this genre, the 'domestic virtues have been the staple of interest; and the decalogue of creative art is summed up in the commands, to be genteel, and marry at the end of the third volume'. Such books naturally leave in the mind 'a craving . . . for something beyond meals, dress, and small talk, . . . the monotony of common things'. Here, according to the *National Review*, was the explanation for the popularity of sensation novels, which tried by any means, usually arson, bigamy, and madness, to excite the jaded attention of their readers.[1]

For *Blackwood's* the English sensation novel was a kind of transplantation of Hawthorne's romances—wild stories 'which smiled at probabilities'. The whole movement was a reaction not only against the dullness of modern realism but against the entire middle-class secularized vision of the universe. As a result of such an official world outlook, it was only natural that some novelists would make 'frantic attempts by any kind of black art or mad psychology to get some grandeur and sacredness restored to life—or if not sacredness or grandeur, at least horror and mystery. . . .' [2]

The *Saturday Review* of May 2, 1863, showed the same kind of dissatisfaction with the idea of the novel as an exact transcription of everyday life: 'a novel is not meant to be a picture of real life, but of something interesting in real life, and the reader expects to have something more concentrated and exciting set before him than fragments of family history'.[3] It was only natural that Trollope's *Rachel Ray* should have been attacked for its prosaic literalness: 'We wish fiction would do something for us besides giving us these accurate likenesses of the common run of those whom we see or know.' This Saturday reviewer found himself tired of

truth of minute description. . . . It seems as if it could hardly be worth while for an able man to go on, year after year, working off little likenesses, more or less exact, of provincial brewers retiring from business and other provincial brewers coming into business. . . . We may hope that the next fashion in fiction will take us to something more exciting and poetical than the domestic sorrows of brewers' wives. . . .[4]

[1] XVI (April, 1863), 360–1.   [2] XCI (May, 1862), 565.
[3] XV, 575.   [4] XVI (October 24, 1863), 555.

But it was not his lower middle-class material that made Trollope's novel uninteresting—though there was a trace of snobbery in the critic's insistence on the word *brewer*. Subject matter alone, according to the critical stand taken by the *Saturday Review* in the sixties, would not make a book uninteresting, and scenes of ordinary life are legitimate material for the novel; but the writer must do something with them. Thus George Eliot 'proved how full of interest a mode of existence might be that had hitherto been held as too homely or prosaic for fiction. . . .'[1] As the reviewer of *Silas Marner* explained, after praising the scene in the Rainbow Tavern, a real group in a pothouse would not amuse us so much, but because George Eliot chose only the most significant remarks, the scene becomes art. In real life the same remarks might be made, but they would be so diluted with banality we would never notice them.[2] In the same year Harriet Beecher Stowe's *The Pearl of Orr's Island* was attacked for its lack of imagination: 'True to nature we doubt not it is; but the nature is plain, dull, and prosy. . . .'[3]

Fraser's Magazine of January, 1860, saw that the attempt made by novelists to create an absolute illusion of reality by the accumulation of detail was in danger of completely stifling the reader's imagination: 'Something must always be left for the reader's imagination to supply; and imitation ceases to please when it assumes [in the sense of replaces] reality and rejects the aid of that imagination which is the surest way of obtaining sympathy.'[4] .

Leslie Stephen too, unlike his brother Fitzjames, thought that verisimilitude, the power of producing the illusion of reality, was too highly valued by many contemporary critics and novelists. As a result, Defoe's novels, which seemed more like genuine history than any other novels, received from most critics 'rather extravagant' praise. 'The trick would be easy enough, if it were worth performing. The story-teller cannot be cross-examined; and if he is content to keep to the ordinary level of commonplace facts, there is not the least difficulty in producing conviction.' As soon as a novelist 'makes a certain attempt at artistic unity' his work will be obviously fictitious,

[1] XII (October 5, 1861), 356.   [2] XI (April 13, 1861), 369.
[3] XI (June 8, 1861), 590.   [4] LXI, 21.

because real life lacks form. Defoe, he found, had not really distinguished between 'the art of lying and the art of fiction'.[1] and his world became a photograph from which 'all confusion was banished' and in which

everything was definite, clear, and precise . . . [a world in which] everything could be accurately measured, and the result stated in figures; by the same parallel, there was a want of perspective, for the distant objects were as precisely given as the nearest; and yet further there was the same absence of colouring which is caused in natural objects by light and heat, and in mental pictures by the fire of imaginative passion. The result is a product which is to Fielding or Scott what a portrait by a first-rate photographer is to one by Vandyke or Reynolds. . . .[2]

Because Defoe was so much interested in producing an absolute illusion of reality, there is no psychological analysis in his novels; all is seen from the outside: 'He never seems to remember that within the mechanism whose working he describes there is a soul very different from that of Daniel Defoe.' His novels therefore lack dramatic power. 'If he had written *Henry IV*, Falstaff, and Hotspur, and the Prince would have all been as like each other as are generally the first and second murderer.' No critic could deny 'the strange appearance of veracity' Defoe could achieve, but 'a story may be truth-like and yet deadly dull'.[3] Behind the dullness is a lack of imagination. 'Defoe, in truth, was little enough of a poet.' And since the novel 'is on the border line between poetry and prose', it should consist of 'as it were, prose saturated with poetry'.[4] For the same reasons that Fitzjames Stephen found *Robinson Crusoe* the greatest English novel, Leslie Stephen pronounced it 'a book for boys rather than men' because of 'the want of power in describing emotion as compared with the amazing power of describing facts'.[5] Defoe's world, in short, was one in which everything is set 'before us in broad daylight; there is too little of the thoughts and emotions which inhabit the twilight of the mind; of those dim half-seen forms which exercise the strongest influence upon the imagination, and are the most tempting subjects for the poet's art'.[6]

The very qualities Defoe lacked were to be most richly found

---

[1] *Hours in a Library* (New York, 1904), I, 11–13.   [2] *Ibid.*, p. 19.
[3] *Ibid.*, pp. 23–4.   [4] *Ibid.*, pp. 28–9.   [5] *Ibid.*, p. 52.   [6] *Ibid.*, p. 28.

in the novels and tales of Hawthorne, and the modern novelist could get more help from Hawthorne than from Defoe in trying to answer the all-important question facing him: how is he to prevent his work from being a 'mere photographic reproduction of this muddy, money-making, bread-and-butter-eating world?' How 'is the novelist who, by the inevitable conditions of his style, is bound to come into the closest contact with facts, who has to give us the details of his heroes' clothes, to tell us what he had for breakfast, and what is the state of his balance at the banker's—how is he to introduce the ideal element which must, in some degree, be present in all genuine art?' [1] In other words, how is he to prevent his work from being commonplace?

Disraeli's solution to this problem, a fusion of the exotic with mundane reality, Stephen found especially *sympathique*: 'The lights and shadows fluctuate, and solid forms melt provokingly into mist; but we must learn to enjoy the uncertain twilight which prevails on the border-land between romance and reality, if we would enjoy the ambiguities and the ironies and the mysteries of *Coningsby*.' [2] Such a method for a critic like G. H. Lewes would be completely out of the question. A work was either realistic or romantic, and each form had its own canons of verisimilitude; any mixing of them outraged his critical sense: 'We are by no means rigorous in expecting that the story is to move along the highway of everyday life . . . [but] if we are to travel into fairy-land, it must be in a fairy equipage, not a Hansom's cab.' [3] Real gardens required real toads. But for Stephen, Disraeli's refusal to commit himself either to realism or romance was of a piece with the essence of his genius, characterized by an 'ambiguous hovering between two meanings, . . . [an] oscillation between the ironical and the serious . . .' 'Simple-minded people' are 'revolted, even in literature by the ironical method; and tell the humourist, with an air of moral disapproval, that they never know when he is in jest or in earnest. To such matter-of-fact persons Disraeli's novels must be a standing offence. . . .' [4]

Literal realism as a doctrine seemed to Stephen particularly foolish in the rendering of character. 'It would . . . be the heigh

---

[1] *Hours in a Library*, I, p. 230.   [2] *Ibid.*, II, 312.
[3] *Edinburgh Review*, XCI (January, 1850), 166.
[4] *Hours in a Library*, II, 290.

of pedantry' to think that 'a fictitious personage were to be in all respects bounded by the narrow limits of human capacity. It is not the object of a really good novelist, nor does it come within the legitimate means of high art in any department to produce an actual illusion.' Rather, Stephen asserted throughout his literary criticism, there must always be essential differences between characters in life and those in literature.[1] *The Caxtons* was a second-rate novel simply because the people in it *were* so life-like, in the wrong sense. 'There is not in it one really living and moving character; but there are a large number of characters, who live and move as much as most of the persons who pass themselves off for real human beings in the course of our daily lives.'[2] Literature, apparently, for Stephen, does not reproduce life but must intensify it.

In our own time Albert Camus, in *The Rebel*, has given an analogous account of the relation between the novel and reality. Quoting from a letter of Van Gogh, 'I believe more and more that God must not be judged on this earth. It is one of his sketches that has turned out badly,' Camus writes: 'Every artist tries to reconstruct this sketch and to give it the style it lacks.' A novel through its stylization of reality becomes 'a universe in which action is endowed with form, where final words are pronounced, where people possess one another completely, and where life assumes the aspect of destiny'. The great characters of fiction are those 'who indulge their passions to the fullest . . . [who] complete things that we can never consummate'. And for that reason these characters—personages like Kirilov, Stavrogin, Julien Sorel—become typical. Each can completely typify one of many conflicting and fluctuating desires of actual people. 'Art disputes reality, but does not hide from it.'[3]

When Leslie Stephen turned to Charlotte Brontë, a much more important novelist than Disraeli or Bulwer, and examined 'the greatest of all her triumphs', the character of Paul Emanuel, he found something lacking. 'A more charming hero was never drawn, or one whose reality is more vivid and unmistakeable.' Yet a comparison with Don Quixote or Uncle Toby would

[1] *Ibid.*, I, 88.
[2] *Cornhill Magazine*, XXVII (March, 1873), 354.
[3] (New York, 1956), pp. 256–64.

reveal Charlotte Brontë's limitations as a creator of character. In one sense, M. Paul is certainly more real than the other two, more like a familiar friend. 'He is so real that we feel at once that he must have been drawn from a living model. . . .' But, as Stephen reiterates from essay to essay, the merit of fiction is not 'simply its approach to producing illusion'; if it were, M. Paul would be 'one of the first characters in the world of fiction. But such a test admittedly implies an erroneous theory of art; and, in fact, the intense individuality of Paul Emanuel is, in a different sense, the most serious objection to him.' He can only be a man who gave lectures at a particular *pension* at Brussels and nothing else, so that he is not 'one of those great typical characters, the creation of which is the highest triumph of the dramatist or novelist. There is too much of the temporary and accidental—too little of the permanent and essential.' [1]

Mr. Rochester, among all Charlotte Brontë's characters, comes closest to the typical rather than the merely individual— 'the personification of a true woman's longing (may one say it now?) for a strong master'. The character is not accurately portrayed, though, because 'the parson's daughter did not really know anything about the class of which he is supposed to be the type, and he remains vague and inconsistent in spite of all his vigour'. She intended him to be a man of the world, surfeited by experience and completely disillusioned, yet 'he really knows just as little of the world as she does'. The account of his adventures is 'taken from the first novel at hand of the early Bulwer school, or a diluted recollection of Byron. . . . He is supposedly to be specially simple and masculine, and yet he is as self-conscious as a lady on her first appearance in society. . . .' [2] Don Quixote, on the other hand, is one of the great typical characters of world literature: 'The most powerful type ever set forth of the contrast between the ideal and the common-place, and his figure comes before us whenever we are forced to meditate upon some of the most vital and most melancholy truths about human life.' A literary character can only be of permanent interest if he is 'the embodiment of one answer to a profound and enduring problem'. [3]

[1] *Hours in a Library*, III, 295–6.　　[2] *Ibid.*, pp. 302–3.
[3] *Ibid.*, p. 296.

9. OBJECTIVE AND SUBJECTIVE NOVELS:
THE REAL AND THE IDEAL

According to Samuel Lucas, a critic who wrote for *The Times* and was the editor of *Once a Week*, there were two classes of novelists, those who paint life 'phenomenally, as the majority would see it' and those who draw 'its presentment of mankind in a large degree from its inner consciousness. . . .' We have here, of course, another variation on those favourite terms of nineteenth-century criticism—*objective* and *subjective*, which, as we have seen, Henry Crabb Robinson said could be equated with the *real* and the *ideal*, and Lucas in an important review in *The Times* of *The Ordeal of Richard Feverel* does just that. It is wrong, Lucas claims, to condemn Meredith's characters by calling them unnatural, since Meredith belongs to the second class of novelists, whom Lucas labels 'humourists'. 'The humourist draws more from his humour than from obvious facts—from his modes of thought than from the manners of the time. He spins his web, like the spider, out of his own bowels. . . .' His characters are not intended to be realistic but are 'symbols and shadows of his thought', and his success is not to be measured 'by the standard relations of novels to life'. Since Meredith's world is of 'his own shaping', all we can fairly question is 'the plan and object of its creation' and then we can demand that 'his world . . . [hold] together on its own principles', which are related to, but not necessarily the same as, the world of our everyday experience.[1] By such canons, Lucas finds the weak spot of the novel in the death of Lucy, for it is not required by the logic of the forces Meredith set in motion, but is 'the pure wantonness of authorship'.[2]

In 1850 Sydney Dobell, best known as the author of *Balder*, a 'spasmodic' poem, used a similar system for classifying novelists, this time to get the Brontë novels out of the procrustean bed of realist criticism. Obviously, figures like Heathcliff and Mr. Rochester were not like 'life', but, Dobell pointed out, there was no reason why they should be. Since the Brontës were not

[1] M. Buxton Forman, ed., *George Meredith, Some Early Appreciations* (New York, 1909), pp. 52–3.
[2] *Ibid.*, p. 66.

'perceptive' writers who, like Thackeray, drew people 'uniformly from without', characters who were merely 'portraits, and limited to the circle of the author's outward experience', but were rather 'ideal' writers, like Dickens, who drew 'from within', 'principally by amplifying and pursuing ideals', their novels were exempt from the test of verisimilitude. For Dobell these two terms—the *perceptive* and the *ideal*—are not merely descriptive; they are also judgments of value. The ideal writer ranks much higher for him than the perceptive, and he includes in this essay a highly rhetorical plea to Thackeray to shift from one class to the other.

Admiring in him a faculty of perception amounting to genius, we have hitherto been unwilling to concede to him the possession of the higher gift. But there is a mellow atmosphere about some of his later scenes, a delicacy of aerial perspective, a depth and purity of tone, a poetic handling and freshness of rosy colour, a 'light that never was on sea or shore', [*sic*] which bespeak that a new faculty is awakening within him. . . . If he will take his stand no longer on the platform of experience, but on the mount of vision; look down, not on park, palace, or kingdom, but on the microcosm, . . . it may be his to give us some ideals which our own times may worthily study. . . .[1]

In other words, if Thackeray ceased to be Thackeray, he might be a major novelist. Such criticism, however barbarously written, is refreshing in the context of the predominantly realistic fifties.

Dobell's very deep-seated dislike of realism and the objective method in literature did enable him to appreciate the genius of Emily Brontë at a time when *Wuthering Heights* was either widely ignored or attacked, even though he denied her existence as a writer. In common with some other contemporary critics, he thought there was only one Bell, Currer—*Wuthering Heights* being her earliest novel, followed by *The Tenant of Wildfell Hall* and then *Jane Eyre*. The qualities he saw in *Wuthering Heights* were those usually associated with great narrative and dramatic poetry rather than with novels:

There are few things in modern prose to surpass these pages for native power. We cannot praise too warmly the brave simplicity,

---

[1] *The Life and Letters of Sydney Dobell*, ed. 'E.' (London, 1878), I, 163-4.

the unaffected air of intense belief, the admirable combination of extreme likelihood with the rarest originality, the nice provision of the possible even in the highest effects of the supernatural, the easy strength and instinct of keeping with which the accessory circumstances are grouped, the exquisite but unconscious art with which the chiaro-scuro of the whole is managed, and the ungenial frigidity of place, time, weather, and persons, is made to heighten the unspeakable pathos of one ungovernable outburst.[1]

David Masson gave another variation of the two classes of novelists that Lucas and Dobell distinguished; only he labelled them the 'real' and the 'ideal' and found both approaches to the art of fiction valid ones.[2] Thackeray and Dickens were the chief exemplars of the two schools, and the essay in which Masson first made this dichotomy was a plea addressed to 'educated readers' for the serious consideration of Dickens as an artist rather than a supremely successful popular entertainer. Dickens' characters, since they are the work of an 'ideal' artist, are

transcendental renderings of certain hints furnished by nature. Seizing the notion of some oddity as seen in the real world, Mr. Dickens has run away with it into a kind of outer or ideal region, there to play with it and work it out at leisure as extravagantly as he might choose, without the least impediment from any facts except those of his own story.

As a result, the 'mixture of good and bad' is not always 'in the same proportions as we find in nature. Some of his characters are thoroughly and ideally perfect; others are thoroughly and ideally detestable; and even in those where he has intended a mingled impression, vice and virtue are mingled in a purely ideal manner.' But Thackeray, as a 'real' artist, 'seems . . . to give the good and the bad together, in very nearly the same proportions that . . . nature herself, uses'. One artist, contrary to current belief, does not negate the other, and Masson's essay is called 'Pendennis and Copperfield: Thackeray and Dickens', not Thackeray or Dickens. 'Now, while, according to Mr. Thackeray's style of art, this is perfectly proper, it does not follow that Mr. Dickens's method is wrong.' Most of the great writers of the past were anything but realistic, Masson points out:

---

[1] *Ibid.*, pp. 169–71. [2] See above, pp. 148–9.

The characters of Shakespeare . . . are grand hyperbolic beings created by the breath of the poet himself out of hints taken from all that is most sublime in nature; they are humanity caught, as it were, and kept permanent in its highest and extremest mood, nay carried forth and compelled to think, speak, and act in conditions superior to that mood. As in Greek tragedy, the character that an artist of the higher or poetical school is expected to bring before us, is not, and never was meant to be, a puny 'Man and brother', resembling ourselves in his virtues and his foibles, but an ancestor and a demigod, large, superb, and unapproachable. Art is called Art, says Goethe, precisely because it is *not* Nature; and even such a department of art as the modern novel is entitled to the benefit of this maxim.[1]

Since Dickens' fiction is 'a world projected imaginatively beyond the real one, or inserted into the midst of the real one, and yet imaginatively moated round from it', only in judging Thackeray is the question of resemblance to actuality a legitimate one to raise.[2]

Much more important critical questions for Masson are those relating to the originality and interest of the characters, the 'moral spirit and sentiment' of the whole novel, and the 'unity of view and aim which pervades it . . . which is the result of all the author's natural convictions and endowments, all his experience of life, and all his intellectual conclusions on questions great and little. . . .'[3] In other words, a novel should be judged by the canons applicable to any other work of literature.

[1] *North British Review*, XV (May, 1851), 75.
[2] *British Novelists and Their Styles* (Cambridge, 1859), p. 250.
[3] *North British Review*, XV (May, 1851), 76-8.

V

THE CHEEK OF THE
YOUNG PERSON

I. THE NOVELISTS

Towards the end of our period, in September, 1867, an anonymous critic in *Blackwood's* wrote: 'English novels have for a long time—from the days of Sir Walter Scott at least—held a very high reputation in the world, not so much for what critics would call the highest development of art, as for a certain sanity, wholesomeness, and cleanness unknown to other literature of the same class.' English novelists, this critic asserted, had 'with a tolerably unanimous consent' agreed to reserve 'the darker problems of the time' to other kinds of literature and keep prose fiction 'pure from all noxious topics' because they realized it was 'the favourite reading matter of the young, . . . one of the chief amusements of all secluded and most suffering people . . . [and an escape] precious to women and unoccupied persons. . . .' This situation, however, had ceased to exist for some time, ever since 'Jane Eyre made what advanced critics call her "protest" against the conventionalities in which the world clothes itself'.[1] The English novel, therefore, for almost twenty years had been in a seriously tainted condition; that is,

[1] CII, 257–8.

novelists had felt free to deal with transgressions of the code governing sexual morality.

It is doubtful if the novelists of the earlier part of the century really acquiesced in the developing prudery of the new middle-class reading public they were so desirous of reaching. Scott, for instance, suggested that the English common reader had become a hypocrite: 'We are not now, perhaps, more moral in our conduct than men were fifty or sixty years since; but modern vice pays a tax to appearances, and is contented to wear a mask of decorum.' [1] John Moore, author of *Zeluco*, likewise noted that readers in the age of Dr. Bowdler were much more squeamish than they had been in the age of Wyclif. 'Whether a greater purity of morals exists in the present age than in the days of Chaucer, some people doubt; but that the same licentiousness which was allowed in the press and on the stage then, would meet with public marks of disapprobation now, cannot be disputed.' [2] (Moore's historical sense was evidently not very accurate.)

In an essay on Fielding in *The Times* in 1840, Thackeray made a similar observation about his own age:

The world does not tolerate now such satire as that of Hogarth and Fielding, and the world is no doubt right in a great part of its squeamishness; for it is good to pretend to the virtue of chastity even though we do not possess it. . . . But any man who has walked through Regent Street of a night, or has been behind the scenes of the Opera . . . must know that the *Rake's* and *Harlot's Progress* is by no means concluded. . . . The same vice exists, only we don't speak about it; the same things are done, but we don't call them by their names.

Hence Fielding cannot properly be accused of immorality; all that one can say is that his age 'was more free-spoken than ours'. Thus, Thackeray implied that values in one hundred years had been so reversed that in 1840 hypocrisy was a virtue and honesty a fault. Far from being immoral, *Tom Jones*, he thought, was a most improving work, if the age would only learn to read it rightly. Fielding

[1] *Miscellaneous Prose Works* (Boston, 1829), III, 319.
[2] 'A View of the Commencement and Progress of Romance', *Works of John Moore, M.D.* (Edinburgh, 1820), V, 49.

gives a strong, real picture of human life, and the virtues which he exhibits shine out by their contrasts with the vices which he paints so faithfully, as they never could have done, if the latter had not been depicted as well as the former. He tries to give you, as far as he knows it, the whole truth about human nature; the good and the evil of his characters are both practical. Tom Jones sins, and his faults are described with a curious accuracy, but then follows the repentance which comes of his very sins, and surely, that is moral and touching.[1]

In the same year, in *Fraser's*, Thackeray described a young thief's mistress he had seen in a crowd at the public hanging of Courvoisier, a notorious murderer:

. . . if attacked, ready to reply without a particle of modesty; could give as good ribaldry as she got; made no secret (and there were several inquiries) as to her profession. . . . But with all this there was something good about the girl; a sort of devil-may-care candour and simplicity that one could not fail to see. Her answers to some of the coarse questions put to her, were very ready and good-humoured.

She was 'ugly, stunted, thick-limbed, and by no means a beauty' and was dressed not in rags but in a greasy cotton shawl and an old faded rag-shop bonnet. Comparing her with Dickens' Nancy, Thackeray thought that Dickens gave us 'the most unreal fantastical personage possible; no more like a thief's mistress' than a Dresden china shepherdess 'resembles a real country wench'. Dickens did not dare 'tell the truth concerning such young ladies. They have, no doubt, virtues . . . that are not called . . . into exercise among other women.' But since Dickens presented 'one or two favourable points as character-izing the whole', the figure of Nancy was hopelessly sentimen-talized. Either give the girl in all her sordidness or 'leave the picture alone altogether'.[2]

Thackeray, however, was nothing if not inconsistent, or rather ambivalent whenever he wrote about sex, and on this subject of the prudery of the Victorian reading public, he wavered very widely. When he came to treat *Tom Jones* again in *The English Humourists of the Eighteenth Century* of 1853, he roundly condemned Fielding's morality, completely reversing

[1] *Critical Papers in Literature* (London, 1904), pp. 203-4.
[2] 'Going to See a Man Hanged', *Thackeray Works*, III, 643.

his earlier statements, those of the 1840 review and the 1851 preface to *Pendennis,* where he had written:

Since the author of 'Tom Jones' was buried, no writer of fiction among us has been permitted to depict to his utmost power a MAN. We must drape him, and give him a certain conventional simper. . . . You will not hear—it is best to know it—what moves in the real world, what passes in society, in the clubs, colleges, messrooms, —what is the life and talk of your sons.[1]

In *The English Humourists* he lectured: 'I can't say that I think Mr. Jones a virtuous character; I can't say but that I think Fielding's evident liking and admiration for Mr. Jones shows that the great humourist's moral sense was blunted by his life, and that here, in Art and Ethics, there is a great error.' Tom Jones, Thackeray held, was too 'flawed' to be considered a hero: 'He would not rob a church, but that is all; and a pretty long argument may be debated, as to which of these old types —the spendthrift, the hypocrite, Jones and Blifil . . .—is the worst member of society, and the most deserving of censure.' In this frame of mind, characteristically, Thackeray much preferred *Amelia:* it is 'perhaps . . . not a better story than "Tom Jones" but it has the better ethics. . . .' [2] His squeamishness manifested itself in its most extreme form in his denunciation of Swift, almost psychotic in its intensity: 'A monster gibbering shrieks, and gnashing imprecations against mankind—tearing down all shreds of modesty, past all sense of manliness and shame; filthy in word, filthy in thought, furious, raging, obscene.' [3] At the end of the lecture on Sterne, which was again almost entirely a denunciation—'the foul satyr's eyes leer out of the leaves constantly' [4]—Thackeray gave Dickens a very dubious compliment: 'I think of these past writers and of one who lives amongst us now, and am grateful for the innocent laughter and the sweet unsullied page which the author of "David Copperfield" gives to my children.' [5] One wonders whether Dickens appreciated this piece of Podsnappery.

In the *Roundabout Papers,* 'De Juventute', he was much more mellow about Sterne, but still thankful he did not live in such a 'free-spoken' age: 'Ah! not against thy genius, O father of

[1] *Thackeray Works,* II, xlviii.
[2] *Ibid.,* VII, 582–4.
[3] *Ibid.,* p. 446.
[4] *Ibid.,* pp. 600–1.
[5] *Ibid.,* p. 601.

Uncle Toby and Trim, would I say a word in disrespect. But I am thankful to live in times when men no longer have the temptation to write so as to call blushes on women's cheeks, and would shame to whisper wicked allusions to honest boys.' [1] This concern with the cheeks of women and young persons, however, was not something Thackeray developed at the latter end of his career. In 1844, for example, he had written in *Fraser's*: 'There is no reader of Mr. Lever's tales but must admire the extreme, almost woman-like, delicacy of the author, who, amidst all the wild scenes through which he carries his characters and with all his outbreaks of spirits and fun, never writes a sentence that is not entirely pure.' [2] And in his early reviews, he consistently attacked Balzac and George Sand for indecency, although ironically, in *Vanity Fair*, he parried the same kind of criticism: '. . . it has been the wish of the present writer, all through the story, deferentially to submit to the fashion at present prevailing and only to hint at the existence of wickedness in a light, easy, and agreeable manner, so that nobody's fine feelings may be offended.' [3]

Again, in *The Virginians*, he returned to the subject of the young person in two characteristic passages. In one, after Dr. Johnson praises Richardson, Thackeray advises parents:

Do not let any young lady trip to her grandfather's bookcase in consequence of this eulogium, and rashly take down *Clarissa* from the shelf. . . . I wonder, are our women more virtuous than their grandmothers, or only more squeamish? . . . Oh, my faithful, good old Samuel Richardson! Hath the news yet reached thee in Hades, that thy sublime novels are huddled away in corners, and that our daughters may no more read *Clarissa* than *Tom Jones*?[4]

In the other passage, he has reversed his position: 'It may be that the novelist's art is injured by the restraints put upon him, as many an honest harmless statue at St. Peter's and the Vatican is spoilt by the tin draperies in which ecclesiastical old women have swaddled the fair limbs of marble. But in your prudery

[1] *Ibid.*, XII, 237. [2] 'A Box of Novels', *ibid.*, XIII, 404.
[3] *Ibid.*, I, chap. LXIV, p. 624. Kathleen Tillotson's thesis that writers during the 1840's did not feel hampered by any restrictions on their subject matter does not seem consistent with Thackeray's statement. See *Novels of the Eighteen-Forties* (London, 1954).
[4] *Ibid.*, X, chap. XXVI, p. 221.

there is reason.' If any page of a novel is dangerous to good morals, 'Out with your scissors, censor, and clip off the prurient paragraph! We have nothing for it but to submit.'[1]

As an editor, Thackeray was extremely cautious about offending his public, and even Trollope and Elizabeth Barrett Browning had manuscripts refused for indecency. When Trollope's short story 'Mrs. General Talboys' was rejected because of an allusion to 'a man with illegitimate children and . . . a woman not as pure as she should be', Trollope answered, 'I will not allow that I am indecent, and profess that squeamishness—in so far as it is squeamishness and not delicacy—should be disregarded by a writer.'[2] To Mrs. Browning, Thackeray wrote upon the rejection of 'Lord Walter's Wife': 'In your poem you know there is an account of unlawful passion felt by a man for a woman—and though you write pure doctrine and real modesty and pure ethics, I'm sure our readers will make an outcry, and so I have not published this poem.' Mrs. Browning, in her answer, was much more indignant than Trollope:

I am not a 'fast woman'—I don't like coarse subjects, or the coarse treatment of any subject—But I am deeply convinced that the corruption of our society requires, not shut doors and windows, but light and air—and that it is exactly because pure and prosperous women choose to *ignore* vice, that miserable women suffer wrong by it everywhere.[3]

Bulwer, in *England and the English* of 1833, saw as one of the direct causes of 'the fearful amount of prostitution which exists throughout England, . . . for which no remedy is ever contemplated' the extreme 'regard for appearance' and the idea that morality only operates in 'the connexions between the sexes'. 'Morality, strictly translated with us, means the absence of licentiousness—it is another word for one of its properties—chastity; as the word profligacy bears only the construction of sexual intemperance.' Bulwer then very shrewdly noted that 'our extreme regard for the chaste induces a contemptuous apathy to the unchaste. We care not how many there are—or how far they descend into the lower abysses of crime.'[4]

---

[1] *Thackeray Works*, X, chap. XLI, p. 345.   [2] *Trollope Letters*, p. 78.
[3] *Thackeray Letters*, IV, 227–8.   [4] (London, 1874), pp. 190–1.

But if society chooses to ignore vice, the novelist, if he is true to his profession, cannot acquiesce. 'It is precisely those offences which society cannot interfere with, that society requires fiction to expose,' Bulwer wrote in the 1848 preface to *Paul Clifford* (the book which Cazamian believed inaugurated the English social novel). 'Fiction follows truth into all the strongholds of convention; strikes through the disguise, lifts the mask, bares the heart, and leaves a moral wherever it brands a falsehood.' [1]

Bulwer's repeated treatment of vice and crime in the thirties and forties was savagely attacked by *Fraser's Magazine*, chiefly for political reasons. (And one of the most severe of the *Fraser's* critics was Thackeray.) [2] On the reiterated charge that his novels were immoral and dangerous to the public welfare because they excited sympathy for and interest in criminals, Bulwer wrote to Forster in 1841: 'To me this dogma seems to strike down . . . the grandest privileges and the greatest masterpieces of Art,' and he gives the examples of *Othello* and *Macbeth*.

The element of the highest genius is not among the village gossips of Miss Austen; it is in crime and passion, for the two are linked together. It is the art of that genius to make you distinguish between the crime and the criminal. . . . It is not immoral, it is moral, and of the most impressive and epic order of morals, to arouse and sustain interest for a criminal. It is immoral when you commend the crime, and this . . . I have never done. [3]

Bulwer was extremely sensitive to criticism of his morality as a writer, and after the publication of *Lucretia*, when the old charges were again repeated, he wrote a fifty-page pamphlet, 'A Word to the Public', which he appended to the 1853 edition of that novel, laying down the principle that the artist should have complete 'liberty in the choice of materials'. This liberty he claimed for all writers, 'from the greatest poet to the meanest novelist', and asserted that the general public as well as the artist would gain if this principle were generally admitted.

It is no less to the interest of the public, that writers should not be scared, by tacit acquiescence in charges most painful to honorable

[1] (London, 1874), p. xi.

[2] See Miriam Thrall, *Rebellious Fraser's* (New York, 1934); and Michael Sadleir, *Bulwer, a Panorama* (Boston, 1931).

[3] The Earl of Lytton, *The Life of Edward Bulwer, First Lord Lytton* (London, 1913), II, 85–6.

men, from whatever exposition of evil as it exists—whatever investigation of the human mind, in its sublimity or its baseness, its
virtues or its guilt, the uniform example of received authorities in
literature has proved it to be salutary or safe to permit to the scope
of the poet and the purpose of the teacher.[1]

Referring to the idea set forth by certain critics that crime
and passion were legitimate subjects for the drama and not the
novel, he retorted:

Much is said about the 'weak minds of circulating library readers'
—'the young' and 'impressionable' etc. As if there were no weak
minds in the pit and the gallery of Drury Lane . . . as if, too, after
all, literature were a kind of medicated farina to be adapted with
the daintiest nicety to the digestion of the weakly and diseased—as
if any man of education and vigour, no matter whether he writes a
novel or a history, must not take it for granted that he addresses
readers of ordinary understanding and healthful comprehension.
. . . As if all grave purpose and tragic end were forbidden to the
compositions of fiction, because they are divided into chapters, not
compressed into acts![2]

Because novelists tacitly agreed to avoid, in the words of the
Blackwood's critic, 'the darker problems of the time' and keep
their works free from 'noxious topics',[3] the contemporary novel,
Bulwer complained, became trivial: 'We have too much neglected the deeper and graver characteristics of our own age;
too much contented ourselves with surveys of the surface,
delineations of manners, fashions, and foibles, and turned to the
past for that sterner poetry which is not less sensibly to be found
in the sorrow and guilt of the life around us.' Contrary to the
usual notions of artistic decorum and propriety, Bulwer declared
there were no low or forbidden subjects:

It is the treatment that ennobles, not the subject. Grant that the
characters are what convention calls *low*—in birth, station, instruction; born in a cellar, dying on the gibbet, they are not one jot,
for those reasons, made *necessarily* low to art. Art can, with Fielding,
weave an epic from adventures with gamekeepers and barbers. Art
can, with Goethe, convert into poetry, the most lofty, the homely
image of the girl condemned for infanticide. . . .[4]

[1] *Lucretia* (Philadelphia, 1878), II, 312–18.   [2] *Ibid.*, pp. 325–6.
[3] See above, p. 191.   [4] *Lucretia*, pp. 334–7.

Bulwer was thus fighting the same battle in Victorian England that painters like Courbet and Manet, poets like Gautier and Baudelaire, and novelists like the Goncourts and Zola were waging in nineteenth-century France—or that D. H. Lawrence would still be fighting in twentieth-century England.

During the fifties and sixties Dickens was essentially in agreement with Bulwer about the freedom of the artist to choose his own subject matter and he ran an article in *All the Year Round*, similar in thesis to Bulwer's 'A Word to the Public', which opposed the view that novelists should avoid crime and the great passions and pretend that there are no 'dark shadows in the world'. The author of this essay, 'The Sensational Williams' (Williams was Dickens' private name for Shakespeare because he had once heard a Frenchman refer to him that way), points out the danger of confusing the vulgar kind of sensational novel with great tragedy: 'The difference between an artist who can look into the psychology of crime and terror, and the botcher who can do nothing more than lay on the carmine with a liberal brush is so great as to be essential.' [1] An essay in *Household Words*, 'Something Shakespeare Lost', shows how certain Victorian critics would have received *Hamlet* had it been a contemporary work: '*Hamlet* is a melodrama of the worst school. Let it suffice to say that of the dozen characters it contains, exclusive of the supernumeraries, eight are killed by sword, drowning, or poison, during the course of the piece. . . .' [2]

Writing to Forster about the Exposition Universelle of 1855 in Paris, where he had a good opportunity to compare contemporary French and English painting, he found the English artist severely hampered by Mr. Podsnap's concern for the cheek of the young person. The English exhibits wanted character, fire, and purpose. 'There is a horrid respectability about most of the best of them. . . .' It was true there was 'no want of bad pictures among the French, but, Lord! the goodness also!—the fearlessness of them; the bold drawing; the dashing conception; the passion and action in them!' Such a response to an exhibition dominated by Delacroix and Ingres was perhaps to be expected, but it was not usual among Englishmen. Dickens concluded that 'mere form and conventionalities usurp, in English art, as in English government and social

[1] XI (February 13, 1864), 14.   [2] XV (January 17, 1857), 51.

relations, the place of living force and truth'.[1] In the same mood of disgust with English conventions he answered a critic who complained that 'the hero of an English book is always uninteresting—too good—not natural, etc.' 'This same unnatural young gentleman . . . whom you meet . . . in books . . . *must* be presented to you in that unnatural aspect by reason of your morality, and is not to have, I will not say any of the indecencies you like, but not even any of the experiences, trials, perplexities and confusions inseparable from the making of all men!'[2]

In Dickens' novels, English respectability found its chief exponents in Pecksniff, Podsnap, and less well known, Mrs. General of *Little Dorrit*. It was she who applied liberal coats of varnish to all the cracked surfaces of the world. 'Mrs. General was not to be told of anything shocking. Accidents, miseries, and offences, were never to be mentioned before her. Passion was to sleep in the presence of Mrs. General, and blood was to change to milk and water.'[3] But although he satirized the conventions, Dickens never defied them in any significant way. In 1840 he wrote: 'Beware of writing things for the eyes of everybody, which you would feel the smallest delicacy in *saying* anywhere,'[4] even apparently in the presence of the young person; and in 1858 he cautioned Wills: 'I particularly wish you to look well to Wilkie's article . . . and not to leave anything in it that may be sweeping, and unnecessarily offensive to the middle class. He always has a tendency to overdo that. . . .'[5] In 1866 during the critical furore caused by Reade's *Griffith Gaunt*, in which the hero deliberately commits bigamy because he suspects his wife of having an adulterous affair with a priest, Dickens wrote to Collins that though he admired the novel, he would refuse it as an editor: 'What was pure to an artist might be impurely suggestive to inferior minds. . . .'[6]

Reade himself sued for libel an American magazine called *The Round Table*, which carried the severest attack made on his book, and he answered his critics with the angry pamphlet 'The Prurient Prude', vindicating his freedom as an artist to treat

[1] *Dickens Letters*, II, 700.   [2] *Ibid.*, p. 797.
[3] *Little Dorrit*, Everyman's Library (London, 1907), Book II, chap. 2, p. 430.
[4] *Dickens Letters*, I, 285.   [5] *Ibid.*, III, 58.   [6] *Ibid.*, p. 510.

violations of the sexual codes of society.[1] Five years after *Griffith Gaunt*, Reade published *A Terrible Temptation*, which stirred up even more controversy in England because of its treatment of the demi-monde and its open recognition that many Englishmen kept mistresses in addition to wives. On August 26, 1871, Reade wrote a letter to *The Times* entitled 'Facts Must Be Faced' (later reprinted in *Readiana*) in response to its protest against the treatment of such subjects in novels. Reade first of all claimed he had gotten all his facts from articles in *The Times*; he then went on to demand at least the same freedom in choice of subject matter that a newspaper enjoyed '. . . That a journalist has the right to put into his leaded type and to amplify, discuss, and dwell upon any subject whatever, and that the poet or novelist has not an equal right to deal with that subject in fiction, this is monstrous and the mere delusion of a rabid egotism.' Just because his novel was 'not adapted to the narrow minds of bread-and-butter misses', it was not immoral. His mission as a writer was 'to weave the recorded facts . . . of this great age, into the forms of Art', and the facts as recorded in the newspaper were 'Lunacy, Prisons, Trades Unions, Divorce, Murder, Anonyma [a Victorian euphemism for a high-class prostitute]'.[2]

Wilkie Collins was as outspoken as Charles Reade about his right and duty to treat what many reviewers called 'unpleasant' subjects, and Dickens, as we have seen, thought Collins inclined to offend his bourgeois audience more than was necessary, as he seemed to in an essay on Balzac in *Household Words*. The reason, Collins wrote, the greatest French writer of the century was completely unknown in England was that he 'lays himself open to grave objection (on the part of that unhappily large section of the English public which obstinately protests against the truth wherever the truth is painful) as a writer who sternly insists on presenting the dreary aspects of human life, literally, exactly, nakedly, as he finds them. . . .' [3] Most of these aspects— which so many magazine editors, reviewers, and owners of circulating libraries did not want to see in novels—were connected with relationships not recognized by law. The idea that 'the novelist is forbidden to touch on the sexual relations which

---

[1] Reprinted in *Readiana*, Library Edition (London, 1896), pp. 296–301.
[2] *Ibid.*, pp. 305–8.   [3] *My Miscellanies* (New York, 1874), p. 155.

literally swarm around him and influence the lives of millions of his fellow creatures' is an 'essentially immoral view of the functions of the novelist' and one which forces the novel to present 'a false reflection of life'.[1] On another occasion when he was requested by his publisher to remove the word *damn* from a story because it might encourage children to swear, he said his novels were '*not* addressed to young people exclusively', and he refused to consider them 'the ultimate court of appeal in English literature'.[2]

The interdicted word *damn* can also be found in *Wuthering Heights*, and Charlotte Brontë, as editor of the second edition, refused to tamper with her sister's text and represent *damn* by the customary 'initial and final letter only', inasmuch as she deemed it

a rational plan to write words out at full length. The practise of hinting by single letters those expletives with which profane and violent persons are wont to garnish their discourse, strikes me as a proceeding which, however well meant, is weak and futile. I cannot tell what good it does—what feeling it spares—what horror it conceals.[3]

Trollope fully recognized the fact that novels were meant to be family reading and would never wilfully offend his public by language that was generally interdicted by the middle class. There is, he wrote in the *Nineteenth Century* in 1879, 'a general conviction that it behoves the English novelist to be pure',[4] and he seemed to approve of the fact that Richardson and Fielding were often frowned upon because 'they describe coarse things in coarse language, and are not in accordance with the tastes or with the sympathies of the age'.[5] He admired 'the strain Scott put upon himself so that he should not be carried away into the seducing language of ill-regulated passion'.[6] The greatest temptation of the novelist, Trollope wrote in his *Auto-biography*, since he wants to interest his readers, is 'to sacrifice something for effect, to say a word or two here, or to draw a picture, for which he feels that he has the power, and which

[1] Kenneth Robinson, *Wilkie Collins* (New York, 1952), p. 259.
[2] *Ibid.*, p. 232. [3] *Wuthering Heights* (New York, 1943), p. xxviii.
[4] V (January, 1879), 32.
[5] *Four Lectures*, ed. Morris L. Parrish (London, 1938), p. 101.
[6] *Nineteenth Century*, V (January, 1879), 32.

when spoken or drawn would be alluring'. This something, of course, in the cliché of much nineteenth-century criticism, is the novelist's 'pure moral tone'. However, he must resist this tempting prospect because 'the regions of absolute vice are foul and odious. The savour of them . . . is disgusting.' So the novelist must keep out, but his biggest danger lies in the 'outskirts on these regions, on which sweet-smelling flowers seem to grow, and grass to be green. . . . The flowers and the grass in these neutral territories sometimes seem to give him so easy an opportunity of pleasing!' [1]

But judging from his correspondence, Trollope loved to stray in this limbo adjoining the region of 'absolute vice' and so had difficulties over more of his works than the story Thackeray refused for the *Cornhill*. When, in 1860, the publisher George Smith objected to something 'indelicate' in the story 'The Banks of the Jordan', Trollope answered: 'You city publishers are so uncommonly delicate. . . . I shall never forget what a terrible and killing correspondence I had with W. Longman because I would make a clergyman kiss a lady whom he proposed to marry. . . .' [2] The book, of course, was *Barchester Towers*, and Longman's reader, in his report, thought the major defects of that work were the 'low-mindedness and vulgarity of the chief actors', the chapter entitled 'Mrs. Proudie's Reception' (one of the greatest comic scenes in Trollope), and the entire character of the Signora Neroni. [3] Trollope, after receiving this report from William Longman, wrote back in 1856:

I beg to assure you that nothing would be more painful to me than to be considered an indecent writer. . . . But I do not think that I can in utter ignorance have committed a volume of indecencies. I do not now remember what can be the sin of the special scene to which you allude. Of course the woman is intended to [appear?] as indifferent to all moralities and decent behaviour—but such a character may I think be drawn without offence if her vice be made not attractive. [4]

For Trollope there were practically no subjects or characters whose presentation in a novel would be immoral *per se*, but the

[1] *Autobiography* (Berkeley and Los Angeles, 1947), pp. 184–5.
[2] *Trollope Letters*, p. 67.
[3] Michael Sadleir, *Trollope: A Commentary* (London, 1945), pp. 170–1.
[4] *Trollope Letters*, p. 25.

base must 'be made to look base', not alluring or noble; virtue must be made 'alluring'; and vice, 'ugly'. Thus 'Gay did injury to morality when he persuaded all the town to sympathize with a thief', and *Roxana* is an example of a thoroughly immoral work. Richardson, on the other hand, even though coarse, was a thoroughly moral writer because he wrote 'to do good'.[1]

Because of his treatment of Lady Glencora Palliser, who through a large part of *Can You Forgive Her?* seriously contemplates an elopement even though she is married, Trollope was taken to task, as he tells it, by 'a distinguished dignitary of our Church' for whom it had been 'one of the innocent joys of his life . . . to have my novels read to him by his daughters. But now I was writing a book which caused him to bid them to close it!' [2] Trollope answered by claiming the same privileges as a moralist that the clergyman enjoyed:

Adultery . . . is a sin against which you are called on to inveigh, (—and I also as I think of my work,). . . . The bible does not scruple to speak to us of adultery as openly as of other sins. You do not leave out the seventh commandment. The young girl for whom I or you are so tender is not ignorant of the sin;—and, as I think, it would not be well that she should be ignorant of it. . . . Thinking as I do that ignorance is not innocence I do not avoid, as you would wish me to do, the mention of things which are to me more shocking in their facts than in their names.[3]

If the clergyman, however, were to assert that to most young ladies, except for the fact that he was financially ineligible (but then Lady Glencora was so rich), Burgo Fitzgerald was a much more attractive suitor than Plantaganet Palliser, one wonders how Trollope would have reconciled that undoubted fact with his belief that virtue must be made alluring and vice ugly.

The Vicar of Bullhampton must have been even more shocking to many readers since it was 'written chiefly with the object of exciting not only pity but sympathy for a fallen women. . . .' In the preface to that novel, which Trollope thought so important as a statement of his literary principles that he inserted it in the *Autobiography*, he brought up the question of

whether a novelist, who professes to write for the amusement of the

---

[1] *Nineteenth Century*, V (January, 1879), 29–30; *Autobiography*, p. 185.
[2] *Autobiography*, p. 153.　　　　　　　　[3] *Trollope Letters*, pp. 173–4.

young of both sexes, should allow himself to bring on his stage a character such as that of Carry Brattle. It is not long since . . . that the very existence of such a condition of life as was here, was supposed to be unknown to our sisters and daughters. . . . Whether that ignorance was good may be questioned; but that it exists no longer is beyond question.[1]

Clearly then, it would make no sense to interdict the subject of prostitution and sexual promiscuity in novels.

If George Eliot were the author of 'The Progress of Fiction as an Art', as Professor Haight believes,[2] then in 1853 she had a rather prim sense of propriety and was inclined to take a very strict view of the boundaries of art. 'Richardson's pictures of life are revolting to our more fastidious tastes,' and Fielding and Smollett 'offend by . . . the studied coarseness of even their best scenes and descriptions. . . . No great author of our time . . . *could* write like Fielding or Smollett; and the work would not be tolerated were it attempted.' [3] Here is Mrs. General with a vengeance. Wilkie Collins, who in *Basil* came too close to the eighteenth century for comfort, is lectured: 'There are some subjects on which it is not possible to dwell without offence,' and the author of this essay advises him to read *The Scarlet Letter* to learn how adultery may be treated so that 'the pure need not turn away'. Collins 'dwells on the details of animal appetite with a persistency which can serve no moral purpose, and may minister to evil passions while professing condemnation of them'.[4] The fact that George Eliot was a great admirer of George Sand, especially her *Lélia*,[5] which was a great stumbling block to prudish reviewers, makes the attribution of this article to George Eliot seem doubtful. If, however, this was her first statement of this major problem for the Victorians, she was never again to adopt such a tone in relation to the treatment of extramarital relationships in fiction. After 1854 her realism, in theory at least, would completely reject the idea that only certain subjects were fit for art and others were beyond the pale. When an editor requested a preliminary sketch of the plot of *Adam Bede*, she refused to tell her story beforehand 'on the

[1] *Autobiography*, p. 273.   [2] See above, pp. 146–7.
[3] *Westminster Review*, LX (October, 1853), 355–6.
[4] *Ibid.*, pp. 372–3.   [5] *George Eliot Letters*, I, 243.

ground that I would not have it judged apart from my *treatment*, which alone determines the moral quality of art. . . .' [1] This surely implies that there are no 'low' *subjects*, although she was 'Victorian' to the extent that she believed art should 'soften' certain facts. But even if reality is to be 'softened', experience is never to be falsified; that is sentimentality. Thus of her story *Janet's Repentance*, she wrote to her publisher: 'Everything is softened from the fact so far as art is permitted to soften, and yet to remain essentially true.' [2] Accordingly, she was firm in resisting editorial protest over a situation in which the heroine is married to a chronic alcoholic and gradually becomes one herself. George Eliot refused to change the story in any way, and to John Blackwood's complaint that it was too 'harsh' ('I should have liked a pleasanter picture'[3]) she replied: '. . . There are too many prolific writers who devote themselves to the production of pleasing pictures, to the exclusion of all disagreeable truths, for me to desire to add to their number.' [4] (Writing almost twenty years later, Henry James still found the story 'scabreuse'.)

Meredith, although he personally disliked the work of the French naturalists because of what he considered their erroneous view of the nature of man[5] was in the sixties one of the chief advocates of more freedom for the artist. To Swinburne he wrote after the storm over the publication of *Poems and Ballads*: 'It has done the critical world good by making men look boldly at the restrictions imposed upon art by our dominating damnable bourgeoisie.' [6] These same restrictions, he believed, ruined a potentially great poet in Tennyson:

The 'Holy Grail' is wonderful, isn't it? The lines are satin lengths, the figures Sèvres china. . . . To think!—it's in these days that the foremost poet of the country goes on fluting of creatures that have not a breath of vital humanity in them, and doles us out his regular five-feet with the old trick of the vowel endings—the Euphuist's tongue, the Exquisite's leg, the Curate's moral sentiments, the British matron and her daughter's purity of tone. . . . The man has got hold of the Muses' clothes-line and hung it with jewelry.

[1] *George Eliot Letters*, II, 503-4.   [2] *Ibid.*, p. 347.   [3] *Ibid.*, p. 344.
[4] *Ibid.*, pp. 348-9.   [5] See above, pp. 170-1.
[6] Siegfried Sassoon, *Meredith* (New York, 1948), p. 61.

'Lucretius' was the only recent poem of Tennyson's he could read:

> I can't say how much I admire it and hate the Sir Pandarus public which has corrupted this fine (natural) singer. In his degraded state . . . he is useful, for he reflects as much as our Society chooses to show of itself. The English notion of passion, virtue, valour is in his pages: and the air and the dress we assume are seen there.—I turn to Rabelais and Montaigne with relief. See what a gentleman Boccaccio is in his narration! and always manly, always fresh.[1]

2. THE CRITICS

Meredith in this letter was perhaps thinking of the treatment his *Modern Love* had received in the *Saturday Review*, usually one of the few magazines favourably disposed towards his work. 'No word-painting or clever analysis', wrote the author of 'Mr. George Meredith's Poems', 'can atone for a choice of subject which we cannot help regarding as involving a grave moral mistake—a mistake so grave as utterly to disqualify the chooser from achieving any great and worthy result in art.' In order to learn how to treat adultery, Meredith was advised to read Tennyson's 'Guinevere'.[2]

Meredith had difficulties with English propriety from the beginning of his career as a novelist. When *Richard Feverel* was first published, Mudie's library, so important for the financial success of a novel, automatically bought three hundred copies, but when it was accused by the *Spectator* of having a 'low ethical tone' and called 'painful' by the *Athenaeum*: 'it affects the reader like a painful reality to see . . . such child's play with the most sacred mysteries of life . . .,' Mudie apparently read the novel and refused to circulate it.[3] The favourable notice in the *Saturday Review* was hardly the sort that would have made him change his mind:

> The merit of Mr. Meredith's book . . . [is] that he has tried to work his subject out to what he thinks its legitimate conclusions, and that there is originality and boldness in the steps he takes to

[1] *Meredith Letters*, I, 197–9.   [2] XVI (October 24, 1863), 562–3.
[3] Sassoon, *op. cit.*, pp. 23 ff.; Lionel Stevenson, *The Ordeal of George Meredith* (New York, 1953), pp. 71 ff.; and Jack Lindsay, *George Meredith, His Life and Works* (London, 1956), pp. 93 ff.

bring about the desired result. . . . He does not allow any conventional notions of impropriety to stand between him and the description of scenes he thinks necessary to carry out his main purpose.

(Here the reviewer is referring to the scenes in which Mrs. Mount, under orders from Sir Austin, sets about in a very deliberate fashion to seduce Richard.) 'There is much that is repulsive' in this section of the novel, but 'it is the repulsiveness of a horrible truth. There is nothing shadowy, vague, or mock-moral about this portraiture of immorality. . . . We do not object to this. It is quite right that there should be men's novels, if only it is understood at the outset they are only meant for men.' The author of this review, on the whole, thoroughly approved of Meredith's intentions: 'There is a great danger in literature altogether shrinking from the topics usually handled among men, for men thus get an impression that all the representations of life given in fiction are hypocritical and superficial.' Yet his insistence that '*The Ordeal of Richard Feverel* is entirely a man's book' and that it contained 'some of the most unflinching sketches of immorality that the pen of a modern Englishman has ventured to draw' [1] did not help the sale of the books among the lending libraries, and it was they who controlled an author's income.

Yet for an author who was supposed to have defied one of the most cherished literary conventions of the period, Meredith did not suffer nearly as much as one would have expected, or as he later led people to believe. As J. A. Hammerton pointed out, Meredith, more than most writers who were consciously *avant-garde*, had 'intelligent and cordial appreciation from the beginning', and after studying the criticism of Meredith's novels, Hammerton concluded that the myth Meredith circulated of 'long years of neglect' was not true. [2] For instance, after Mudie refused to circulate *Richard Feverel*, which was very favourably reviewed in the *Saturday Review*, the *Westminster Review*, and *The Times*, Meredith's second novel, *Evan Harrington*, was serialized in *Once a Week*, a magazine intended to rival Dickens' *Household Words* in popularity. In the same year, 1860, he also became literary adviser and reader for Chapman and Hall, one of the most important publishers of the period, in

[1] VIII (July 9, 1859), 48–9.
[2] *George Meredith in Anecdote and Criticism* (London, 1909), p. 131.

which position he succeeded the extremely influential John
Forster. It seems strange today that such a responsible job,
equivalent to that of chief editor, should have been held by a
man considered to be a dangerous innovator subversive of
public morals. In 1866 Meredith's fourth novel, *Vittoria*, was
serialized in the *Fortnightly Review*, and in 1870 *Harry Richmond*,
in the magazine that had one of the largest circulations of the
period, the *Cornhill*. In a decade three out of the six novels he
published were serialized in important periodicals.

In July, 1864, the *Westminster Review* carried an article by
Justin MacCarthy, 'Novels with a Purpose', devoted chiefly to
Meredith. The author's chief point was that

the world of fiction is still, for the most part, a nursery and bread-
and-butter world. Terrible dangers no doubt are described as
therein to be met. . . . But the familiar, homely, real, seductive
dangers of grown-up human life are not to be talked of there. The
heroine of the modern novel seems always as if she ought to wear
short-clothes and trousers with frills on them.

MacCarthy asserted that, as a critic, he would give 'a friendly
reception' to Meredith 'were it for nothing but the mere fact
that conventionality might be inclined to shriek' out against
him. 'While it is coldly, stiffly, prudishly agreed to paint for us
as a rule only such life as might be lectured on in a young ladies'
boarding-school, we feel thankful to the novelist who has the
courage to approach some of the great problems of existence. ...'[1]

Outside literature the situation, however, MacCarthy noted,
was very different in the England of 1864. There

the institution of marriage might almost seem to be . . . just now
upon its trial. What English people used to think Madame Sand
very wicked years ago for saying, newspapers, books, and even
sermons, not uncommonly say now. It is discovered that throughout
English social life immorality is a much more general institution
than successful and satisfactory marriage. Leading newspapers have
admitted grave and earnest argument to prove that the mistress is a
far cheaper, more convenient, and agreeable companion than the
wife. Fashionable young ladies in London are reputed to make no
secret that they dress and get themselves generally up after the
pattern of certain more successful sisters, whom it was once accounted a vice to know.[2]

[1] LXXXII, 47-9.   [2] *Ibid.*, p. 40.

(Mrs. Lynn Linton, in a series of extremely successful articles in the *Saturday Review* entitled 'The Girl of the Period', had been saying much the same thing.)[1]

In the same article, MacCarthy also noticed an anonymous novel, *Recommended to Mercy*, about the life of the demi-monde (a subject which seemed quite popular in the sixties). The book itself was not very good, but MacCarthy thoroughly approved of the author's intention:

> The best justification for the adoption of such topics as the ground-work of novels destined for general reading [not just for men, as the *Saturday Review* wanted] assuredly is that women may perhaps be thus redeemed from the possibility of remaining in that imbecile and ignorant condition which the romancist commonly regards as innocence, and which woman is so generally encouraged to cherish as her special virtue, even by those who are so in earnest in describing it as the principal cause of her ruin.[2]

It was during the eighteen-sixties that the question of the subject matter of fiction was most thoroughly debated, because of the rise of the sensational novel, and on the whole, two of the leading weekly reviews, the *Saturday Review* and the *Spectator*, were inclined to allow the novelist a much greater degree of freedom than were the editors of most family magazines and the leading publishers of books. On March 9, 1861, for example, one Saturday reviewer lamented, 'Nothing is more common than to complain that all novels are vapid because they are all alike. . . . Yet when a novelist leaves the beaten track and constructs a romance out of the results of special experience, he is exposed to criticism that he is bringing in things and persons of a kind which ought not to be touched on in fiction.' The moral quality of any work, this reviewer concludes, has nothing to do with an author's subject matter *per se* but 'will depend almost entirely on the mode in which the story is told. . . .'[3] Mrs. Norton's *Lost and Saved*, a novel about adultery in high society, is thus defended in the *Saturday Review* on May 30, 1863. 'These things go on in the world, and although such very plain accounts of adulterous connexions as are given in *Lost and Saved* are not quite the thing for family reading, yet, if that is once understood,

---

[1] Merle M. Bevington, *The Saturday Review, 1855–1868* (New York, 1941), pp. 110–12.

[2] *Westminster Review*, LXXXII (July, 1864), 45.   [3] XI, 248.

it is no use being mealy-mouthed, and Mrs. Norton may call a spade by its name if she pleases.' [1] The author of an article on George Sand, long a *bête noire* to many English reviewers, grants that the English atmosphere of respectability, with all its prohibitions, is 'probably quite right', 'but all people do not submit quite calmly to this control', and as a result they turn 'to a foreign literature in which there is no reticence'. In *Lélia*, George Sand has set forth with the great 'attraction of genuineness and of ardour, both in feeling and expression', her 'sense of pain at the mystery of things. . . . If literature sets itself to record all vivid human feeling, why not these among others?' George Sand, this reviewer recognizes, has many faults: 'She has often written too much, too inconsiderately and too stupidly'—but her choice of subjects is not open to attack. [2]

So eager was the *Saturday Review* to get rid of puritanical restrictions on the novel that it enthusiastically welcomed *Rhoda Fleming*, probably the weakest of all Meredith's early novels, for its 'large and liberal observation of life'. And Meredith's treatment of the seduction of Dahlia and her subsequent refusal to marry Edward Blancove, her seducer, was especially praised because the author neither condemned nor sentimentalized the 'fallen woman'. [3]

One of the strongest protests that the *Saturday Review* printed against the prudery of a large part of the reading public appeared on July 11, 1857, in a review of *Madame Bovary* written by Fitzjames Stephen. *Paradise Lost* and *Othello*, he observed, contain passages 'which could not be read aloud to English ladies', and if it were not from force of habit, the same condition would apply to the Bible. 'Surely it is very questionable', Stephen asserted, 'whether it is desirable that no novels should be written except those fit for young ladies to read.' If the other branches of literature—'theology, history, philosophy, morality, law, and physical science'—are all to be studied 'at the reader's peril', why should 'works of imagination . . . [be considered] such mere toys that they ought always to be calculated for girlish ignorance?' Novelists, in acquiescing in the crippling

---

[1] XV, 701-2. The same permission, with the same proviso, had been granted to Meredith in 1859 (see above, p. 208).

[2] *Saturday Review*, XIV (August 16, 1862), 194.

[3] XX (October 14, 1865), 489.

restrictions placed upon them, seem 'to think that . . . [their] highest function . . . is the amusement of children; but we are by no means prepared to say that, in literature, emasculation produces purity'. But in spite of his attack on current novelistic conventions, Stephen still did not approve of Flaubert's novel. The character of Emma Bovary, he found 'one of the most essentially disgusting that we ever happened to meet with' because the 'notion of duty or responsibility never seems to cross her mind'. The novel itself Stephen declared to be immoral, but not for the reasons usually given or those for which Flaubert had to stand trial in France. *Madame Bovary* is really immoral not because Flaubert gives 'full-length descriptions of vice' but because, except for the last few chapters, 'the author rather sympathizes with his heroine'. He does not hate adultery so much as he shows it has bad consequences. In addition to not disapproving of Flaubert's subject matter, Stephen refused 'to make use of any very indignant expressions. There is no fear that our novelists will outrage public decency. Their weaknesses forbid such dangerous eccentricity quite as much as their virtues.' [1]

But with *Salammbô*, the *Saturday Review* lost the usual *sang froid* it managed to display when faced with French novels. Flaubert was the representative of a school of writers in France who 'think they have an indisputable right to describe whatever exists. No matter how loathsome and repulsive an object may be, it is enough for them to know, or believe, that it either has been or is. Fair or foul, good or bad, it falls equally in the domain of their art.' The length to which Flaubert carried this principle seemed to the reviewer 'positively incompatible with soundness of mind', and *Salammbô* could excite, even in France, no feeling 'but that of unmitigated contempt and disgust'. [2] On February 13, 1864, in an article called 'Novels and Life', the *Saturday* reiterated the same argument, with one very curious exception. Vice cannot be made a subject of interest to people with healthy minds and so should never be treated in a novel; 'immoral subjects', however, *are* permissible if set back in the distant past. [3] An earlier article in the *Saturday Review* asked the novelist not to introduce 'into the pleasant fields of literature, wherein the heart and the imagination seek emotion and recrea-

[1] IV, 40–1. [2] XV (March 7, 1863), 309. [3] XVII, 188–9.

tion, the hideous vices which gangrene society. . . .' [1] But even though the *Saturday Review* was inconsistent on the question of freedom of subject matter, still it was basically a force for liberality.

The *Spectator*, the other leading weekly review, announced rather dramatically in 1862 that English readers 'of sufficient age and moral stability' should read French novels, and that they should realize what 'a rare advantage [it was] to find in a highly civilized age a really *frank* literature. . . .' (One wonders whether this pun was intentional, since humour was not the *Spectator's* forte.) In England the growth of civilization only succeeded in making its literature 'cramped'; 'the fetters of a propriety are laid upon it, which our fathers had not to bear, and which hamper half its movements'. The writer goes on to state as a principle: 'Hardly any part of life can be well comprehended unless it is imaginatively delineated,' and thus Englishmen can learn much more from French literature than their own, since there are almost no restrictions across the Channel. But when the question comes up of sullying the purity of the English novel, the writer is not too sure. 'Divorce and adultery are, perhaps, within the present limits of English art, if treated with rapidity and delicacy, and if admitted to be immoral.' [2]

Griffith Gaunt, which Dickens said he would reject as editor of *All the Year Round*, is a good example of how the *Spectator* thought such matters should be treated. Its 'delicate plainness' and 'reserved simplicity' are apparent even though it 'has of necessity, once or twice, to touch . . . on scenes over which a prurient writer would have gloated. . . .' Reade cannot ignore such scenes since 'they are necessities to his moral', but he 'instantly escapes without a smirch'. [3]

The *Spectator's* very uncertain attitude towards the rules of conventional delicacy in literature was quite apparent in an article of October 20, 1866. A writer can break them, but he must show cause. 'If he is fulfilling an adequate purpose, such as the removal or diminution of human suffering, or obeying some necessity in art, the right of objection drops, but the burden of proof rests upon him, not upon the critics.' The creation of Mistress Quickly, the reviewer continues in explanation, is

[1] I (April 5, 1856), 461. [2] XXXV (September 13, 1862), 1029–30.
[3] XXXIX (October 27, 1866), 1198.

'one proof of Shakespeare's genius. . . .' Her creation was 'not only right, but a bounden duty in the dramatist, and yet . . . her perfection could only have arisen from some base sympathy or regrettable experience in her author'.[1] Here a sense of propriety became inextricably entangled with that widespread English vice, snobbery.

The *Spectator* of March 31, 1866, analysed one of the favourite strategies English writers used to have their cake and eat it, the 'attempt to depict passions which . . . [they] are unwilling to follow out to their natural development', so as not to offend their largest customer, Mudie's library. Phemie Keller, the heroine of a novel by Mrs. Trafford, much praised by serious critics in the sixties, falls in love with her husband's heir and then draws back, yet she expiates the rest of her life for the uncommitted sin. (George Eliot, in the last part of the *Mill on the Floss*, used a very similar theme.) 'If the climax had been what it would have been in a French novel, we could make excuses for the heroine; but a woman who goes to the very verge of sin, and yet is always collected and high-principled enough to resist all attempts . . . cannot command either our respect or our compassion.' The whole point of the Bible story of the woman taken in adultery, this reviewer exclaimed, would have been sacrificed if she had been true to her husband. 'Yet this is what our English passion novelists are always doing.' If adultery is to be treated at all, let us at least have the real thing: 'We are not sure that morality gains by the Platonic character given to . . . [its] development.'[2]

By 1868, the *Spectator* seemed quite certain that 'Illicit love is, of course, a fair subject for both novelist and dramatist, for both novelist and dramatist must alike deal with human passions', and, as we have seen before,[3] Hutton, the editor, complained that Trollope did not allow his heroine, Lady Glencora, an honest illicit love affair, but instead only led her to the brink of adultery.

The predominant attitude of the reviews during the fifties and sixties in regard to so-called proscribed subjects, was not, of course, that of the *Saturday Review* or the *Spectator*; yet surely the extent of the demand for more freedom has not been fully recognized by literary historians. As one looks through Vic-

[1] XXXIX, p. 1171.   [2] *Ibid.*, p. 361.   [3] See above, p. 57.

torian periodicals, he soon discovers that the supposed unanimity on the question of the 'young person' has been very much exaggerated and that the protests against English prudery by no means began in the seventies and eighties with Henry James and George Moore.

There were indeed many foolish and often hysterical outbursts, chiefly against French novels.[1] All French fiction was often lumped together and characterized as 'diseased to its very core'.[2] John Morley in *Macmillan's* was speaking for many of his fellow critics when he said that realism in France is 'only another name for a steady and exclusive devotion to a study of all the meanest or nastiest elements in character and conduct'.[3] For W. K. Gregg, in an essay entitled 'French Fiction: the Lowest Deep', all current French novels conveyed a 'vivid impression' of 'the abandonment of all self-control or self-respect, the surrender of all manliness, dignity, reticence, the hunger after the most diseased, unholy, extravagant excitement. . . .'[4] The novels he was writing about were so bad, he could not even give examples or quotations to prove his point. There were, however, many protests against this critical hysteria. G. H. Lewes, for example, in the *Leader* of December 31, 1853, complained of 'the stupid cant about French novels—a cant which extends to all the reprobation deserved only by a few'.[5] According to the author of 'Balzac and His Writing',[6] the English seemed to care for 'nothing more elevated than Eugène Sue, or more decent than Paul de Kock',[7] since there were so many of their works translated. As a matter of fact the popularity of French novelists appeared to be in inverse proportion to their merit: very few of George Sand's works were translated, only two of Mérimée's and not one of Balzac's. A later essay, 'The

[1] Since this phase of Victorian criticism has been the one most fully studied heretofore in works like *The Victorian Conscience* by Clarence Decker, *The Fortunes of Victor Hugo in England* by Kenneth Hooker, and 'Flaubert in English Criticism' by Desmond Pacey, it will not be necessary in this study to repeat that material.

[2] *Edinburgh Review*, CI (January, 1855), 115.

[3] XIV (August, 1866), 276.

[4] *National Review*, XI (October, 1860), 400 (reprinted in *Literary and Social Judgements* [Boston, 1873]).

[5] IV, 1265.   [6] See above, p. 148.

[7] *Westminster Review*, LX (July, 1853), 201.

Life and Writing of Stendhal', complained of the unmerited neglect of another fine French novelist, Henri Beyle.[1]

Hutton, writing on George Sand in the *National Review*, tried to account for the hostility shown to French fiction in England as objectively as he could:

> We cannot judge by their standard, or feel with their feelings. There are whole portions of thought in which our minds run in an entirely distinct channel. More especially with regard to those two cardinal points of human society, religion and the relations of the sexes, we seem to think with irreconcilable difference—our right is not their right, nor their wrong our wrong. . . . We talk as if the whole of French fiction was a vast mass of corruption. . . . What we call licence, they think the honest obedience to a divine passion. What we consider delicacy, they consider the affectation of prudery.[2]

And the language of George Sand's novels which Englishmen would call 'coarse', the French call 'plainspoken'. 'They call a spade a spade,' and even more horrifying for the English is the fact that the French 'do not distinguish between the passions, and speak of the physical symptoms and issues of love as they would of those of fear'.[3]

Comparing French and English novels in their ability to hold the reader's interest, the author of 'English Novels' in *Fraser's*, October, 1851, finds the French decidedly superior: 'Whatever sins against taste or morality may be chargeable upon French novels, it cannot be denied that they possess in a high degree the power of fascinating the attention.' Of course, if the critic were forced 'to make a choice between prosy decent books, and vicious books that are written with sprightliness and skill', he is bound to prefer the former. 'But we cannot help regretting at the same time, that our English novelists, who, for the most part, write unexceptionable morality, should not be able to make it a little more amusing.' In the end, however, the interest of French fiction almost becomes a function of its immorality or, as this critic calls it, 'the almost unbounded latitude allowed the French novelist. . . .' Opposed to this freedom are the

[1] *Edinburgh Review*, CIII (January, 1856), 203–34.

[2] VI (January, 1858), 37. For the attribution of this essay to Hutton see *Love-Letters of Walter Bagehot and Eliza Wilson*, ed. Mrs. Russell Barrington (London, 1933), p. 97.

[3] *National Review*, VI (January, 1858), 54.

'restraints and prejudices of our state of society' which seem to prevent the English novel from being 'made a pleasanter and more enjoyable book than it is'.[1]

Some critics, however, were not too certain of the 'purity' of the English novel. As we have already seen, a writer in *Blackwood's* in 1867 complained that since the publication of the Brontë novels, fiction had been too much concerned with 'noxious topics',[2] and seven years before that an essay in *Fraser's* complained that British fiction was being ruined by 'the tendency of the present age towards investigation, the determination at all hazards to call a spade a spade [it is remarkable how frightened many Victorians were of shovels], to *ventilate* every question thoroughly. . . .' Because of the intrusion of the scientific spirit into literature—we must remember that this essay followed shortly on the publication of *The Origin of Species*—'We are losing, if not modesty, at least refinement; not so much refinement of expression, though that is often wanting, but refinement of thought and mind. The faults of the French school are creeping into our literature, and threaten to flourish there.' [3]

Every important novelist of the period, as we have seen in the course of this study, was attacked, most novelists more than once, for lowering the standard of 'purity' of the English novel: Dickens and Bulwer for their treatment of crime and extra-marital unions; Thackeray for his fondness in general for 'unpleasant' subjects, especially the suggestion of incest in *Henry Esmond*; Mrs. Gaskell for dealing with such social questions as the plight of the unmarried mother in *Ruth*, prostitution in *Mary Barton*, and the condition of the Manchester factory hands in both *North and South* and *Mary Barton*; and George Eliot for allowing Maggie Tulliver to run off with Stephen Guest, and for her portrayal of the seduction of Hetty Sorrel. Even the Reverend Charles Kingsley, chaplain to Queen Victoria, who avowedly wrote didactic and improving novels that were always in danger of becoming tracts, had several of his novels branded as immoral. *Blackwood's*, for instance, found that the plot of *Yeast*, in which the daughter of a landowner falls in love with her father's gamekeeper, was 'really a little too much; for, if

[1] XLIV, 375. [2] See above, p. 191.
[3] LXII (August, 1860), 210.

we consider it rightly, it implies an entire departure from the modesty of woman, not to say a depraved instinct'. It almost sounds as if Kingsley had written *Lady Chatterley's Lover*, even though his heroine dies before anything 'dangerous' could happen. 'Such things, doubtless, have taken place, but they are not to be mentioned with honour, or judged with leniency; and we cannot help thinking that the writer who unnecessarily brings forward such aberrations, and who treats them as if society were at fault in not recognizing unions of that kind, ought to be treated with severest censure.' [1] This review makes very clear how close was the relationship in the mid-nineteenth century between political conservatism, snobbery, and literary prudery (and it also shows how right was Lawrence's instinct in choosing the same subject as the *donnée* for his most revolutionary novel).

All the more important critics of fiction during this period by no means agreed with the *Blackwood's* reviewer who wanted novels free from 'the darker problems of the time' because they were 'the favourite reading matter of women, children, and invalids'.[2] David Masson, answering the often repeated charge that Fielding and Smollett were immoral and indecent writers, asserted, 'There are, doubtless, passages in them which we should not like to see read by "young ladies in white muslin", and this is a pity. But, if the test of endurable literature were that it should always and in every part be fit to be read, or to be fancied as read, by young ladies in white muslin, what a bonfire of books there would have to be. . . .' [3]

John Skelton, one of the chief critics of *Fraser's*, writing under his usual pseudonym of 'Shirley', in May, 1857, vehemently defended the morality of *Jane Eyre*: 'It speaks freely of many questionable matters on which our sanctimonious society closes its eyes or passes by on the other side; and it exhibits a freedom and latitude in discussing difficult questions which have struck many pious souls with consternation.' And he asks very rhetorically: 'Why should not holy hypocrisy be unmasked and scarified? Why should not the struggle between virtue and vice be chronicled? Why should it not be said—She was tempted and she overcome; nay, even—She was tempted, and she fell?' Concerning the charge made by 'austere critics' that the interest of

[1] LXXVII (June, 1855), 629. [2] See above, p. 191.
[3] *British Novelists and Their Styles* (Cambridge, 1859), p. 134.

the Brontë novels depended on 'the terrible and the immoral, two elements which cannot be rightly appropriated by fiction', Skelton asks, 'Why not?' and answers, 'The old dramatists, at least, did not judge so; and the result was that they evoked "high passions and high actions" which stir our hearts to the core.' Where in modern literature 'with its guarded touch and surface propriety' shall we find the same kind of appeal 'to our deepest feelings' that we find in the Elizabethan drama?[1] Nassau Senior made a very similar comment in the *North British Review* in August, 1855, on the attacks against the subject matter of Bulwer's novels of the thirties and forties. Evil, crime, and vice are the necessary subject matter of 'serious fiction', and they must arise from 'human wickedness or folly'. Any branch of literature which avoids such subjects inevitably becomes superficial. Hence, Senior explained, he refused to 'join in the outcry which has been raised against "Lucretia" as a tale of crime'.[2]

Some of the most interesting discussions of just how far the writer may go in his treatment of evil and human depravity appeared in criticisms of *Wuthering Heights*. Charlotte Brontë raised the question in her preface to the second edition but refused to answer it: Emily followed the dictates of her inspiration and that was all there was to it. Sydney Dobell, however, in almost the only appreciative notice of the novel in the early fifties, although he admitted the conception of Heathcliff was 'wonderfully strong and original', declared that Emily Brontë had overstepped the limits of art since she 'has too often disgusted, where she should have terrified, and has allowed us a familiarity with her fiend which has ended in unequivocal contempt'.[3] After Mrs. Gaskell's *Life of Charlotte Brontë* appeared in 1857, *Wuthering Heights* received its first really widespread critical attention in the English periodical press, and one can, in reading discussions of the book, see the dilemma many critics were in: they strongly admired the power and language of the novel and yet they had very definite ideas about the treatment of evil in literature. Thus W. C. Roscoe, in the *National Review*, declared that 'in force of genius, in the power of conceiving and

[1] LV, 577–8.
[2] XXIII, 365 (reprinted in *Essays in Fiction* [London, 1864]).
[3] *The Life and Letters of Sydney Dobell*, ed. 'E' (London, 1878), I, 170.

uttering intensity of passion', Emily Brontë surpasses her more
famous sister, and so almost every contemporary novelist.
'But', he insisted, 'it is idle to deny the book is revolting. . . .
The author drives her plough through the worst recesses of
human nature. . . .' He especially instances the narrator's
dream of rubbing the wrists of a child against the broken
windowpane. 'Art throws aside her prerogative to dwell on
beautiful and hint at hideous things. . . .' [1]

Peter Bayne also admired in the book 'evidence of powers it
were perhaps impossible to estimate, and mental wealth which
we might vainly attempt to compute'. But again, in spite of the
'tremendous strength and maturity of the style' and the 'ability
to conceive and depict, with a strength so unwavering and
clearness so vivid, that wild group of characters', 'true tastes and
natural instincts', expressing themselves in 'canons of art sound
and imperative', 'unite in pronouncing it [*Wuthering Heights*]
unquestionably and irremediably monstrous'. The whole atmosphere of the novel is 'distempered, disturbed, and unnatural'. [2]
John Skelton was one of the very few who did not seem to be
revolted or frightened by the uncompromising rigour of Emily
Brontë's imagination. Although every other critic clearly preferred Charlotte's novels, Skelton was alive to the complexity of
Emily's genius. In *Wuthering Heights* we meet 'with more subtle
diversities of character than we do in any of them [Charlotte's
novels]. Charlotte Brontë's heroes are all broad and emphatic;
marked types not delicate suggestions . . . no attempt is made
to explain conflicting motives, to assimilate complex passions.
There is a certain immobility and hardness in the outline.'
After explaining just how 'subtly conceived' is the figure of
Cathy, with her 'fire, and tenderness, and vanity, and perversity, and the untutored grace of her free moorland nature',
Skelton remarks on the 'richness and affluence of poetic life in
which Emily invests the creations of her brain, . . . [the] deli-
cacies and subtleties of insight' which are 'all the more striking,
from the grave, sombre, and resolutely homely form in which the
tale is narrated. She may describe abnormal characters; but whatever they are, she describes them with startling genuineness.' [3]

[1] V (July, 1857), 134–5 (reprinted in *Poems and Essays* [London, 1860], II).
[2] *Essays in Biography and Criticism, First Series* (Boston, 1857), 398–400.
[3] *Fraser's*, LV (May, 1857), 574–5.

Fraser's mentioned *Wuthering Heights* again in July, 1859, in an article called 'Thoughts on Modern English Literature'. *Jane Eyre* was 'the *best novel* of our century', and the only novel equal in power is *Wuthering Heights,* which 'considering its authorship . . . [is] the greatest intellectual prodigy the world has ever seen'. Even though it is 'a fearful picture', it is a great book because the picture is 'drawn with a deep miraculous knowledge of the human heart'.[1] *Blackwood's* called *Wuthering Heights* 'the nearest approach that has been made in our time to the pitiless fatality which is the dominant idea of Greek tragedy'.[2] Thus there were literary qualities much more important than pleasantness, and the question of *Wuthering Heights* presented a powerful challenge to prevailing criticism to examine many of its long-accepted premises. The characters of that novel were much more relentless than any the reviewers knew in everyday experience and the action was hardly what they would call 'realistic'; yet the book had something that many of the novels of the century lacked.

Another major critical stumbling block was *Wilhelm Meister.* The work was translated by Carlyle, and Goethe, as interpreted by Carlyle, was supposed to be one of the great moral teachers of the century; yet the hero of the novel had at least one illegitimate child and a succession of mistresses, not to mention the fact that Goethe also treated the incest motif, so dear to the romantic movement. Here was the case of *Tom Jones* or *Roderick Random* all over again. As a result, G. H. Lewes, in his *Life of Goethe,* first published in 1856, felt himself forced to defend the morality of *Wilhelm Meister*:

All that can be said is that the Artist has been content to paint scenes of life, *without comment*; and that some of these scenes belong to an extensive class of subjects, familiar indeed to the experience of all but children, yet by general consent not much talked of in society. If any reader can be morally injured by reading such scenes in the novel rather than in the newspaper, his moral constitution is so alarmingly delicate . . . that he is truly pitiable. Let us hope the world is peopled by robuster natures. . . .[3]

The *Wahlverwandtschaften* also received its share of moralistic criticism, since it dealt with the theme of love in conflict with

[1] LX, 102.   [2] LXXXII (July, 1857), 90.
[3] (Leipsig, 1864), II, 157.

marriage, a theme common to many of the great nineteenth-century novels: for example, *Anna Karenina*, *Madame Bovary*, and *Middlemarch*. Lewes defended Goethe's choice of subject and treatment by declaring that those who 'look at life as it *is*, and not as it ought to be, and demand that Art should represent reality—consider this situation as terribly true, and although tragic, by no means immoral'. Since Goethe as an objective novelist set as his aim the delineation of human life, the avoidance of such subjects would considerably impoverish his created world.[1] An essay on 'The Morality of Wilhelm Meister', probably by Lewes, originally appearing in the *Leader* and later reprinted in an American edition of George Eliot's essays, declared that the true morality of Goethe's novels lay in 'his large tolerance', his ability to comprehend so much of life. '. . . The sphere of art extends wherever there is beauty either in form, or thought, or feeling.'[2] Hence the usual proscriptions of subject matter have nothing to do with true aesthetic principles.

Most of the important mid-Victorian novelists and many of the critics of novels would have agreed with Henry James' advice to the young writer of fiction:

All life belongs to you, and do not listen either to those who would shut you up into corners of it, and tell you that it is only here and there that art inhabits. . . . There is no impression of life, no manner of seeing and feeling it, to which the plan of the novelist may not offer a place; you have only to remember that talents so dissimilar as those of Alexandre Dumas and Jane Austen, Charles Dickens and Gustave Flaubert have worked in this field with equal glory. . . . Remember that your first duty is to be as complete as possible—to make as perfect a work.[3]

It seems fitting to end a study of mid-Victorian theory of the novel with James' 'The Art of Fiction', a classical critical document which seems to grow so clearly from the chief preoccupations of the critical discussions of this period. It also seems very right that James opposed Walter Besant's foolish attempt to codify and so make rigid the very flexible and sug-

[1] *Life of Goethe*, II, 273.
[2] *Essays and Uncollected Papers* (Boston and New York, 1908), pp. 308-9.
[3] *Op. cit.*, pp. 407-8.

gestive principles set forth in the three preceding decades. As Delacroix wrote in his journal with reference to his own attempt to construct a systematic exposition of his theory of painting:

> If a man of talent wishes to write down his thoughts on the arts, he had better express them in the order in which they come to him. He should not be afraid of contradicting himself; there is more fruit to be harvested from a rich profusion of ideas, however contradictory, than from the neat, constricted, clipped pattern of a work in which a writer has concentrated upon the form.[1]

Here, if anywhere, we have the clearest answer to those who would characterize the mid-nineteenth century, in its criticism of the novel, as a wasteland, because it produced no systematic treatise on the art of fiction, of the sort that Percy Lubbock wrote. But, as we have seen, there was, during this period, a very full discussion of the purpose of fiction, in which every important novelist felt called upon to assert the dignity of his chosen form. Each in turn from Bulwer to Meredith clearly distinguished between art and entertainment on the one hand and art and didacticism on the other. From Bulwer's 'Art in Fiction' of 1838 to James' 'Art of Fiction' in 1885, a common theme runs through every important discussion of the novel form: the novel is a serious work of art, and reader and novelist should consider it as important as, if not more important than, any other literary genre. The important technical problems specifically concerning the novel as such—the author's position in regard to his own work, point of view, the dramatic presentation of character and scene in a work predominantly narrative, structure and unity—were all rather fully treated during the years 1850–70. These discussions, many of which Henry James certainly read, since the James family were ardent readers of the English periodical press during this period,[2] gave the young Henry James, together with his reading of French novels and criticism, a firm basis from which to construct his own critical position, which so decisively influenced the novel of the twentieth century.

[1] *The Journal of Eugène Delacroix*, trans. Lucy Norton (London, 1951), p. 165.
[2] Leon Edel, *Henry James, The Untried Years* (Philadelphia and New York, 1953), pp. 91, 150, 157, 213, and *passim*.

James' position as the major theorist of the novel remains unique. Nevertheless, many of his statements were anticipated by earlier critics and novelists, and by tracing the English background of his theories, we are better able to evaluate him as the most important link in the history of what he called 'the great form', from his Victorian past to the present.

BIBLIOGRAPHY

I. GENERAL WORKS ON THE HISTORY OF THE NOVEL AND NOVEL CRITICISM

ALLEN, WALTER. *The English Novel, A Short Critical History*. New York: Dutton, 1955.

AUERBACH, ERICH. *Mimesis; The Representation of Reality in Western Literature*, tr. Willard R. Trask. Princeton: Princeton University Press, 1953.

BAKER, ERNEST A. *The History of the English Novel*. 10 vols. London: Witherby, 1924–39.

BLANCHARD, FREDERICK T. *Fielding the Novelist; A Study in Historical Criticism*. New Haven: Yale University Press, 1926.

BOEGE, FRED W. *Smollett's Reputation as a Novelist*. Princeton: Princeton University Press, 1947.

CROSS, WILBUR. *The Development of the English Novel*. New York: Macmillan, 1923.

DAVIS, ROBERT GORHAM. 'The Sense of the Real in English Fiction', *Comparative Literature*, III (Summer, 1951), 200–17.

DEVONSHIRE, M. G. *The English Novel in France*. London: University of London Press, 1929.

FORD, FORD MADOX. *The English from the Earliest Days to the Death of Joseph Conrad*. London: Constable, 1930.

HILLHOUSE, JAMES T. *The Waverley Novels and Their Critics*. Minneapolis: University of Minnesota Press, 1936.

HOOKER, KENNETH WARD. *The Fortunes of Victor Hugo in England*. New York: Columbia University Press, 1938.

LEAVIS, F. R. *The Great Tradition*. New York: Doubleday Anchor Books, 1954.

LEAVIS, Q. D. *Fiction and the Reading Public*. London: Chatto and Windus, 1932.

LEVIN, HARRY. 'What Is Realism?' *Comparative Literature*, III (Summer, 1951), 193–9.

MACDOWALL, ARTHUR. *Realism: A Study in Art and Thought*. London: Constable, 1908.

SAINTSBURY, GEORGE. *A History of English Criticism.* Edinburgh and London: William Blackwood and Sons, 1949.

WASHBURN, CAROLYN. 'The History, from 1832 to 1860, of British Criticism of Narrative Prose Fiction.' Unpublished Ph.D. dissertation, University of Illinois, Urbana, Illinois, 1937.

WEINBERG, BERNARD. *French Realism: The Critical Reaction 1830–1870.* Chicago: The Modern Language Association of America, 1937.

2. BACKGROUND. MATERIAL BEFORE 1850

ABRAMS, MEYER H. *The Mirror and the Lamp: Romantic Theory and the Critical Tradition.* New York: Oxford University Press, 1953.

BARBAULD, LAETITIA. 'An Essay on the Origin and Progress of Novel-Writing'. *The British Novelists,* Vol. I. London: Rivington, 1810.

BEATTIE, JAMES. 'On Fable and Romance', *Dissertations, Moral and Critical,* Vol. II. Dublin: Exshaw, Walker, Bently . . ., 1783.

BISSELL, FREDERICK OLDS. *Fielding's Theory of the Novel.* Ithaca: Cornell University Press, 1933.

CARLYLE, THOMAS. *Thomas Carlyle's Works.* Ashburton Edition. 20 vols. London: Chapman and Hall, 1885–8.

CAZAMIAN, LOUIS. *Le Roman social en Angleterre, 1830–1850.* Paris: Librairie George Bellais, 1904.

'Charles Chesterfield', *The Athenaeum,* September 25, 1841, p. 740.

[DE QUINCEY, THOMAS]. 'Forster's Life of Goldsmith', *North British Review,* IX (May, 1848), 187–251.

DUNLOP, JOHN C. *The History of Fiction.* 2 vols. Philadelphia: Carey and Hart, 1842.

FIELDING, HENRY. *Joseph Andrews.* New York: Century, 1906.

—— *Tom Jones.* New York: The Modern Library, 1943.

GIBSON, BYRON HALL. 'The History from 1800 to 1832 of English Criticism of Prose Fiction.' Unpublished Ph.D. dissertation, University of Illinois, Urbana, Illinois, 1931.

GUNNELL, DORIS. *Stendhal et l'Angleterre.* Paris: Bouvalet-Jouve, 1908.

[HAZLITT, WILLIAM]. 'The History of Fiction', *Edinburgh Review,* XXIV (November, 1814), 38–58.

—— *Lectures on the English Comic Writers.* Philadelphia: Carey, 1819.

—— 'Standard Novels and Romances', *Edinburgh Review,* XXIV (February, 1815), 320–32.

HEIDLER, JOSEPH B. *The History, from 1700 to 1800, of English Criticism of Prose Fiction.* University of Illinois Studies in Language and Literature, Vol. XII, No. 2. Urbana: University of Illinois, 1928.

HILDYARD, M. CLIVE, ed. *Lockhart's Literary Criticism.* Oxford: Basil Blackwell, 1921.

HORNE, RICHARD HENGIST. *A New Spirit of the Age.* The World's Classics. London: Oxford University Press, 1907.

HOWE, SUSANNE. *Wilhelm Meister and His English Kinsmen.* New York: Columbia University Press, 1930.

HUET, PIERRE. *A History of Romances, An Inquiry into Their Original; Instructions for Composing Them* . . ., tr. Stephen Lewis. London: J. Hooke and T. Caldecott, 1715.

JEFFREY, FRANCIS. *Contributions to the Edinburgh Review.* 4 vols. London: Longmans, Brown, Green and Longmans, 1844.

JOHNSON, R. BRIMLEY, ed. *Novelists on Novels.* London: Noel Douglas, n.d.

MCKILLOP, ALAN DUGALD. *The Early Masters of English Fiction.* Lawrence: University of Kansas Press, 1956.

A. A. MENDILOW. *Time and the Novel.* London: Peter Nevill, 1952.

MILL, JOHN STUART. 'Thoughts on Poetry and Its Varieties', *English Critical Essays (Nineteenth Century).* The World's Classics. London: Oxford University Press, 1947.

MOORE, JOHN. 'A View of the Commencement and Progress of Romance', *The Works of John Moore, M.D.,* ed. Robert Anderson, Vol. V. Edinburgh: Stirling and Slade, 1820.

PATTERSON, CHARLES I. 'Coleridge's Conception of Dramatic Illusion in the Novel', *ELH,* XVIII (June, 1951), 123–37.

—— 'De Quincey's Conception of the Novel as Literature of Power', *PMLA,* LXX (June, 1955), 375–89.

QUINLAN, MAURICE. *Victorian Prelude: A History of English Manners, 1700–1830.* New York: Columbia University Press, 1941.

REYNOLDS, SIR JOSHUA. *Discourses on Art.* Chicago: Packard, 1945.

SCOTT, SIR WALTER. *Introductions to the Waverley Novels.* 3 vols. Edinburgh: Robert Cadell, 1833.

—— *Miscellaneous Prose Works.* 6 vols. Boston: Wells and Lily, 1829.

TAYLOR, HOUGHTON W. 'Modern Fiction and the Doctrine of Uniformity', *PQ,* XIX (July, 1940), 225–36.

—— ' "Particular Character": An Early Phase of a Literary Evolution'. *PMLA,* LX (March, 1945), 161–74.

TAYLOR, JOHN TINNON. *Early Opposition to the Novel (1760–1830).* New York: King's Crown Press, 1943.

THRALL, MIRIAM. *Rebellious Fraser's: Nol Yorke's Magazine in the Days of Maginn, Thackeray, and Carlyle.* New York: Columbia University Press, 1934.

TIEJE, A. J. *The Theory of Characterization in Prose Fiction Prior to 1740.* Studies in Language and Literature, No. 5. Minneapolis: University of Minnesota, 1916.

TILLOTSON, KATHLEEN. *Novels of the Eighteen-Forties.* Oxford: Clarendon Press, 1954.

WATT, IAN. *The Rise of the Novel; Studies in Defoe, Richardson, and Fielding.* London: Chatto and Windus, 1957.

WELLEK, RENÉ. *A History of Modern Criticism: 1750–1950,* Vols. 1 and 2. New Haven: Yale University Press, 1955.

3a. 1850–1870. PERIODICALS

(Articles in this section are listed by periodical. In the cases of weekly reviews, I have not attempted to list articles separately, except for those of exceptional importance to my subject. To do so would have made this bibliography too long.)

BIBLIOGRAPHY

All the Year Round (Successor to *Household Words*), Vols. I–XXIV (1859–1870), *passim*. See especially:
'The Sensational Williams.' XI (February 13, 1864), 14–17.
'The Spirit of Fiction.' XVIII (July 27, 1867), 118–20.

The Athenaeum

Nos. 1158–2253 (1850–1870), *passim*.

Bentley's Miscellany

'Of Novels, Historical and Didactic.' XLVI (1859), 42–51, 135–47.

Bentley's Quarterly Review

'Novels by Sir Edward Bulwer Lytton.' I (March, 1859), 73–105.
'Adam Bede and Recent Novels.' I (July, 1859), 433–72.
'George Sand.' II (January, 1860), 369–403.

Blackwood's Edinburgh Magazine

'Alton Locke.' LXVIII (November, 1850), 592–610.
'Mr. Thackeray and His Works.' LXXVII (January, 1855), 86–96.
'Bulwer.' LXXVII (February, 1855), 221–33.
'Charles Dickens.' LXXVII (April, 1855), 451–66.
'Modern Novelists—Great and Small.' LXXVII (May, 1855), 554–68.
'The Rev. Charles Kingsley.' LXXVII (June, 1855), 621–43.
'Remonstrance with Dickens.' LXXXI (April, 1857), 490–503.
'Currer Bell.' LXXXII (July, 1857), 77–94.
'The Novels of Jane Austen.' LXXXVI (July, 1859), 99–113 [George Henry Lewes].
'A Word about *Tom Jones*.' LXXXVII (March, 1860), 331–41 [George Henry Lewes].
'The Mill on the Floss.' LXXXVII (May, 1860), 611–23.
'The Works of Charles Lever.' XCI (April, 1862), 452–72 [Robert Lytton].
'Sensation Novels.' XCI (May, 1862), 564–85.
'Caxtoniana; A Series of Essays on Life, Literature and Manners.' XCII (August, 1862), 163–71 [Bulwer-Lytton].
'Mr. Thomas Trollope's Italian Novels.' XCIII (January, 1863), 84–98.
'Caxtoniana; A Series of Essays on Life, Literature, and Manners.' XCIII (May, 1863), 545–60 [Bulwer-Lytton].
'Novels.' CII (September, 1867), 257–80.

British Quarterly Review

'Hypatia.' XVIII (August, 1853), 123–70.
'Kingsley's *Two Years Ago*.' XXV (April, 1857), 399–420.
'Novels and Novelists.' XXX (October, 1859), 443–69.
'The Works of Charles Dickens.' XXXV (January, 1862), 135–59.
'*Romola*.' XXXVIII (October, 1863), 448–65.
'Lawrence Sterne.' XL (July, 1865), 152–74.
'The Author of *John Halifax*.' XLIV (July, 1866), 32–58.

'George Eliot.' XLV (January, 1867), 141–78.
'The Works of Mrs. Gaskell.' XLV (April, 1867), 399–429.
'Works by George MacDonald.' XLVII (January, 1868), 1–34.
'Nicholas Gogol.' XLVII (April, 1868), 327–45 [C. E. Turner].
'Works by Mrs. Oliphant.' XLIX (April, 1869), 301–29.
'*He Knew He Was Right.*' L (July, 1869), 263–4.
'Works by Ivan Serguevitch Tourgéneff.' L (October, 1869), 423–47 [C. E. Turner].

Cornhill Magazine

'In Memoriam.' IX (February, 1864), 129–34. Charles Dickens.
'Sentimentalism.' X (July, 1864), 65–75 [Sir James Fitzjames Stephen].
'Richardson's Novels.' XVII (January, 1868), 48–69 [Leslie Stephen].
'Defoe's Novels.' XVII (March, 1868), 293–316 [Leslie Stephen].
'Hours in a Library. No. III.—Some Words about Sir Walter Scott.' XXIV (September, 1871), 278–93 [Leslie Stephen].
'Hours in a Library. No. VI.—Nathaniel Hawthorne.' XXVI (December, 1872), 714–34 [Leslie Stephen].
'The Late Lord Lytton as a Novelist.' XXVII (March, 1873), 345–54 [Leslie Stephen].
'Art and Morality.' XXXII (July, 1875), 91–101 [Leslie Stephen].
'Hours in a Library. No. XIV.—Fielding's Novels.' XXXV (February, 1877), 154–71 [Leslie Stephen].
'Hours in a Library. No. XVII.—Charlotte Brontë.' XXXVI (December, 1877), 723–39 [Leslie Stephen].
'Hours in a Library. No. XXII.—Sterne.' XLII (July, 1880), 86–106 [Leslie Stephen].
'The Moral Element in Literature.' XLIII (January, 1881), 34–50 [Leslie Stephen].

Dublin Review

'Novel-Morality.' XXXIV (March, 1853), 174–202.

Edinburgh Review

'Shirley.' XCI (January, 1850), 153–72 [George Henry Lewes].
'Recent Classical Romances.' XCII (October, 1850), 468–91.
'Traits of the Irish Peasantry.' XCVI (October, 1852), 384–403.
'Recent Novels: *Agatha's Husband.*' XCVII (April, 1853), 380–90.
'Thackeray's Works.' XCIX (January, 1854), 196–243 [Nassau Senior].
'Modern French Literature.' CI (January, 1855), 92–120.
'The Life and Writings of Stendhal.' CIII (January, 1856), 203–34.
'The Licence of Modern Novelists.' CVI (July, 1857), 124–56 [Sir James Fitzjames Stephen].
'*Guy Livingstone.*' CVIII (October, 1858), 532–40 [Sir James Fitzjames Stephen].
'*Adam Bede.*' CX (July, 1859), 234–46.
'The Virginians.' CX (October, 1859), 438–53.
'Felix Holt.' CXXIV (October, 1866), 435–49.

BIBLIOGRAPHY

Fortnightly Review

'Causerie' and 'Varia'. Vols. I–VI (May 15, 1865–December 1, 1866), *passim*. George Henry Lewes.

'Criticism in Relation to Novels.' III (December 15, 1865), 352–61. George Henry Lewes.

'Victor Hugo's New Novel.' V (May 15, 1866), 30–46. George Henry Lewes.

'Immorality in Authorship.' VI (September 15, 1866), 289–300. Robert Buchanan.

'Mr. Anthony Trollope's Novels.' XI (February 1, 1869), 188–98. J. Herbert Stack.

'Richardson, as Artist and Moralist.' XII (October 1, 1869), 428–43. H. Buxton Forman.

'Dickens in Relation to Criticism.' XVII (February 1, 1872), 141–54. George Henry Lewes.

Fraser's Magazine

'Recent Novels: French and English.' XXXVI (December, 1847), 686–695 [George Henry Lewes].

'Sir E. B. Lytton and Mrs. Grundy.' XLI (January, 1850), 98–111.

'A Triad of Novels.' XLII (November, 1850), 574–90.

'Charles Dickens and *David Copperfield*.' XLII (December, 1850), 698–710.

'W. M. Thackeray and Arthur Pendennis, Esquires.' XLIII (January, 1851), 75–90.

'English Novels.' XLIV (October, 1851), 375–91.

'New Novels.' XLVI (December, 1852), 622–36.

'*Heartsease*.' L (November, 1854), 489–503.

'The Art of Story Telling.' LIII (January, 1856), 722–32.

'*Tristram Shandy* or *The Caxtons?*' LIII (March, 1856), 253–7.

'On the Treatment of Love in Novels.' LIII (April, 1856), 405–18.

'Literary Style.' LV (March, 1857), 249–64.

'Charlotte Brontë.' LV (May, 1857), 569–82 [John Skelton].

'On the Life and Writings of Henry Fielding.' LVII (February, 1858), 205–17. Thomas Keightly.

'Thoughts on Modern English Literature.' LX (July, 1859), 97–110. 'H.'

'British Novelists—Richardson, Miss Austen and Scott.' LXI (January, 1860), 20–38.

'Novels of the Day: Their Writers and Readers.' LXII (August, 1860), 205–18. 'M—M.'

'The Popular Novels of the Year.' LXVIII (August, 1863), 253–69.

'Mr. Thackeray.' LXIX (April, 1864), 401–18.

'Fiction and Its Uses.' LXII (December, 1865), 746–60. 'Decem.'

'A Spanish and a Danish Novel.' LXVI (August, 1867), 190–202.

'Victor Hugo's *L'Homme qui rit*.' LXXX (December, 1869), 798–805.

Gentlemen's Magazine

'The Novels of M. Alexandre Dumas.' CXCVI (September, 1854), 230–4.

Household Words

Vols. I–XVIII (1850–1858), *passim*. See especially:
'Old Lamps for New Ones.' I (June 15, 1850), 265–7.
'A Curious Misprint in the *Edinburgh Review*.' XVI (August 1, 1857), 97–100.
'An Idea of Mine.' XVII (March 13, 1858), 289–91.

Leader

Vols. IV, V, VII, and VIII, *passim*. See especially:
'*Ruth*.' IV (January 23, 1853), 89–90 [George Henry Lewes].
'Two Novels.' IV (July 23, 1853), 739–40 [George Henry Lewes].
'*Hide and Seek*.' V (June 24, 1854), 591–3 [George Henry Lewes].
'*The Shaving of Shagpat*.' VII (January 5, 1856), 15–17 [George Eliot].
'*Rachel Gray*.' VII (January 5, 1856), 19 [George Eliot].
'Imaginative Artists.' VII (June 7, 1856), 545–6 [George Henry Lewes].
'Charles Reade's New Novel.' VII (August 23, 1856), 809–10 [George Henry Lewes].
'*Kathie Brand*.' VII (November 15, 1856), 1097 [George Henry Lewes].
'*The Mildmays*.' VIII (January 3, 1857), 18–19 [George Henry Lewes].

Macmillan's Magazine

'To Novelists—And a Novelist.' III (April, 1861), 441–8.
'*Elsie Venner* and *Silas Marner*.' IV (August, 1861), 305–8. J. M. Ludlow.
'Thackeray.' IX (February, 1864), 356–63. Henry Kingsley.
'Thackeray.' IX (February, 1864), 363–8. David Masson.
'Recent Novel Writing.' XIII (January, 1866), 202–9. Thomas Arnold.
'Penny Novels.' XIV (June, 1866), 96–105.
'George Eliot.' XIV (August, 1866), 272–7. John Morley.

National Review

'The Novels and Poems of the Rev. Charles Kingsley.' I (July, 1855), 124–61.
'A Novel or Two.' I (October, 1855), 336–50 [Walter Bagehot].
'W. M. Thackeray, Artist and Moralist.' II (January, 1856), 177–213 [William Caldwell Roscoe].
'The Hard Church Novel.' III (July, 1856), 127–46 [Richard Holt Hutton].
'Aurora Leigh.' IV (April, 1857), 239–67.
'Miss Brontë.' V (July, 1857), 127–64 [William Caldwell Roscoe].
'George Sand.' VI (April, 1858), 37–68 [Richard Holt Hutton].
'The Waverley Novels.' VI (April, 1858), 442–72 [Walter Bagehot].
'Mr. Trollope's Novels.' VII (October, 1858), 415–35.
'The False Morality of Lady Novelists.' VIII (January, 1859), 144–67 [William Rathbone Gregg].
'Sir E. B. Lytton, Novelist, Philosopher, and Poet.' VIII (April, 1859), 279–313 [William Caldwell Roscoe].
'Peasant Life in Russia.' VIII (April, 1859), 469–87.

'Mr. Kingsley's Literary Excesses.' X (January, 1860), 1–24.
'The Novels of George Eliot.' XI (April, 1860), 191–219 [Walter Bagehot].
'French Fiction: The Lowest Deep.' XI (October, 1860), 400–27 [William Rathbone Gregg].
'Nathaniel Hawthorne.' XI (October, 1860), 453–81 [Richard Holt Hutton].
'*Martin Chuzzlewit*.' XIII (July, 1861), 130–50.
'Mr. Charles Reade's Novels: *The Cloister and the Hearth*.' XIV (January, 1862), 134–49.
'*Orley Farm*.' XVI (January, 1863), 27–40.
'*The Chronicles of Carlingford*.' XVI (April, 1863), 350–62.
'Distortions of the English Stage: *Macbeth*.' XVII (October, 1863), 292–322.
'Sterne and Thackeray.' XVIII (April, 1864), 523–53 [Walter Bagehot].

Nineteenth Century

'Novel Reading.' V (January, 1879), 24–43. Anthony Trollope.

North British Review

'*Pendennis* and *Copperfield*: Dickens *and* Thackeray.' XV (May, 1851), 57–89 [David Masson].
'Recent Works of Fiction.' XV (August, 1851), 419–41.
'*Ruth*.' XIX (May, 1853), 151–75.
'American Novels.' XX (November, 1853), 81–109.
'Sir E. Bulwer-Lytton.' XXIII (August, 1855), 339–92 [Nassau Senior].
'Fielding and Thackeray.' XXIV (November, 1855), 197–216.
'Religious Novels.' XXVI (November, 1856), 209–27.
'Novels by the Authoress of "John Halifax".' XXIX (November, 1858), 466–80.
'Recent Publications.' XXX (May, 1859), 562–76.
'Novels—*Geoffrey Hamlyn* and *Stephen Langton*.' XXXI (November, 1859), 384–406.
'Imaginative Literature: The Author of *Adam Bede* and Nathaniel Hawthorne.' XXXIII (August, 1860), 165–85.
'Novels and Novelists of the Day.' XXXVIII (February, 1863), 186–90.
'Thackeray.' XL (February, 1864), 210–65.
'Mr. Trollope's Novels.' XL (May, 1864), 369–401.
'Sensation Novels: Miss Braddon.' XLIII (September, 1865), 180–205.
'George Eliot's Novels.' XLV (September, 1866), 197–232.
'Jane Austen.' LII (April, 1870), 129–52.

Prospective Review

'*David Copperfield* and *Pendennis*.' VII, No. 26 (1851), 157–91.
'*Ruth*. By the Author of *Mary Barton*.' IX, No. 34 (1853), 222–47.
'The Author of *Heartsease* and the Modern School of Fiction.' X, No. 40 (1854), 460–82.

BIBLIOGRAPHY

Quarterly Review

'The Newcomes.' XCVII (September, 1855), 350–78 [Whitwell Elwin].
'Henry Fielding.' XCVIII (December, 1855), 100–48 [Whitwell Elwin].
'Tobias Smollett.' CIII (January, 1858), 66–108 [Whitwell Elwin].
'Fictions of Bohemia.' CIII (April, 1858), 328–46.
'Eliot's Novels.' CVIII (October, 1860), 469–99.
'Les Misérables.' CXII (October, 1862), 271–305.
'Sensation Novels.' CXIII (April, 1863), 481–514 [Margaret Oliphant].
'Sir Walter Scott.' CXXIV (January, 1868), 1–54.
'Jane Austen.' CXXVIII (January, 1870), 196–218.

Saturday Review

Vols. I–XXX (1856–1870), *passim*. See especially:
'A Forbidden Novel.' I (April 5, 1856), 461–2.
'Mr. Dickens as a Politician.' III (January 3, 1857), 8–9.
'Little Dorrit.' IV (July 4, 1857), 15–16 [Sir James Fitzjames Stephen].
'Light Literature and the *Saturday Review*.' IV (July 11, 1857), 34–5 [Sir James Fitzjames Stephen].
'Madame Bovary.' IV (July 11, 1857), 40–1 [Sir James Fitzjames Stephen].
'The *Edinburgh Review* and the Modern Novelists.' IV (July 18, 1857), 57–8 [Sir James Fitzjames Stephen].
'The Ordeal of Richard Feverel.' VIII (July 9, 1859), 48–9.
'The Virginians.' VIII (November 19, 1859), 610–12.
'The Mill on the Floss.' IX (April 14, 1860), 470–1.
'Artist and Craftsman.' X (July 7, 1860), 22–4.
'The Woman in White.' X (August 25, 1860), 249–50.
'The Tragedy of Life.' XI (March 9, 1861), 248–9.
'Silas Marner.' XI (April 13, 1861), 369–70 [John Morley].
'Who Breaks—Pays.' XII (September 7, 1861), 251–2.
'A Great Sensation.' XIII (March 8, 1862), 276–7.
'George Sand.' XIV (August 16, 1862), 193–4.
'Verner's Pride.' XV (February 28, 1863), 279–80.
'Salammbô.' XV (March 7, 1863), 309–11.
'Lost and Saved.' XV (May 30, 1863), 701–2.
'Rachel Ray.' XVI (October 24, 1863), 554–5.
'Tara: A Mahratta Tale.' XVI (October 31, 1863), 587–8.
'Novels and Life.' XVII (February 13, 1864), 188–9.
'Poetical Justice.' XVII (April 2, 1864), 407–8.
'Taine's *Contemporary English Literature*.' XIX (January 7, 1865), 22–3.
'Novels, Past and Present.' XXI (April 14, 1866), 438–40.
'Novel-Reading.' XXIII (February, 1867), 196–7.

Spectator

Vols. XXIII–XLII (1850–70), *passim*. See especially:
'My Novel.' XXVI (February 19, 1853), 178–9 [George Brimley].
'Bleak House.' XXVI (September 24, 1853), 923–4 [George Brimley].
'It Is Never too Late to Mend.' XXIX (August 16, 1856), 877–8.

'Unctuous Sentiment.' XXXV (March 15, 1862), 298–300 [Richard Holt Hutton].

'La Griffe Rose.' XXV (September 13, 1862), 1029–30.

'Orley Farm.' XXXV (October 11, 1862), 1136–8 [Richard Holt Hutton].

'Two New Novels.' XXXV (December 27, 1862), 1447–8.

'Aurora Floyd.' XXXVI (January 31, 1863), 1586–7 [Richard Holt Hutton].

'Lost Sir Massingberd.' XXXVII (June 18, 1864), 715–17 [Richard Holt Hutton].

'Can You Forgive Her?' XXXVIII (September 2, 1856), 978–9 [Richard Holt Hutton].

'Phemie Keller.' XXXIX (March 31, 1866), 360–1.

'For Ever and Ever.' XXXIX (October 20, 1866), 117.

'Vittoria.' XL (February 9, 1867), 161–3 [Richard Holt Hutton].

'The Last Chronicle of Barset.' XL (July 13, 1867), 778–80 [Richard Holt Hutton].

'The Moonstone.' XLI (July 25, 1868), 881–2 [Richard Holt Hutton].

'Sensation Novels.' XLI (August 8, 1868), 931–2 [Richard Holt Hutton].

'Nathaniel Hawthorne's Notebooks.' XLII (January 2, 1869), 14–15 [Richard Holt Hutton].

'The Empire of the Novel.' XLII (January 9, 1869), 43–4 [Richard Holt Hutton].

'Phineas Finn.' XLII (March 20, 1869), 356–7 [Richard Holt Hutton].

'He Knew He Was Right.' XLII (June 12, 1869), 706–8 [Richard Holt Hutton].

Train

'Mr. Dickens and His Critics.' IV (August, 1857), 76–9. John Hollingshead.

Westminster Review

'Contemporary Literature of England.' LVII (January, 1852), 247–88 [George Eliot].

'Retrospective Survey of American Literature.' LVII (January, 1852), 288–305.

'Contemporary Literature of England.' LVII (April, 1852), 625–62.

'The Lady Novelists.' LVIII (July, 1852), 129–41 [George Henry Lewes].

'Contemporary Literature.' LVIII (July, 1852).

'Contemporary Literature of England.' LVIII (October, 1852).

'Contemporary American Literature.' LVIII (October, 1852).

'Thackeray's Works.' LXIX (April, 1853), 363–88.

'Ruth and *Villette.'* LIX (April, 1853), 474–91.

'Balzac and His Writings.' LX (July, 1853), 199–214.

'The Progress of Fiction as an Art.' LX (October, 1853), 342–74.

'Belles Lettres.' Vols. LXI–XCII (1854–70), *passim.* See especially: Vols. LXIV (July, 1855)–LXVII (January, 1857) (George Eliot), and LXVII (April, 1857) and LXVIII (October, 1857) (George Meredith).

BIBLIOGRAPHY

'Woman in France: Madame de Sablé.' LXII (October, 1854), 448–73 [George Eliot].
'The Natural History of German Life.' LXVI (July, 1856), 51–79 [George Eliot].
'Silly Novels by Lady Novelists.' LXVI (October, 1856), 442–61 [George Eliot].
'Worldliness and Otherworldliness: The Poet Young.' LXVII (April, 1857), 1–41 [George Eliot].
'Realism in Art: Recent German Fiction.' LXX (October, 1858), 488–518 [George Henry Lewes].
'*Adam Bede*.' LXXI (April, 1859), 486–512.
'*The Mill on the Floss*.' LXXIV (July, 1860), 24–33.
'W. M. Thackeray as Novelist and Photographer.' LXXIV (October, 1860), 500–23.
'The Literature of Bohemia.' LXXIX (January, 1863), 32–56.
'*Les Misérables* by Victor Hugo.' LXXIX (January, 1863), 77–114.
'*Romola*.' LXXX (October, 1863), 344–52.
'Novels with a Purpose.' LXXXII (July, 1864), 24–49. [Justin Mac-Carthy].
'Modern Novelists: Charles Dickens.' LXXXII (October, 1864), 414–41.
'Modern Novelists: Sir Edward Bulwer-Lytton.' LXXXIII (April, 1865), 468–503.
'American Novelists: Theodore Winthrop.' LXXXIV (July, 1865), 163–85.
'Felix Holt—The Radical.' LXXXVI (October, 1866), 200–7.
'Spielhagen's Novels.' XC (October, 1868), 334–73.
'Richardson's *Clarissa*.' XCI (January, 1869), 48–75.

3b. PRIMARY MATERIAL, 1850–1870: BOOKS

BAGEHOT, WALTER. (See 3a. *1850–1870. Periodicals: National Review*.)
—— *The Love Letters of Walter Bagehot and Eliza Wilson*, ed. Mrs. Russell Barrington. London: Faber and Faber, 1933.
—— *The Works of Walter Bagehot*, ed. Mrs. Russell Barrington. 9 vols. London: Longmans, Green, 1915.
BARRINGTON, MRS. RUSSELL. *The Life of Walter Bagehot*. London: Longmans, Green, 1915.
BAYNE, PETER. *Essays in Biography and Criticism, First Series*. Boston: Gould and Lincoln, 1857.
BOOTH, BRADFORD A. 'Trollope on Scott', *NCF*, V (December, 1950), 223–30.
BRIMLEY, GEORGE. (See 3a. *1850–1870. Periodicals: Spectator*.)
—— *Essays*, ed. William George Clark. London: Macmillan, 1868.
BRONTË, CHARLOTTE. Novels. Everyman's Library.
BRONTË, EMILY, *Wuthering Heights*. New York: The Modern Library, 1943.
BULWER-LYTTON, EDWARD GEORGE. (See 3a. *1850–1870. Periodicals: Blackwood's Edinburgh Magazine*.)
—— *The Critical and Miscellaneous Writing of Sir Edward Lytton Bulwer*. 2 vols. Philadelphia: Lea and Blanchard, 1841.

BULWER-LYTTON, EDWARD GEORGE. 'A Word to the Public.' Appended to *Lucretia, Or the Children of the Night*. Philadelphia: J. B. Lippincott, 1878.

—— *The Works of Lord Lytton*. Knebworth Edition. London: George Routledge and Sons, 1874.

'Charles Reade's Opinion of Himself and His Opinion of George Eliot', *Bookman*, XVIII (November, 1903), 252–60.

COLEMAN, JOHN. *Charles Reade as I Knew Him*. London: Treherne, 1903.

COLLIER, WILLIAM FRANCIS. *A History of English Literature*. London: T. Nelson and Sons, 1870.

COLLINS, WILKIE. *Novels*. 29 vols. New York: Harper, 1873–1915.

COOLIDGE, BERTHA. *A Catalogue of the Altschul Collection of George Meredith in the Yale University Library*. Boston: The Merrymount Press, 1931.

DALLAS, ENEAS SWEETLAND. *The Gay Science*. 2 vols. London: Chapman and Hall, 1866.

DICKENS, CHARLES. (See 3a. *1850–1870. Periodicals: Cornhill Magazine, Household Words*, and *All the Year Round*.) For the novels I have used the Oxford edition when it was available; otherwise I have used Everyman editions.

—— *The Heart of Charles Dickens*, ed. Edgar Johnson. New York: Duell, Sloan and Pearce, 1952.

—— *The Letters of Charles Dickens*, ed. Walter Dexter. 3 vols. London: Nonesuch, 1938.

DOBELL, SYDNEY. *The Life and Letters of Sydney Dobell*, ed. 'E.' 2 vols. London: Smith, Elder, 1878.

DRUMMOND, JAMES. *The Life and Letters of James Martineau*. 2 vols. New York: Dodd, Mead, 1902.

ELIOT, GEORGE. (See 3a. *1850–1870. Periodicals: Leader* and *Westminster Review*.)

—— *Essays and Uncollected Papers*. Boston and New York: Houghton Mifflin, 1908.

—— *The George Eliot Letters*, ed. Gordon S. Haight. 7 vols. New Haven: Yale University Press, 1954–5.

—— *The Works of George Eliot*. Cabinet Edition. 24 vols. London and Edinburgh: William Blackwood, 1878–85.

ESPINASSE, FRANCIS. *Literary Recollections and Sketches*. New York: Dodd, Mead, 1893.

FORMAN, MAURICE BUXTON, ed. *George Meredith, Some Early Appreciations*. New York: Scribner, 1909.

FORSTER, JOHN. *The Life of Charles Dickens*, ed. J. W. T. Ley. New York: Doubleday, n.d.

FORSYTHE, WILLIAM. *The Novels and Novelists of the Eighteenth Century*. New York: Appleton, 1871.

FRISWELL, J. HAIN. *Modern Men of Letters Honestly Criticized*. London: Hodder and Stoughton, 1870.

GASKELL, ELIZABETH CLEGHORN. *The Life of Charlotte Brontë*. London: John Murray, 1929.

—— *The Works of Mrs. Gaskell*. Knutsford Edition. 7 vols. London: John Murray, 1906.

BIBLIOGRAPHY

GILFILLAN, GEORGE. *A Third Gallery of Literary Portraits.* Edinburgh: James Hogg, 1854.

GREEN, THOMAS HILL. *An Estimate of the Value and Influence of Works of Fiction in Modern Times,* ed. Fred Norton Scott. Ann Arbor: George Wahr, 1911.

GREGG, WILLIAM RATHBONE. (See 3a. *1850–1870. Periodicals: National Review.*)

—— *Literary and Social Judgements.* Boston: James R. Osgood, 1873.

HAMMERTON, J. G. *George Meredith in Anecdote and Criticism.* New York: Mitchell Kennerley, 1909.

HANNAY, JAMES. *A Course of English Literature.* London: Tinsley, 1866.

—— *Studies on Thackeray.* London: George Routledge and Sons, 1869.

HUTTON, RICHARD HOLT. (See 3a. *1850–1870. Periodicals: National Review* and *Spectator.*)

—— *Brief Literary Criticisms, Selected from the Spectator,* ed. Elizabeth M. Roscoe. London: Macmillan, 1906.

—— *Criticisms on Contemporary Thought and Thinkers, Selected from the Spectator.* 2 vols. London: Macmillan, 1906.

—— *Essays on Some of the Modern Guides to English Thought in Matters of Faith.* London: Macmillan, 1900.

—— *Literary Essays.* London: Macmillan, 1892.

—— *Sir Walter Scott.* 'English Men of Letters.' New York: Harper, 1879.

HUXLEY, LEONARD. *The House of Smith, Elder.* London: Printed for private circulation, 1923.

JEAFFRESON, J. CORDY. *Novels and Novelists from Elizabeth to Victoria.* 2 vols. London: Hurst and Blackett, 1850.

KINGSLEY, CHARLES. *His Letters and Memories of His Life,* ed. his wife. 4 vols. London: Macmillan, 1902.

—— *The Works of Charles Kingsley.* 19 vols. London: Macmillan, 1901–03.

LEWES, GEORGE HENRY. (See 3a. *1850–1870. Periodicals: Blackwood's Edinburgh Magazine, Edinburgh Review, Fortnightly Review, Fraser's Magazine, Leader, Westminster Review.*)

—— *The Life of Goethe.* 2 vols. Leipsig: F. A. Brockhaus, 1864.

—— *Principles of Success in Literature.* London: Walter Scott, n.d.

LEY, J. W. T. *The Dickens Circle.* London: Chapman and Hall, 1919.

LINTON, MRS. LYNN. *My Literary Life.* London: Hodder and Stoughton, 1899.

LUCAS, SAMUEL. *Eminent Men and Popular Books.* London: Warnes and Routledge, 1859.

LYTTON, THE EARL OF. *The Life of Edward Bulwer, First Lord of Lytton.* 2 vols. London: Macmillan, 1913.

MARTINEAU, HARRIET. *Autobiography,* ed. Maria Weston Chapman. 2 vols. Boston: James R. Osgood, 1877.

MASSON, DAVID. (See 3a. *1850–1870. Periodicals: North British Review* and *Macmillan's Magazine.*)

—— *British Novelists and Their Styles.* Cambridge: Macmillan, 1859.

—— *Wordsworth, Shelley, Keats, and Other Essays.* London: Macmillan, 1870.

MEREDITH, GEORGE. (See 3a. *1850–1870. Periodicals: Westminster Review.*)

—— 'Essay on Comedy', in *Comedy,* ed. Wylie Sypher. New York: Doubleday Anchor Books, 1956.

MEREDITH, GEORGE. *Letters of George Meredith*, ed. William Maxse Meredith. 2 vols. New York: Scribner, 1912.

—— *The Works of George Meredith*. Memorial Edition. 29 vols. New York: Scribner, 1909–12.

MILLER, HUGH. *Essays, Historical, Biographical, Political, Social, Literary, and Scientific*. Boston: Gould and Lincoln, 1865.

MORGAN, CHARLES. *The House of Macmillan (1843–1943)*. New York: Macmillan, 1944.

OLIPHANT, MARGARET. *Annals of a Publishing House*. 3 vols. Edinburgh: William Blackwood, 1897.

PHILLIPS, SAMUEL. *A Second Series of Essays from 'The Times'*. London: John Murray, 1855.

READE, CHARLES. *The Works of Charles Reade*. Library Edition. 17 vols. London: Chatto and Windus, 1883–96.

READE, CHARLES L. and REVEREND COMPTON READE. *Charles Reade, A Memoir*. 2 vols. London: Chapman and Hall, 1887.

'Romance', *Encyclopedia Britannica*, Vol. XIX, pp. 253–93. 8th ed. Boston: Little, Brown.

ROSCOE, WILLIAM CALDWELL. (See 3a. *1850–1870. Periodicals: National Review*.)

—— *Poems and Essays*, ed. Richard Holt Hutton. 2 vols. London: Chapman and Hall, 1860.

SENIOR, NASSAU. (See 3a. *1850–1870. Periodicals: Edinburgh Review* and *North British Review*.)

—— *Essays in Fiction*. London: Longmans, Green, Longmans, 1864.

SMITH, GEORGE BARNETT. *Poets and Novelists; A Series of Literary Studies*. New York: Appleton, 1876.

SHORTER, CLEMENT. *The Brontës: Life and Letters*. 2 vols. New York: Scribner, 1908.

SPALDING, WILLIAM. *A History of English Literature*. New York: Appleton, 1853.

STEPHEN, SIR JAMES FITZJAMES. (See 3a. *1850–1870. Periodicals: Cornhill Magazine, Edinburgh Review* and *Saturday Review*.)

—— 'The Relation of Novels to Life', *Cambridge Essays*. London: Parker, 1855.

STEPHEN, LESLIE. (See 3a. *1850–1870. Periodicals: Cornhill Magazine*.)

—— *George Eliot*. 'English Men of Letters.' London: Macmillan, 1940.

—— *Hours in a Library*. 4 vols. New York: Putnam, 1904.

—— *The Life of Sir James Fitzjames Stephen*. London: Smith, Elder, 1895.

THACKERAY, WILLIAM MAKEPEACE. *Contributions to the 'Morning Post'*, ed. Gordon N. Ray. Urbana: University of Illinois Press, 1955.

—— *Critical Papers in Literature*. London: Macmillan, 1904.

—— *The Letters and Private Papers of William Makepeace Thackeray*, ed. Gordon N. Ray. 4 vols. Cambridge: Harvard University Press, 1945–6.

—— *The Works of William Makepeace Thackeray*. Biographical Edition. 13 vols. New York and London: Harper, 1898–9.

TROLLOPE, ANTHONY. (See 3a. *1850–1870. Periodicals: Nineteenth Century*.)

—— *An Autobiography*, ed. Bradford A. Booth. Berkeley and Los Angeles: University of California Press, 1947.

—— *The Eustace Diamonds*. New York: The Modern Library, n.d.

—— *Four Lectures*, ed. Morris L. Parrish. London: Constable, 1938.

—— *The Letters of Anthony Trollope*, ed. Bradford A. Booth. London: Oxford University Press, 1951.

—— *Thackeray*. 'English Men of Letters.' New York: Harper, n.d.

—— *The Works of Anthony Trollope: The Barsetshire Novels*. Shakespeare Head Edition. 14 vols. Stratford-upon-Avon: Shakespeare Head Press, 1929. (Other novels in World's Classics.)

WAUGH, ARTHUR. *A Hundred Years of Publishing, Being the Story of Chapman and Hall, Ltd.* London: Chapman and Hall, 1930.

3C. 1850–1870. SECONDARY MATERIAL

ANNAN, NOEL. *Leslie Stephen, His Thought and Character in Relation to His Time*. Cambridge: Harvard University Press, 1952.

BEACH, JOSEPH WARREN. *The Comic Spirit in Meredith, An Interpretation*. New York: Longmans, Green, 1911.

BETHELL, S. L. 'The Novels of George Eliot', *Criterion*, XVIII (October, 1938), 39–57.

BEVINGTON, MERLE. *The Saturday Review, 1856–1868*, New York: Columbia University Press, 1941.

BISSON, L. A. 'Proust, Bergson, and George Eliot', *MLR*, XL (April, 1945), 104–14.

BOEGE, FRED W. 'Point of View in Dickens', *PMLA*, LXV (March, 1950), 90–105.

BOOTH, BRADFORD A. 'Trollope on the Novel', *Essays Critical and Historical Dedicated to Lily B. Campbell*. Berkeley and Los Angeles: University of California Press, 1950.

—— 'Wilkie Collins and the Art of Fiction', *NCF*, VI (September, 1951), 131–43.

BROWNELL, W. C. *Victorian Prose Masters*. New York: Scribner, 1902.

BUCKLEY, JEROME H. *The Victorian Temper, A Study in Literary Culture*. Cambridge: Harvard University Press, 1951.

BULLETT, GERALD. *George Eliot, Her Life and Her Books*. New Haven: Yale University Press, 1948.

CECIL, LORD DAVID. *Early Victorian Novelists*. Harmondsworth, Middlesex: Penguin Books, 1948.

CHESTERTON, GILBERT KEITH. *Charles Dickens, A Critical Study*. New York: Dodd, Mead, 1906.

COCKSHUT, A. O. J. *Anthony Trollope, A Critical Study*. London: Collins, 1955.

COLBY, ROBERT A. 'How It Strikes a Contemporary: The "Spectator" as Critic', *NCF*, XI (December, 1956), 182–206.

CRUSE, AMY. *The Victorians and Their Reading*. London: Allen, 1935.

DECKER, CLARENCE R. *The Victorian Conscience*. New York: Twayne, 1952.

DONOVAN, ROBERT A. 'Trollope's Prentice Work', *MP*, LIII (February, 1956), 179–86.

ELWIN, MALCOLM. *Charles Reade*. London: Jonathan Cape, 1934.

ENGEL, MONROE E. 'Dickens on Art', *MP*, LIII (August, 1955), 25–38.

ENZINGER, PHILLIP. 'Thackeray, Critic of Literature', *University of North*

Dakota Quarterly Journal, XX (1930–1), 318–33; XXI (1931–2), 52–65, 145–60.

EVERETT, EDWIN MALLARD. *The Party of Humanity: The Fortnightly Review and Its First Contributors, 1865–1874*. Chapel Hill: University of North Carolina Press, 1939.

GARY, FRANKLIN. 'Charlotte Brontë and George Henry Lewes', *PMLA*, LI (June, 1936), 518–42.

GETTMANN, ROYAL A. 'Serialization and *Evan Harrington*.' *PMLA*, LXIV (December, 1949), 963–75.

—— 'Meredith as a Publisher's Reader', *JEGP*, XLVIII (January, 1949), 45–56.

—— *Turgenev in England and America*. Illinois Studies in Language and Literature, Vol. XXVII, No. 2. Urbana: University of Illinois Press, 1941.

GREENHUT, MORRIS. 'G. H. Lewes as a Critic of the Novel', *SP*, LXV (July, 1948), 491–512.

HAIGHT, GORDON S. *George Eliot and John Chapman*. New Haven: Yale University Press, 1940.

HARRISON, FREDERIC. *Studies in Early Victorian Literature*. London: E. Arnold, 1906.

HOPKINS, ANNETTE B. 'Dickens and Mrs. Gaskell', *Huntington Library Quarterly*, IX (August, 1946), 357–85.

JOHNSON, EDGAR. *Charles Dickens: His Tragedy and Triumph*. 2 vols. New York: Simon and Schuster, 1952.

JUMP, J. D. 'Weekly Reviewing in the 1850's', *RES*, XXIV (January, 1948), 42–57.

—— 'Weekly Reviewing in the 1860's', *RES*, n.s., III (July, 1952), 244–62.

KAMINSKY, ALICE R. 'George Eliot, George Henry Lewes, and the Novel', *PMLA*, LXX (December, 1955), 997–1013.

KITCHEL, ANNA THERESA. *George Eliot and George Lewes, A Review of Records*. New York: John Day, 1933.

LEAVIS, Q. D. 'Leslie Stephen: Cambridge Critic', *Scrutiny*, VII (March, 1939), 404–14.

LESTER, JOHN A., Jr. 'Thackeray's Narrative Technique', *PMLA*, LXIX (June, 1954), 392–409.

LINDSAY, JACK. *Charles Dickens, A Biographical and Critical Study*. London: Andrews Dakers, 1950.

—— *George Meredith, His Life and Work*. London: The Bodley Head, 1956.

MARCHAND, LESLIE ALEXIS. *The Athenaeum: A Mirror of Victorian Culture*. Chapel Hill: University of North Carolina Press, 1941.

MAURER, OSCAR. 'Froude and *Fraser's Magazine*', *University of Texas Studies in English*, XXVII (1949), 213–43.

—— 'Leslie Stephen and the *Cornhill Magazine*, 1871–1882', *University of Texas in English*, XXXII (1953), 67–95.

O'CONNOR, FRANK. *The Mirror in the Roadway*. New York: Knopf, 1956.

OSBOURNE, R. V. 'The British Quarterly Review', *RES*, n.s., I (April, 1950), 147–52.

PACEY, DESMOND. 'Flaubert and His Victorian Critics', *University of Toronto Quarterly*, XVI (October, 1946), 74–84.

PHILLIPS, WALTER C. *Dickens, Reade, and Collins, Sensation Novelists: A Study in the Conditions and Theories of Novel-Writing in Victorian England.* New York: Columbia University Press, 1919.

PRAZ, MARIO. *The Hero in Eclipse in Victorian Fiction*, trans. Angus Davidson. London: Oxford University Press, 1956.

POPE HENNESY, UNA. *Canon Charles Kingsley, A Biography.* New York: Macmillan, 1949.

RAY, GORDON N. *Thackeray: The Uses of Adversity, 1811–1846.* New York: McGraw-Hill, 1955.

ROBINSON, E. A. 'Meredith's Literary Theory: Realism vs. the Comic Spirit', *PMLA*, LIII (September, 1938), 857–68.

ROBINSON, KENNETH. *Wilkie Collins.* New York: Macmillan, 1952.

RUST, JAMES D. 'The Art of Fiction in George Eliot's Reviews', *RES*, n.s., VII (April, 1956), 164–72.

SADLEIR, MICHAEL. *Bulwer, a Panorama.* Boston: Little, Brown, 1931.

—— *XIX Century Fiction; A Bibliographical Record Based on His Own Collection.* 2 vols. London: Constable, 1951.

—— *Trollope, a Commentary.* London: Constable, 1945.

SASSOON, SIEGFRIED. *Meredith.* New York: Viking, 1948.

STEVENSON, LIONEL. *The Ordeal of George Meredith.* New York: Scribner, 1953.

TILLOTSON, GEOFFREY. *Criticism and the Nineteenth Century.* London: The Athlone Press, 1951.

—— *Thackeray.* Cambridge: Cambridge University Press, 1954.

TILLOTSON, KATHLEEN and JOHN BUTT. *Dickens at Work.* London: Methuen, 1957.

WATTS, HAROLD H. 'Lytton's Theories of Prose Fiction', *PMLA*, L (March, 1935), 274–89.

WRIGHT, WALTER F. *Art and Substance in George Meredith: A Study in Narrative.* Lincoln: University of Nebraska Press, 1953.

4. ALL OTHER MATERIAL

ALDRIDGE, JOHN W., ed. *Critiques and Essays on Modern Fiction.* New York: Ronald Press, 1952.

'American Novels', *Quarterly Review*, CLV (January, 1883), 202–29.

AMES, VAN METER. *The Aesthetics of the Novel.* Chicago: University of Chicago Press, 1928.

ARNOLD, MATTHEW. 'Count Leo Tolstoi', *Essays in Criticism: Second Series.* London: Macmillan, 1888.

BAKER, HOWARD. 'An Essay on Fiction with Examples', *Southern Review*, III (Autumn, 1941), 385–406.

BAUDELAIRE, CHARLES. 'Madame Bovary', trans. William Troy, *Partisan Review*, XIII (November–December, 1946), 568–76.

—— *The Mirror of Art*, trans. Jonathan Mayne. New York: Doubleday Anchor Books, 1956.

BEACH, JOSEPH WARREN. *The Method of Henry James.* New Haven: Yale University Press, 1918.

—— *The Twentieth Century Novel; Studies in Technique.* New York: Appleton, 1932.

BENNETT, ARNOLD. *Fame and Fiction; An Enquiry into Certain Popularities.* London: Grant Richards, 1901.

BESANT, SIR WALTER. *The Art of Fiction.* London: Chatto and Windus, 1884.

BLACKMUR, R. P. *The Lion and the Honeycomb; Essays in Solicitude and Critique.* New York: Harcourt, Brace, 1955.

BOWRON, BERNARD R., Jr. 'Realism in America', *Comparative Literature,* III (Summer, 1951), 268–85.

BROWN, MALCOLM. *George Moore: A Reconsideration.* Seattle: University of Washington Press, 1955.

BRUNETIÈRE, FERDINAND. *Le Roman naturaliste.* Paris: Calmann, Lévy, 1883.

CAMUS, ALBERT. *The Rebel: An Essay on Man in Revolt,* trans. Anthony Bower. New York: Vintage, 1956.

CRANE, R. S., ed. *Critics and Criticism, Ancient and Modern.* Chicago: University of Chicago Press, 1952.

DELACROIX, EUGÈNE. *The Journal of Eugène Delacroix,* trans. Lucy Norton. London: Phaidon, 1951.

DONELLY, MABEL COLLINS. *George Gissing, Grave Comedian.* Cambridge: Harvard University Press, 1954.

DUPEE, F. W. *Henry James.* 'American Men of Letters.' New York: Sloane, 1951.

—— *The Question of Henry James; A Collection of Critical Essays.* New York: Holt, 1945.

EDEL, LEON. *Henry James, The Untried Years.* Philadelphia: Lippincott, 1953.

EGERTON, HUGH E. 'The Scientific Novel and Gustave Flaubert', *National Review,* I (August, 1883), 894–907.

FLAUBERT, GUSTAVE. *The Selected Letters of Gustave Flaubert,* trans. and ed. Frencis Steegmuller. New York: Farrar, Straus and Young, 1953.

FORSTER, E. M. *Aspects of the Novel.* New York: Harcourt, Brace, 1927.

FRIERSON, WILLIAM C. *The English Novel in Transition, 1885–1940.* Norman: University of Oklahoma Press, 1942.

GISSING, GEORGE. *Charles Dickens, A Critical Study.* New York: Dodd, Mead, 1898.

—— *Letters to Members of His Family,* ed. Algernon and Ellen Gissing. London: Constable, 1927.

—— *New Grub Street.* New York: The Modern Library, n.d.

GOSSE, EDMUND. *Questions at Issue.* London: William Heinemann, 1893.

HARDY, THOMAS. *Life and Art: Essays, Notes, and Letters,* ed. Ernest Brennecke, Jr. New York: Greenberg, Publisher, 1925.

HENLEY, WILLIAM ERNEST. *Views and Reviews; Essays in Appreciation.* New York: Scribner, 1890.

HOWELLS, WILLIAM DEAN. *Criticism and Fiction.* New York: Harper, 1891.

—— 'Henry James, Jr.', *Century Illustrated Monthly Magazine,* III (November, 1882), 24–9.

JAMES, HENRY. *The Art of the Novel: Critical Prefaces*, ed. R. P. Blackmur. New York: Scribner, 1934.

—— *French Poets and Novelists*. London: Macmillan, 1884.

—— *The Future of the Novel: Essays on the Art of Fiction*, ed. Leon Edel. New York: Vintage, 1956.

—— *The Letters of Henry James*, ed. Percy Lubbock. 2 vols. London: Macmillan, 1920.

—— *Notes and Reviews*, ed. Pierre de Chaignon la Rose. Cambridge, Mass.: Dunster House, 1921.

—— *Notes on Novelists, with Some Other Notes*. New York: Scribner, 1914.

—— *Novels and Tales*. New York edition. 24 vols. New York: Scribner, 1907–17.

—— *Partial Portraits*. London: Macmillan, 1911.

—— *Selected Letters*, ed. Leon Edel. New York: Farrar, Strauss and Cudahy, 1955.

—— *Views and Reviews*, ed. LeRoy Phillips. Boston: Ball, 1908.

KELLEY, CORNELIA PULSIFER. *The Early Development of Henry James*. Urbana: University of Illinois Press, 1930.

LATHROP, G. P. 'The Growth of the Novel', *Atlantic Monthly*, XXXIII (June, 1874), 684–97.

—— 'The Novel and Its Future', *Atlantic Monthly*, XXXIV (September, 1874), 313–24.

LAWRENCE, D. H. *Assorted Articles*. London: Martin Secker, 1930.

—— *Phoenix; The Posthumous Papers of D. H. Lawrence*, ed. Edward D. McDonald. New York: Viking, 1936.

LUBBOCK, PERCY. *The Craft of Fiction*. New York: Scribner, 1921.

MATTHIESON, F. O. *Henry James, The Major Phase*. London: Oxford University Press, 1944.

MAUPASSANT, GUY DE. 'Sur le roman', Preface to *Pierre et Jean*. Paris: P. Ollendorff, 1895.

'Mr. Howells' Novels', *Westminster Review*, CXXII (October, 1884), 347–75.

MOORE, GEORGE. *Avowals*. New York: Boni & Liveright, 1919.

—— *Confessions of a Young Man*. New York: The Modern Library, n.d.

—— *Conversations in Ebury Street*. New York: Boni & Liveright, 1928.

—— 'Some Characteristics of English Fiction', *North American Review*, CLXX (April, 1900), 504–17.

MUIR, EDWIN. *The Structure of Fiction*. London: Hogarth, 1946.

MURRAY, DONALD M. 'Henry James and the English Reviewers', *American Literature*, XXIV (March, 1952), 3–20.

MYERS, WALTER L. *The Later Realism: A Study of Characterization in the British Novel*. Chicago: University of Chicago Press, 1927.

O'CONNOR, WILLIAM VAN, ed. *Forms of Modern Fiction: Essays Collected in Honor of Joseph Warren Beach*. Minneapolis: University of Minnesota Press, 1948.

ORTEGA Y GASSET, JOSÉ. 'Notes on the Novel', *The Dehumanization of Art and Other Writings on Art and Culture*. New York: Doubleday Anchor Books, 1956.

PERRY, THOMAS SARGENT. 'Ivan Tourgénièff', *Atlantic Monthly*, XXXIII (May, 1874), 565–75.

RAHV, PHILLIP. 'Fiction and the Criticism of Fiction', *Kenyon Review*, XVIII (Spring, 1956), 276–99.

ROBERTS, MORRIS. *Henry James' Criticism*. Cambridge: Harvard University Press, 1929.

SHORT, R. W. 'Some Critical Terms of Henry James', *PMLA*, LXV (September, 1950), 667–80.

SCHERER, EDMOND. *Essays in English Literature*, trans. George Saintsbury. New York: Scribner, 1891.

STEVENSON, ROBERT LOUIS. *Essays in the Art of Writing*. London: Chatto and Windus, 1908.

—— *Familiar Studies of Men and Books*. New York: Scribner, 1910.

SULLIVAN, EDWARD D. *Maupassant the Novelist*. Princeton: Princeton University Press, 1954.

TAINE, HIPOLYTE. *History of English Literature*, trans. H. Van Laun. 4 vols. Philadelphia: Gebbie, 1896.

THOMPSON, DAVID GREENLEAF. *The Philosophy of Fiction in Literature*. New York: Longmans, Green, 1890.

TILLEY, ARTHUR. 'The New School of Fiction', *National Review*, I (April, 1883), 257–68.

TRAILL, H. D. *The New Fiction*. London: Hurst and Blackett, 1897.

TRILLING, LIONEL. *The Liberal Imagination; Essays on Literature and Society*. New York: Viking, 1950.

—— *The Opposing Self; Nine Essays in Criticism*. New York: Viking, 1955.

TURNELL, MARTIN. *The Novel in France*. New York: New Directions, 1951.

WILDE, OSCAR. 'The Decay of Lying', *Intentions*. New York: Brentano's, 1907.

WILSON, EDMUND. *The Wound and the Bow; Seven Studies in Literature*. New York: Oxford University Press, 1947.

ZOLA, ÉMILE. *The Experimental Novel and Other Essays*, trans. Belle M. Sherman. New York: Cassell, 1894.

INDEX

INDEX